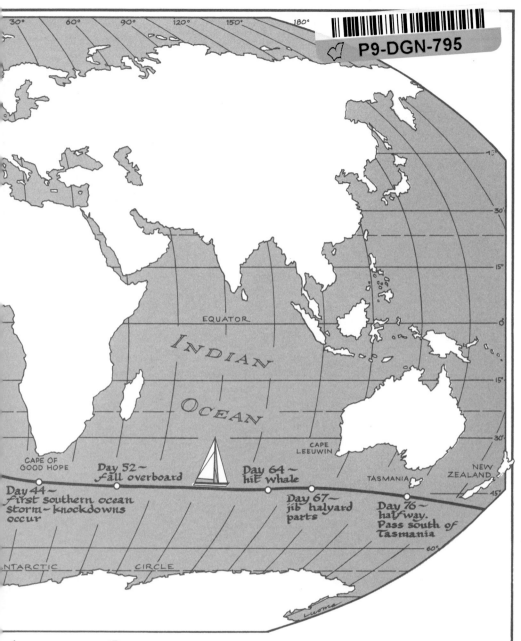

American Promise

Day 44	42°S/19°45′E	Pass south of Cape of Good Hope. Knockdowns occur
Day 52	42°S/50°40′E	Fall overboard
Day 64	42°11′S/99°20′E	Hit whale
Day 67	42°20′S/113°E	Jib halyard parts
Day 76	45°20′S/148°E	Halfway — south of Tasmania
Day 104	54°S/88°W	Tropical cyclone "Ima"
Day 108	56°S/67°45′W	Round Cape Horn
Day 135	0°/30°48′W	Cross equator on return leg
Day 145	22°28′N/54°11′W	"tie the knot"
Day 150		Arrive home – April 11, 1986

The Voyage of
AMERICAN PROMISE

The
Voyage of
AMERICAN
PROMISE ~~~

Dodge Morgan

Houghton Mifflin Company   Boston

1989

For information about permission to reproduce selections
from this book, write to Permissions, Houghton Mifflin Company,
2 Park Street, Boston, Massachusetts 02108.

Library of Congress Cataloging-in-Publication Data

Morgan, Dodge.
    The voyage of American Promise / Dodge Morgan.
        p.   cm.
    ISBN 0–395–44096–3
    1. American Promise (Sailboat).   2. Sailing, Single-handed.
I. Title.
GV822.A54M67   1989
797.1'24—dc19   89-31007
                        CIP

Book design by Anne Chalmers

Printed in the United States of America

V 10 9 8 7 6 5 4 3 2 1

Endpaper map by Jon Luoma
Boat plan drawings courtesy Little Harbor Custom Yachts, Inc.
Chapter-opening drawings by David Moffet, Little Harbor Custom Yachts, Inc.:
1. Custom Fuel Manifold Valve. 2. Hood Yacht Systems Seafurl (R). 3. Steering
Pedestal. 4. Emergency Rudder Steering Quadrant. 5. Barient, Inc. 36 ST PW C
Vertical Drive Winch. 6. Emergency Retractable Rudder. 7. Hood Yacht Systems
Dorade and Guard. 8. Steaming Light. 9. Custom Preventer Hawser. 10. Max-
Prop (TM) Feathering Propeller. 11. Custom Spinnaker Pole Articulating End Fitting.
12. Harken (R) Small Boat Block.

PHOTO CREDITS
Black and white insert: Wide World Photos, p. 4 bottom and p. 5 top;
Curtis Ackerman, p. 5 bottom; Jim Davis, p. 6; all others by Richard Howard.
Color insert: Richard Howard, pp. 2, 3, and 4; Sally Reiley, p. 1 bottom, p. 6 top,
p. 7, and p. 8 bottom; Curtis Ackerman, p. 8 top; all others by Dodge Morgan.

To Manny, Hoyt, and Kim

~~~ CONTENTS

The Voyage of

AMERICAN PROMISE

$\sim\!\!\sim I \sim\!\!\sim$

Midmorning, October 14, 1985,
at Portland, Maine

This is a day of marauding emotion for me. Today, at last, *American Promise* and I depart on our nonstop sail around the world. This should be done quietly, but, instead, I find myself caught up in a spectacle. My senses are under siege. I must deal with the barrage by gun-barreling my attention to the one simple, single task at hand. Get on the boat. Get out to sea.

It is beaming bright sunlight outside my Cape Elizabeth home. I am inside, surrounded by family and close friends and straining to get through last-minute good-byes so that I can go down to Portland Harbor, where *Promise* is waiting.

Down at DiMillo's Marina and Restaurant, the parking lot and the docks are jammed with people. I feel detached, and I see myself not responding sensibly to these people. I hear my own nervous laugh. I watch my embarrassment at the carnival atmosphere, even though I realize I have added to it by wearing my old tuxedo. Yesterday I felt it would help me celebrate the dream come true, going off to sea alone in my special boat. The familiar faces become blurred in a sea of strangers. The real sea is out there, too, I know, but I can't see it through the crowd and the chaos.

In this world that now seems so out of control, I repeat over and over to myself, "Get *Promise* offshore, Dodge. Just hurry up and get her offshore alone with you."

This is not an easy task because *Promise* is a sailboat and there is no wind in Portland today. None. Ernie Burgess and Michael

Porter from Chebeague Island tow us out into the harbor with Ernie's lobster boat, the *Susan Adams*. The lobster boat is dwarfed by my big, new, red, white, and blue sailboat. Halfway out of the harbor, I am suddenly possessed by the need to do something. With a sense of urgency, I cast off Ernie's towline and rush to the foredeck to set *Promise*'s huge, light-air headsail, more than two thousand square feet of featherweight nylon. The sail, a third larger in area than my first house, is designed to gather up any breaths of wind. Any. But now the sail hangs limp because there are no breaths to catch.

I am surrounded by a fleet of wallowing spectator boats, perhaps forty, including the new Chebeague Island ferry, *Islander*, packed with my island friends, and the ancient island ferry, *Longfellow*, now a Casco Bay tourboat filled to heeling with mainland friends. Horns are blatting and heads are grinning and arms are waving and a helicopter is blathering close overhead. The sea is chopped up into disarray. The whole commotion mocks the absence of wind — everyone is just moving up and down. I am growing weary of smiling and waving. I sense a mood of aging anticipation. I feel like a poster that has sold out the house for a show that didn't make town.

More than an hour after leaving the dock, *Promise* is still in the harbor. The event is beginning to take on the air of a comedy. "How in hell can he sail around the world if he can't sail out of Portland Harbor?" "At this rate of speed, let's see, one knot for twenty-seven thousand nautical miles, it will take him one thousand one hundred twenty-five days. Dodge, old boy, we'll see you sometime before the end of the decade."

Ted Hood, *Promise*'s designer, succumbs to the strain of seeing his boat sit still and calls for one more assist from the *Susan Adams*. "Pick up another tow, Dodge," he calls, "it's getting late." Ernie throws his towline back to me, I make it fast, and *Promise* glides another half mile in the lobster boat's wake. I cast off Ernie's line for the final time just as *Promise* drifts over her official (if arbitrary) starting line off Portland Head Light at 1245 hours Eastern Standard Time. A cannon fires to mark the moment.

One by one, the boats of the spectator fleet file up the channel toward home. *Promise* and I are relieved to be without our audience. We are sailing slowly, still within sight of Cape Elizabeth, and I think I can see my house in the trees over the rocks, a home where I have not yet really lived because my *American Promise* dream has consumed me for the past two years.

I concentrate very hard to burn into my memory the last image I have of my family: Manny, Hoyt, and Kim, smiling together on the deck of the *Islander*. It will be so long before I see them again. My thoughts keep *Promise* and me from breaking away. I feel held in a powerful magnetic field cast by loved ones and land.

By sunset, only the empty sea is visible and *Promise* makes three knots on a light southeast breeze. I feel solemn, alone now and on my way, a hollowness in my gut, my mind swelling with the awareness that I have traded comfort and safety for the unknown.

Just as I think *Promise* and I are escaping the pull of the land, a chickadee flies on board and flits her way into the pilothouse with me. The little creature stares me straight in the eye, looking as apprehensive as I feel. She will not live long aboard the boat, I know, and I wonder if she can make the fifteen-mile flight back to land.

"None of us lives forever." I speak aloud for the first time since departing.

The night passes slowly with *Promise* in and out of the calms, her sails slapping and her masthead drawing lazy circles overhead. After a nap, I awake to find that the chickadee has gone. She has decided to try for it. I give her a spontaneous word, part toast, part prayer, and then turn my attention to the chart and the late weather briefing that Bob Rice gave me at DiMillo's dock.

I liked Rice from our first meeting, when I enlisted him for the planning stage of the voyage. Although it was his credentials that brought me to him — he had forecast the weather for Phil Weld, the winner of the 1980 OSTAR solo transatlantic race, for Joe Kittinger's epic balloon flight across the Atlantic, and for countless other ocean-racing sailors and America's Cup campaigners — it was his open self-confidence and dry sense of humor that really won me.

Rice also endeared himself to me by showing no qualms about my plan to sail alone, nonstop, around the world. He reacted as if such a voyage was both interesting and reasonable — a refreshing change from the oblique glances and patronizing smiles I had gotten from most people since making my plans public. Before our meeting, I had sent Rice strong evidence that those plans were serious. He got a ten-page specification for the voyage, including my own evaluations of my experience and capabilities, a seven-page specification for the design of the boat hull, rig, and layout, estimates for stores and supplies to be carried, and a computer analysis of wind directions and speeds over the proposed route.

A nonstop circumnavigation from Newport to Newport (my original planning port), sailing in an easterly direction on the traditional great circle sailing routes, is a voyage of just under 27,500 nautical miles. (One nautical mile equals 6,076 feet, so my voyage would be equivalent to 31,645 land or statute miles. All references to miles in this book are to nautical miles.) The traditional sailing route is taken from *Ocean Passages of the World*, published by the Hydrographer of the Navy (British, of course). This volume, in print since 1895 and still only in its second edition, is a treasure trove of precise global routes for sail and power vessels. It expresses firm conclusions on the seasonal climatologies of all navigable waterways and oceans and includes ample charts and maps and graphs, distances and sailing days and headings.

It is an astonishingly direct and honest book, as shown by this sentence describing a summer Indian Ocean crossing at the higher latitudes: "Tempestuous gales, sudden, violent and fitful shifts of wind, accompanied by hail or snow, and terrific and irregular seas are often encountered in the higher latitudes; moreover, the islands in the higher latitudes are frequently so shrouded in fog that often the first sign of their vicinity is the sound of the surf beating against them." Damned if this isn't a government publication written without bureaucratic language, disdaining qualification and caveats, and wallowing in judgments and conclusions, correct and romantic at the same time.

Using the traditional sailing routes from *Ocean Passages* as a guide, but taking into account the better windward performance of a modern sailing craft, I plotted courses on the U.S. Defense Mapping Agency Pilot Charts for the appropriate months. I then divided the trip into twenty-seven segments. Each segment was defined by relatively uniform wind conditions — that is, the wind speed and direction for the projected time of year were historically the same throughout the length of each segment when I would be sailing through. Course headings and distances were taken for

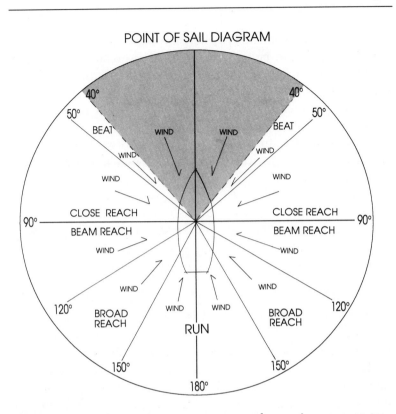

POINT OF SAIL DIAGRAM

these segments. A computer program was then written to compare the course heading and distance with the prevailing wind direction for each segment to project sailing conditions, particularly the number of miles to be sailed on each of the five points of sail. The point of sail is the angle of the wind over the boat when it is on course. The five points of sail are beating, close reaching, beam reaching, broad reaching, and running. The point-of-sail definitions I used for my computer analysis are as follows: Beating is sailing into the wind, 50 degrees off the bow or less; close reaching is sailing on a wind from 51 to 90 degrees from dead ahead; beam reaching is sailing on a wind that comes broad on the side from 91 to 120 degrees; broad reaching is sailing with a wind that comes over the boat from 121 to 150 degrees; and running is sailing with a following wind from 151 degrees to dead astern.

There is no matter more important to a sailor than the direction of the wind. The point-of-sail conditions to be met have a great bearing on almost all aspects of the voyage, from the selection of the route to hull and rig design. A boat designed to sail into the wind is going to be quite different from one designed to run with the wind. Of course, sailors regard a proper wind as one that is behind them. That's why they say "fair winds and following seas" to each other and admonish that "gentlemen do not sail to weather" (i.e., into the wind).

Taking the data from my wind analysis, I divided the circumnavigation into six logical passages. (All numbers are nautical miles.)

Point-of-Sail Summary for an Easterly Circumnavigation

PASSAGE	BEAT	CLOSE REACH	BEAM REACH	BROAD REACH	RUN	TOTAL NM
Newport–Equator	574	1,094	1,249	0	568	3,485
Equator–Cape of Good Hope	504	1,067	1,414	838	1,037	4,860
Good Hope–Tasmania	285	529	794	2,382	1,914	5,904
Tasmania–Cape Horn	328	429	791	1,870	1,772	5,190
Cape Horn–Equator	1,014	474	979	1,601	532	4,600
Equator–Newport	357	386	1,192	1,166	319	3,420
Total NM	3,062	3,979	6,419	7,857	6,142	27,459

For an easterly circumnavigation on the traditional sailing routes, then, I would travel 27,500 miles and have the wind behind the beam for a full 75 percent of those miles; only 25 percent of the voyage would be sailed on the wind. This would seem to be close to sailing bliss, but there are two very good reasons why such a voyage would be far from blissful: the doldrums and the Southern Oceans.

The dreaded calms of the doldrums occupy a moving, changing band of latitude across the Atlantic Ocean near the equator. It is where the contrary weather systems of the Northern and Southern hemispheres meet, called the intertropical convergence zone (ITCZ) by climatologists. Sailing ships have been known to be gripped in the vise of these calms for weeks at a time, and *Promise* would have to pass through them twice during her circumnavigation.

There are no travel folders promoting the Southern Oceans to tourists. Nothing I had read or heard made them sound anything less than intimidating to a sailor. For fifteen thousand miles, the Southern Oceans encircle the world unimpeded by landmasses, driven into enormous seas and gale-force winds by a relentless march of storms attacking from the west. These are the latitudes of the "roaring forties" and "ferocious fifties," aptly named by the comparatively few sailors who have ventured there. *Promise* would sail more than eleven thousand miles of the Southern Oceans, crossing the Indian Ocean and the Southern Pacific Ocean and passing south of their five notorious capes: Cape of Good Hope, South Africa; Cape Leeuwin, Australia; Southeast Cape, Tasmania; South Cape, New Zealand, and Cape Horn, South America.

Few sailors have passed south of these great capes, fewer still have done so alone, and only a couple have sailed below them alone and nonstop.

The first man history records as having circumnavigated the world alone under sail was Joshua Slocum, a Canadian turned American, who left Boston, Massachusetts, on April 24, 1895, in the thirty-six-foot yawl *Spray* and returned on June 27, 1898. By 1983, about eighty-five solo sailors had circumnavigated, according to D. H. "Nobby" Clarke, the Englishman who authenticates sailing exploits for *The Guinness Book of World Records*.

The first sailor to circumnavigate without stopping was the Englishman Robin Knox-Johnston. He sailed from Falmouth, England, and returned in 313 days in the thirty-two-foot gaff-rigged wooden ketch *Suhaili* and was the only finisher of nine starters in the Golden Globe race of 1968–69. In fact, he was one of only three sailors in that race who got as far as the Southern Oceans. Another, Donald Crowhurst, was so afraid of those waters that he remained in the South Atlantic sailing circles off South America. He radioed false positions and kept two schizophrenic ship's logs, an accurate one going nowhere and a false one documenting a sail around the world. While the world believed he was sailing a competitive race, Crowhurst went mad and finally stepped from his boat into the sea.

In 1982–83, the BOC Challenge, another solo around-the-world race, began and ended in Newport, Rhode Island, with scheduled stops in Cape Town, Sydney, and Rio de Janeiro. Seventeen boats started this race and ten finished. Two sailors didn't reach the Southern Oceans and five didn't succeed in crossing them. Two boats were torn apart at sea and sunk; two were driven ashore with one of those lost.

The winner of that race was the Frenchman Philippe Jeantot, who sailed his lightweight fifty-six-foot aluminum cutter, *Crédit Agricole,* to a record 159 days, 2 hours, and 6 minutes. (Times given for circumnavigations include sailing times only; time taken for stops is not counted.) Jeantot bettered the record of his fellow countryman Alain Colas by nine days. Sailing without the benefit of a race in 1973–74, in his sixty-seven-foot trimaran *Manureva,* Colas had stopped only once, in Australia.

Curiously, the solo nonstop record, 292 days, was a different order of magnitude. It was set in 1970–71 by the Englishman Chay Blyth. Blyth sailed in the westerly direction, definitely the more difficult one, and rounded all but one of the five great southern capes.

I had puzzled over the huge difference in times for single-handed circumnavigations with stopovers compared to those without, 159 days of sailing to 292 days. One explanation was that so few sailors had succeeded in completing a nonstop voyage. Nobby Clarke had recorded only eight true single-handed nonstop circumnavigations as of 1985: Robin Knox-Johnston, Bernard Moitessier, and Nigel Tetley in 1968–69, Chay Blyth in 1970–71, Henry Jaskula in 1979–80, Leslie Powles in 1980–81, Wilfried Erdmann in 1984–85, and, possibly, Peter Freeman in 1984–85. Nearly a hundred sailors had made it around with stops as of 1985.

Other obvious reasons for the difference, I thought, would be the need for the nonstop sailor to conserve strength, to take fewer risks so as not to damage the boat critically, and to sail a heavier boat, with a larger supply of stores and spare parts. There was also powerful evidence that solo sailors lose their competitive edge after a long time at sea, particularly without the benefit of a race. They assume the what-the-hell attitude of a person who has lost his drive and sense of time.

It seemed reasonable to me that it would be difficult for anyone to continue performing at a high level over a long period of time without some outside praise or encouragement. A psychologist once asked me, "How many times do you think a tight end would cut hard and stretch out for the football if he were invisible to the fans?"

Based on what I felt were sensible criteria, my original target for a solo nonstop circumnavigation was 180 days at an average speed of about six and a quarter knots. When I mentioned that target to people who had reason to know something about the subject — circumnavigators, naval architects, and sailing historians — the responses ranged from "very ambitious" to "physically cannot be done" to "you're nuts." As a result, I changed my target arbitrarily to less than 220 days and I signaled my resolve by ordering the number "211" for *Promise*'s mainsail.

Sunrise breaks on a gray and rainy first day at sea. Rice's short-term weather forecast is spread on top of the charts in front of me. The barely legible scrawl, hurried in the frenzy of departure, tells me to expect some heavy wind as a frontal system passes, then clearing with high pressure for half a day, and then the threat of some major storm centers meandering down from the Grand Banks off Newfoundland.

My course from Portland is east-southeast, passing sixty miles below Cape Sable, the southernmost tip of Nova Scotia, to a waypoint in the middle of the North Atlantic at 34° north latitude and 45° west longitude. At that point, I should be far enough east to pass by the calms prevalent in the Azores high pressure zone and put the high's clockwise circulating wind behind me as I head south-southeast to cross the equator at 26° west longitude. "The wind to your back," as sailors say.

On this first morning, however, *Promise* and I have the wind rising and the seas lifting right on our starboard bow, a chilly, bumpy beat into the weather that has me wearing a sweater under heavy foul weather gear and eating hot oatmeal. And for some reason I am continually sleepy. Even the cold sting of mixed rain and spray fails to keep me alert. By noon, the wind is thirty-five knots and the seas ten feet. Lightning splits the eastern horizon. *Promise* slams heavily into the waves at speeds ranging up to ten knots. In spite of our limp start, we sail 172 miles in our first day, noon to noon.

I am worried, though, because the two autopilots are operating erratically. Neither one, Murphy or Carlos, likes the heavy going, and I am forced to stay close to one of the two helms to steer the boat when a pilot loses control. I begin to run on granola bars and nervous energy.

By midnight of day 2 we are in a whole gale. I struggle to stay awake and steer the boat and don't have time to think through the autopilot problems, much less fix them. At 0400, I am nodding at the inside helm when an abrupt change in the boat's motion jerks me alert. Instinctively I rush out on deck and look up. I am stunned. *Promise*'s big headsail has disappeared. The stay is still there, but the sail is gone. Gone. Then I notice a white flag lying over the leeward lifeline at the bow and a huge white snake squirming in the wake. The sail is dragging its eighty-foot length in the sea behind us, holding to the bow by one corner, the tack. My mouth goes dry with the premonition of what I see next, one of the sights I have feared the most. The jib halyard and the upper assembly of the sail's roller furling system are high above me, at the top of the mast. I must climb the mast to retrieve them.

This is the one job that has intimidated me more than any other. I must pull myself up eighty feet over the ocean while the boat is pitching and wallowing in heavy seas. This would be a difficult enough feat for an experienced mountain climber; I have only practiced it at a mooring in a quiet harbor.

Promise is lugging through the water like a log. The drag from the huge jib takes all the life from her, in spite of thirty-five knots of wind in the mainsail. Getting the jib back aboard takes instant priority. I furl the main to kill our way. The autopilots seem to operate reliably at the slower speed, which, even with no sail, remains nearly two knots in this gale.

I struggle to haul the 1,300-square-foot, 285-pound sail out of the sea a few inches at a time. The water pulls against me as if we were in a tug-of-war. Several times I consider cutting the $6,000 sail loose, but I keep hauling because no amount of money can get me another sail out here. It takes two hours to get it lashed down on deck with a web of line. When the job is complete, the sail and I are both red, the sail from *Promise*'s bottom paint, I from the effort.

I see the fitting that failed — a snap shackle, a quick-release piece of hardware that holds the peak of the sail to the halyard. A roll pin, a small piece of stainless sheet metal rolled into a pin shape and forced into a hole through a threaded bolt and barrel, has somehow disintegrated. The fancy shackle has unscrewed itself and screwed me. I learn again that knots are better than fancy fittings.

As I examine the sail for tears, I wonder what the fates are telling me. Is this the way the whole trip is going to be? Only two days into a seven-month voyage, and I'm already faced with two serious problems. A critical operating system, the autopilot, goes undependable the first day and a halyard parts on the second. I will never make it like this. I had so hoped for the first few weeks to be easy, to break me in slowly.

It's time to climb the mast. As I contemplate this dreaded trip, I am hit hard by homesickness. Oh, how I envy all those people back there, sitting in comfort at their desks and dinner tables, their worlds tacitly under control, problems postponable, threats softly vague. For the first time, for one sickening, fleeting moment, I sense the shadow of failure.

Waiting for my pulse rate to get back to normal and my sweat to dry from hauling the jib aboard, I stare up at the mast and plan how to scale this peak. All the gear I need is stowed in a large plastic tub in the aftermost compartment. There is a bosun's chair, a three-part tackle with four hundred feet of three-eighths-inch line, a mountain climber's Jumar ascender line clamp, a two-foot section of sail luff tape with grommets punched in it, and a large, two-handled canvas bag. I wonder whatever possessed me not to insist that steps be built on this mast.

Midmorning on day three, I am ready to climb. The wind has abated to ten knots and veered south, but lumpy seas roll the boat and whip the masthead over a fifteen-foot arc. It looks like a very rough ascent. As I make my way across the cockpit with an armful of tools, I hear the aft movie camera trigger in automatic mode. The sound infuriates me. I don't like to be peeped at, particularly not now. I know filmmaker Chris Knight would want me to carry a camera aloft with me, to record my climb for his documentary. The thought of it makes me laugh. I remember when a United Press bureau chief once told me that he paid three bucks for pictures, four bucks if the parachute didn't open. I also remember that Steve Callahan watched as water filled his holed boat and shorted out the circuitry, automatically turning on *his* Chris Knight camera to film the sinking. Will there ever be a documentary about *Promise?* I wonder.

I lay the gear out in the cockpit and check every line, every fitting. Then I raise the tackle to the masthead on a spare main halyard; it will give me some mechanical advantage while lifting my weight. I lash the Jumar ascender, a kind of hand-operated jam cleat, to my bosun's chair; it will put a handle on my hauling line and hold me in place, hands free, as I pause during the climb. I then lash the section of sail luff tape to the chair; it will ride up the mast in the groove for the main trysail (a storm sail), stopping me from swinging away from the mast like a pendulum. This is vital because the mast is too big for me to lock my legs around it. The canvas bag will stow the extra hauling line as I gather it in during the climb. It would be easier to allow the line to drop to the deck, but if it snagged around something I would be trapped aloft. I buckle myself into the chair, pull on the gear and pocket the tools, and look up. The climbing rig sways back and forth against the boat's motion. I start the climb.

Haul, clamp, stuff line, pause, check gear, haul, clamp, stuff. A half hour of this work and I am at the first mast spreaders, about twenty-five feet above the deck, sweating heavily and jerking on my short tether like a man having a violent fit. My legs are bruised from the slamming on the mast. One shoe has dropped off and a toenail has been bloodied.

Haul, clamp, stuff line, pause, check gear, haul. I leave the relatively safe perch on the spreaders and look only up as I climb. The higher I reach, the wilder the motion, and the wilder the motion, the harder the work. The upper spreaders are a welcome haven, providing a platform for a rest. Just twenty-five feet more to climb.

I begin to time my hauls with the wave troughs, and as I look, one wave becomes curiously circular, turns dark gray, and then shows a huge eye. The damned thing blows and rolls over and, I swear, grins at me not ten feet off my port bow. I can't help but grin back at the whale. I must be a comical sight, dangling up here like a puppet being jerked around by an angry child.

When I look back to haul, the trigger of my ascender jams, and in the struggle to free it I watch, fascinated, as a fingernail lifts painlessly from a finger and drops down to the deck. The finger is slippery with new blood. While sucking it clean, I realize it would pay to hurry. The bag of line swaying under me is getting heavy. But the heavy-rod standing rigging is coming within reach as it closes in at the top of the mast.

My tackle is two-blocked before I reach the masthead. The halyard has worked down more than a foot, and I can't reach my target on the forward side of the mast while in the bosun's chair. I wiggle out of it to free climb the rest of the way. The rod shrouds are close enough to the mast now for me to get my hands on them. Hanging on is very tough work: I am a nuisance the mast wants to flick away.

My legs are pretzeled around one rod shroud. I free one hand and stretch toward the errant halyard and swivel assembly. Half a dozen times I try to lasso the thing. Finally I get it and make it fast to a spare hundred-foot length of line. The boat is small under me and the horizon is far away. I don't like the view.

I begin the trip down without delay. The ascender is more difficult to operate descending and my fingers take more punishment. But the trip down is faster and easier; it takes only fifteen minutes. Back on the stable platform of the deck, I am very unsteady on my legs but do not pause to rest. I haul the upper swivel assembly back down to the deck on my long lasso — and get some bad news. The foredeck pedestal winch — used to raise *Promise*'s big headsails — is jammed. But I can't stop this job now, and I raise the sail with a makeshift rig of snatchblocks to a winch on the mast. This takes me half an hour, running back and forth from the headstay to the winch.

With the big sail back on, *Promise* leans back with the wind and accelerates to eight knots. I realize that two and a half hours have passed since I lifted off the deck. I also notice that I am beat up and bloody and sore and sweating and breathing hard and thirsty as hell and not at all feeling like a victory celebration.

My special reward for this day's hard work is company. First, a school of bottle-nose dolphins surrounds *Promise*, squirting, bouncing, coughing in formation with her. Next, we are buzzed twice by the Canadian Air Force in a twin-engine prop airplane. Then the air force leaves me to watch whales in a magnificent spouting and belly-flopping display I can see a mile north.

Curiously, I am not cheered by all this, but saddened. It reminds me of the companionship I don't have and I find myself dropping into a hole of loneliness. I am aware that I am now coming to be owned by my problems — rigging failure, jammed winch, malfunctioning autopilots, sleep deprivation, bloodied appendages, and sore muscles.

The next three days are the worst of my life as I am slowly hammered into the shape of failure. I am struck repeatedly by small defeats, and each new one seems to hit me while I am still stunned from the last. The wind is up to forty knots, with gusts to fifty. The seas are ten to twelve feet high and breaking green water over the deck, filling the cockpit faster than the scuppers can empty it.

Autopilot Murphy goes out again while I am nodding at the helm, and *Promise* falls downwind into a flying jibe that parts the main boom preventer and tears a foot-long hole in the mainsail. The computerized alarm, designed to set off buzzers with selected changes in wind speed, wind direction, boat speed, and boat heading, becomes useless because it buzzes all the time from false alerts. The port-tack wind indicator fails. The mainsheet traveler, two massive cars on a track bolted to the top of the pilothouse, flies apart, showing the fitting's weak link: four small metal straps holding the huge hunks of hardware together.

But it is my futile struggle with the autopilots that really chips away at my self-confidence. In these heavy conditions, they both show the same random, intermittent operation. They will steer the boat for no more than half the time and shut down completely and without warning the other half.

Once more I read the manuals and learn nothing helpful. Once more I replace a component of the system to find that nothing changes — control heads, sensing compass, pump set, rudder feedback assembly. Once more I run through the hydraulic plumbing, looking in vain for leaks or incorrect valve positions or anything unusual. I have to cycle my time: sail for two hours, heave to for thirty minutes. I navigate and eat and read equipment service manuals during the sailing time and nap, cook, and attempt repairs while hove to.

I decide to try the emergency mechanical autopilot, Manny, named for my wife because she is always at the helm when we sail the old schooner together. But Manny doesn't live up to her name and is a smoking pile of junk within a few hours. I go back to Murphy, whose operation is now erratic as well as intermittent.

Promise is careening along on a close reach under reefed main-sail alone. We are in a whole gale, but the weather is the least of my problems. The boat cannot run effectively single-handed over long periods of time without reliable self-steering. I know I can't go on with the voyage, but I can't bring myself to admit it. That, by God, is the measure of the emotional pain that has transformed me into a waking death. I can't admit my defeat to myself even as I am so clearly aware of it. Everything in me rejects the failure.

I am shocked by my reflection in the mirror below. It is not a determined, clear-eyed, young adventurer I see but a fifty-three-year-old man the color of despair. What has happened to those years? The dream, the dream has not grown old and ugly as I have.

2

*T*he decision to quit and sail *Promise* to Bermuda is made — or perhaps, more correctly, is recognized — six days after leaving Portland. I am 603 miles from Bermuda, 1,075 from the Azores, and 781 from Portland. I have actually made the turn toward Bermuda before I can acknowledge that this is without question the most difficult decision I have ever made in my life. I feel like a complete fool as well as a failure. All those years of dreaming and all those months of preparation and all the efforts of so many others — and here *Promise* and I sail from Maine to Bermuda, a passage that has been accomplished by a guy on a sailboard!

This defeat makes a mockery of my whole life, I feel. The only way I can accept the decision, the only way I can write down the latitude and longitude of Bermuda and plot a course there, is to make myself another promise:

"You will start again, Dodge. You will start again if you have to row the sonofabitch around," reads my log. As I become more and more deprived of sleep, however, I am drawn further and further into my dejection, mindlessly and masochistically role-playing the future of the loser I know I have become. When I seek relief from this agony, it is in daydreams of the past.

From an early age, I was surrounded by boats I could not use. I worked on other people's boats at my uncle's boatyard in Harwich Port, Massachusetts. That was what a male member of my family got to do in the summers. My brother Russ worked there, too, and so did my grandfather, John "Cap" Dodge. Russ, fourteen years older than I, really filled the role of my father, who died when

I was two. He and Cap were my male role models, and no one ever had anyone more male than they. I worshiped Russ. He was handsome, strong, athletic, decisive, competent in so many ways, and headstrong and combative and hell-raising, too. Cap simply was hell-bent and eccentric. He drank hard, did all the male things hard. And he spoke in maxims. "Whiskey drinking's a man's duty, getting drunk is his damnation," he would say. "Money's simple. If you've got ten dollars and what you want costs nine, you're wealthy. If what you want costs eleven, you're broke." "My father taught me how to work, not to like it." "The four most beautiful things in the world are a ship under sail, a full bottle of rum, a woman's body, and a field of wheat."

I spent a great deal of time in the shadows of Russ and Cap, watching others sail off and wishing I could. I used my boatyard pay to rent a small catboat an hour's walk up the coast, and what I loved most about the sailing was to go alone beyond the tether. And the tether grew longer as I grew older and more experienced. The seeds of solo sailing were planted deep.

The schooner *Coaster* and I were both thirty years old when we met in 1963. The first coasting-type schooner yacht designed by the world-renowned, traditional yacht designer Murray G. Peterson, she was launched in 1931, when Murray was just twenty-three. Murray's boats were like his life, beautiful poems of individuality and truth and conviction and kindness. In the two and a half years *Coaster* and I lived together — and in that time I never slept ashore — she taught me bluewater sailing, shorthanded sailing, and solo sailing. She also ignited in me the dream of one day making a very significant sail alone with a boat built specifically for the job. It was a dream that burned in me over the years and became a promise that I knew I had to keep. By 1983, the vague old dream had evolved into a hardened, precise decision to sail alone around the world without stopping.

Six years after my affair with *Coaster,* following a short career as a writer and three glorious years working with a man who became my mentor in the business world, I was back working for myself. Bob McCray, my mentor, hired me in the first place because I gave him no option. He certainly didn't hire me for my résumé, which read like a work of fiction: college split by a five-year air force stint, eleven months as a reporter for the *Anchorage*

Daily News, three years doing advertising work in Alaska's oil industry, two and a half years sailing *Coaster,* a year of writing that was largely unpublished. I was in my mid-thirties and not especially marketable — except to myself and McCray. I worked like hell for McCray and took from him all I could of his knowledge and understanding of business matters. He was as enthusiastic a teacher as I was a student. He even gave me my own laboratory, an electronics manufacturing division of his Worcester Controls Corporation. The fact that this division was ill conceived and deeply troubled only enhanced the value of his gift for me. But my real opportunity came when his board of directors convinced him he had to get rid of the division and I got the job of selling it. I bought it instead and set up shop in a garage with three employees.

Controlonics Corporation was a textbook example of the ultimate power of determination and persistence, a testament to the Woody Allen adage that "ninety percent of life is showing up." The company was started with $10,000 of capital, $20,000 of debt to a silent partner, and one product, a voice scrambler for use on two-way police radios. Our total sales in the first year were $127,000. It took three years to break a half million in annual sales. But, growing on the cash from earnings only, no bank loans and no recapitalizations, Controlonics passed $20 million in sales, with two hundred employees, by the time it was ten years old. We made the *Inc.* magazine list of fastest-growing American companies and were extremely profitable. The company was a wonderful and exciting world unto itself and my years there were all encompassing.

It was also solid proof, in all the traditional ways businesses measure success, that we were correct in our operating philosophies: Focus everyone's attention personally and intensely and positively on the customer as our products and services relate to him. Constantly measure our performance against that of our competitors. Forever fight to simplify procedures and systems and slay the dragon of bureaucracy. Do not allow the trappings of rank within the company, starting with no private offices. Celebrate frugality, yet give people the best tools to do their job. Encourage an open environment in which people say what they mean with due attention to the opinions and feelings of others. Decentralize decision making, putting the authority where the knowledge is. Foster an atmosphere of honesty, integrity, and ability in which people make commitments and keep them. Do not require conformity. Have fun at work, with relevant hijinks and eccentric celebrations. Remind one another that people are fundamentally honest and compassionate and have the same desires for success. Share the material fruits of the company's success with everyone in the company.

Twelve years after the start in the garage, I decided to sell Controlonics, the principal reason being so I could carry out my old dream. The company was growing rapidly, was extraordinarily profitable, and possessed a gorgeous balance sheet. I knew then that I would be able to make my solo sail first class and became purposeful in my planning.

The company was sold in 1984. As often in my life, I was astounded by my good luck. I have known men with the desire, but not the means, to sail around the world alone, and I have known other men with the means to do it but not the desire. And here I was with both. Money was certainly needed in order to build a special, one-of-a-kind, around-the-world sailboat. The next two years were to immerse me in a period of intense preparation that included a major restructuring of my life. They culminated with *American Promise*.

In the fall of 1983 I began my rounds, speaking to naval architects and sailboat designers and listening carefully to their reaction to my seventeen-page treatise describing the voyage and the single-purpose, no-compromise boat that would accomplish it. The treatise began:

"The objective is to accomplish a solo, nonstop, easterly circumnavigation by sail in 180 to 220 days. The boat design challenges are implicit: A boat to bear the rigors of six months' continuous sailing in varied weather conditions, much of it heavy; a boat to average 6.25 knots or better over that span of time; a boat that will match the age and physical condition of the skipper; a boat that will accept the required stores and equipment and kindly give up those stores one day at a time; a boat that has as few structural and mechanical weak links as possible; a boat that is planned with redundancy in key systems and equipment; a boat that uses mechanical and electrical advantages, proven engineering solutions, yet can be sailed without them."

I contacted Guy Ribadeau Dumas, the young French architect who had designed the boat that then held the solo circumnavigating record, *Crédit Agricole*, winner of the 1982–83 BOC Challenge, in which she was sailed so well by Philippe Jeantot. *Crédit* was a very light-displacement (twenty-two thousand pounds), fifty-six-foot aluminum cutter. She depended on proper placement of seawater ballast to sail well and remain stable; tanks on either side of the boat, each holding four thousand pounds of seawater, were filled to keep her upright sailing on the wind and in trim sailing off the wind. The boat had a lofty rig, and the headsails and mainsail could be reefed by the single sailor from the cockpit.

Although there was much I admired about *Crédit*, I was wary of her light displacement, both because I had been brought up in the "heavier is better at sea" school and because a light boat would have difficulty carrying the supplies required for a nonstop circumnavigation. I was also wary of the whole idea of water ballast.

By the time I finished my dialogue with Dumas in Paris (slowed but not halted by our language barrier), I also knew that *Crédit* had had trouble tracking straight when sailing downwind in the heavy Southern Oceans conditions. And I knew that Dumas would design me a boat very much like *Crédit*, an ultralight aluminum boat with some hull, keel, and rudder changes to improve heavy downwind work. My own provincialism and age bias left me feeling less enthusiastic about the very young-looking designer after our meeting. (When Dumas first introduced himself, I actually asked if I could see his father, thinking that the boy before me couldn't possibly be the famous yacht designer I had crossed an ocean to meet.) He did get my full attention, however, when he said he could promise to deliver in France a completed boat, rigged and ready to sail, in six months for less than 350,000 American bucks.

Germain Frers, the internationally acclaimed designer from Argentina, spoke flawless English and met me in Newport. He was handsome, graceful, sophisticated, and accommodating, but acted irritatingly preoccupied during our visit. He may have been put off by my abundant enthusiasm and bluster. But there were other reasons for his inattention to me and my concerns. Our waitress at lunch insisted that he was a movie star and, despite his denials, organized a gawking and guessing contest among the patrons and help. And a Newport sailing type stopped our conversation again when he accosted Frers on the street for some classic celebrity treatment.

There was no question in my mind that Frers could design a first-rate boat, that he would build the boat wherever it suited me, and that he would integrate my wishes into it, but I couldn't pin him down hard on his concept of what the right boat would be. I would suggest light, and he would amiably agree. Then I would propose heavy, and he would again agree. I was beginning to sense something wrong in my pursuit of these big-name sailboat designers. Maybe it was too feverishly intense. Maybe our first meeting was weighed down too much with heavily worded documents and statistical analyses. Maybe I was expecting more than I should from these men.

Bill Peterson was a friend and the son of a friend, *Coaster*'s designer Murray Peterson, and he designed boats himself. Bill signed on early to work as my technical representative for the design and construction of *Promise*. His role was to be the tough one of playing devil's advocate on a team of strong-willed people, and it would put him on the firing line in a year when personal tragedy battered him with a vengeance. I knew that Bill wanted the design job but also that he, as a friend, did not want me to risk the voyage in the first place. This negative attitude, ironically born of friendship, made him the wrong man to design the boat but just the right man to play the adversarial role. While he was testing the attitudes and interest of several more top American designers, I was getting to know F. E. "Ted" Hood in Marblehead, Massachusetts.

I was introduced to Hood by Per Hoel, a mutual friend. Hood and Hoel fit together as opposites often do, and it sure as hell took both of them for me to decide that Hood would be the designer of *Promise*. Our first meeting on this project was prelude. Per talked. Ted grunted. I listened or delivered short sermons. And we got on together just fine.

Ted Hood talks little, and when he does it is about things, particularly things having to do with boats and sails. Per Hoel talks about people and does so skillfully and incessantly. Ted is a graceful bear of a man; Per is precise and meticulous. Ted takes no notes; Per writes down or tape-records every thought he has in a meeting. Ted is direct, sometimes ponderously so; Per can be cal-

culating and manipulative. To Ted, *Promise* was an interesting design project that should be started immediately to make the target
schedule; he was scribbling sketches by himself at our first meeting.
Per, like Bill Peterson, did not want me to attempt this voyage and
said so. It was not a project to him but the life of a friend being
placed at risk.

"Please do not go," he said simply. "You have enough money
to do anything you want to do and do not have to prove yourself.
Buy one of Ted's seventy-five-footers, hire a crew and tutors, and
cruise the islands of the world with Manny and the kids."

"Get off it, Per, I'm going," I told him. "No more contrary
advice, please. It's time to be with me on this matter or be gone."

He was with me, just as I knew he had to be. And the role he
played between Ted and me was not delicate. Although into the
project up to his skin head, Per periodically reminded us that he
wanted no responsibility for results, no blame. Ted did not carry
the burden of anyone's life on his mind. People are supposed to
take care of their own lives. He had a boat to make.

And there are predictable elements of a boat designed by Ted
Hood. It will have medium to heavy displacement and be shaped
underwater like a whale, round and full with clean, unbroken lines,
a delight to the eye. Ted believes in the power of engineering to
solve a problem, almost any problem, but at the same time he is
intuitive and empirical rather than theoretical. He has an absolute
belief in his own judgment, and he will, on occasion, emphasize
his confidence with displays of temper that are almost pyrotech-
nical, his huge arms and hands waving wildly overhead, his body
crouched as if ready to spring, his eyes wide and blazing, his voice
up an octave. Ted is not a trendy man in any way, nor is he a
contrarian. He simply operates on a gyro of his own, and if you
do not agree with him, then, in his words, "you just do not understand."

Hood brings some major assets to a design challenge. One of
them is the depth of his design experience in the three fundamental
aspects of sailboat performance: hull, rig, and sails. Another is the
huge number of hours he has spent sailing boats. He began his
professional career as a sailmaker, adding engineering value to an
old art and becoming in a short time the dominant sailmaker in
the world. He brought the same engineering thrust to the design of
spars and sail handling systems, and he became one of the world's

leading manufacturers of roller furling and reefing systems for headsails and mainsails.

He began designing hulls when he was still in short pants and became a true professional in 1959, when he was thirty and launched his first and very successful racing machine, *Robin*. With Ted at the helm, *Robin* was still winning races in the eighties. Subsequent Hood designs include the two twelve-meter yachts *Nefertiti* and *Independence,* a redesign of the America's Cup defender *Courageous,* and the Little Harbor line of luxury sailing yachts. As a sailor, Ted Hood has filled a room with more than a hundred trophies. But as a sailmaker, a more significant experience to him, he sailed trials on perhaps a thousand different boats from a hundred different designers.

He began designing *Promise* at his Little Harbor yard in June of 1984. My goal of a mid-October 1985 departure became the fixed moment from which all schedules and events flowed backward. We selected May 1, 1985, as the launch date for this not-yet-designed sailboat. The skeptics howled. They were silenced on a high tide on May 7, 1985, when *American Promise* hit the water for sea trials just six days late. A boat-building miracle was witnessed. But the miracle did not come easy, and the eleven months between the design assignment and the launching stretched the capabilities and tempers of many men and pulled at the fabric of several lives.

The question of how much this boat should weigh, the displacement, arose immediately and became the continuing storm center of the design process. Whenever a major conflict flared anew over some aspect of the design, it could be traced almost directly to the disagreement over weight. When you think of it, it's not surprising because, particularly for a single-handed boat, weight relates to sail area (and the relative difficulty of sail handling), to carrying capacity, to boat speed in different wind conditions, and to seakindliness. Ted wanted a heavy boat for the job, whereas Bill Peterson led the fight for light, certainly the more popular position in an age of ultralight racing machines. I argued light to Ted and heavy to Bill. It was my job to sweat out the evidence from each of them and test the resolve behind their stands.

"A light boat can't carry the stores and spares you'll need for that prolonged a voyage," said Ted.

"A heavy boat will require huge sails and a big rig and I'm

afraid will be too much for one man to handle in heavy conditions or when there is gear failure," said Bill.

"Roller reefing headsails and a Stoway roller reefing main will allow Dodge to handle the sails for the right-size boat," said Ted.

"A big, heavy boat will be dead in light airs . . . it will give Dodge a slow circumnavigation," said Bill.

"A well-designed heavy boat will be faster than a light one in light airs and more comfortable, if not as fast, in heavy wind," Ted said. This was the surprise statement that I would remember so very well in the doldrums a year and a half later.

Bill wanted a relatively light, deep, narrow hull. He wanted a boat that could be easily driven with sails small enough for one man to handle in a blow without depending on roller reefing systems. He warned, too, that weight costs money and adds man-hours of building time and invites complexity; ultimately, it could jeopardize the very tight schedule. He argued his case with the grim resignation of a man who, convinced he is right, senses he is outgunned. He quoted the specifications of recent successful single-handed boats. He unreeled a study, called TREP-Line (Time Related and Equivalent Performance), which analyzed long passages at sea by a large number of sailing vessels over a long span of time to determine key variables in performance. He concluded that ideally, *Promise* should displace about thirty thousand pounds to accomplish the nonstop voyage in less than two hundred and twenty days. But he took his stand at forty-five thousand pounds, feeling, perhaps, that his only hope was to lighten up Hood's fifty-thousand-plus thinking, and for that he needed an easier number to sell.

The interpreter and translator of Ted's design ideas, his drafting arm, and his alter ego was Ted Fontaine, a young design school graduate who had spent his entire professional career with Hood. Fontaine had learned well how to measure his mentor in matters of design, mood, and strength of conviction. And he knew how to use this knowledge to play to his boss, even, on occasion, getting his own way. His defense against Hood's heavy and inflexible creative dominance was a cavalier insouciance, an abrupt rudeness that Ted often found humorous.

It was Fontaine's work on the drawing board that communicated the mind's eye of Hood to Bill and me. I was fascinated as the form emerged in soft, graceful lines from Fontaine's pencil. The only hard angles were at the bow and stern, which rose up sharply to give the hull almost as much length on the waterline as it had on deck. Much attention was also paid to track this hull straight when running in heavy wind and big seas, a requirement I emphasized after my talks with the designer of *Crédit Agricole*. Her forward sections were shallow and round so that she would not dig in and trip and broach when surfing or exceeding hull speed down the backs of large seas. Her aftersections, however, were slightly V'd to stabilize her stern. The fin keel was oversize, sixteen feet in cord length and smoothly raked on the forward edge — partly, I was sure, because I had asked that she be able to strike and ride over a submerged shipping container at eight knots. The rudder was balanced, with the rudder blade on both sides of the rudder post and as far aft as it could be placed. And on one drawing, between the keel and the rudder, were sketched three fins spearing down like triple pelvics on a fish. The center fin was an intermediate centerboard that, when lowered its full four and a half feet, became an emergency or second rudder. It was flanked on each side by daggerboards angled out at twenty-two degrees, which could be lowered to a depth of four feet. The drawing told me that this was a shape that would move easily and only in one direction.

We began our Wednesday meetings in July with Ted, Per, Bill, Fontaine, and me. They were supposed to be design review sessions for "the owner" but soon became the key communications event for the project internally as well as externally. *Promise* had obviously come to dominate the Hood design office. These meetings were played against a backdrop of resolute war waged by Bill to influence Ted to reduce *Promise*'s displacement. But other battles and skirmishes flared continuously, almost as if to give an innocent relief valve to the tension that was to be expected in a project of such dimension and haste. We battled over the use and placement of deck hatches and got Ted to allow for two forward of the cockpit. We skirmished over titanium or stainless steel for the six-inch-diameter main rudder post; the titanium won on what had become a common procedure of opting for the lower risk rather than the lower cost. (The titanium post cost almost twice what I paid for my precious schooner *Eagle* in 1969.) We fought over calculations on ballast ratio and the size and shape of the keel and ended up with a proposed ratio of three to one and a deep keel with an erotic, flared, bulb shape, the sight of which might bring some ladies to a blush. We battled over the demand for electricity and options for charging, over the storage and amount of diesel fuel required for a two-hundred-twenty-day voyage, over calculations on the flotation from the five watertight compartments, over mast height and sail area and lifelines and antenna tower and righting moment, and we argued over arguing itself.

On and on the battles raged. Between them were periods of enthusiastic peace, and through it all, almost always, Ted enigmatically followed the course he had already chosen, his instinct, his gyre. What we were getting for a boat was clearly very special, requiring more and more design time and planning and technical analysis. The project was becoming alarmingly complex.

It was not unusual for Ted to inadvertently disarm a sullen mood with one of his famed displays of temper. He does not like to be opposed but likes even less being ignored. One of those times came on a Wednesday when we were all in a sullen mood. The problems had to do with *Promise*'s pilothouse, and some key decisions had not been made because no one was yet committed enough to sell the others. It was a grumpy group walking through a wet, late summer easterly wind to the "White House," Hood's design office, after lunch.

Ted was mumbling mostly to himself about why the pilothouse windshield should be slanted in reverse, with the bottom in and the top of the window out, the way it is on some modern trawlers. Suddenly I realized that his temper had snapped. He had fallen into his wild-eyed, arm-waving crouch and was running in speed bursts up to and back from an office window and bellowing, "Can't you understand that I can see almost nothing from back here and almost everything from up here!" The rest of us clustered and gave him, finally, our rapt attention. He was showing us how much his field of view increased when he was close to the window. He was showing us the value of reverse-slanting a windshield.

What Ted didn't see that we did, however, was the panic of the secretary seated just inside the window, who obviously assumed she was somehow playing an active role in his wild demonstration. Bill erupted in laughter, and he ignited the rest of us. The tension deflated. By the time we climbed back to the second-floor conference room, decisions were popping, and Ted, whose temper cools as fast as it heats up, had determined to add another character to our cast. Paul Wolter, for nearly twenty years the captain of the *Palawan* yachts designed by Sparkman and Stevens for IBM's chairman, Tom Watson, would be brought to Little Harbor to build a full-size mock-up of the cockpit and pilothouse. Thus ended the crisis of the pilothouse, which became the best-designed such area I have ever seen on a single-handed boat.

I had rented an apartment overlooking Marblehead Harbor's town landing to be close to the Little Harbor yard and to deal in solitude with the myriad other preparations for the voyage, such as food, clothing, medical supplies, tools, spare parts, charts, and electronic equipment. These should be jobs for me to do alone, I thought, because I needed the practice.

I like to practice, to role-play anticipated important events over and over in my mind until the actual event becomes almost déjà vu. I had gotten by the terrifying late night awakenings that immediately followed my commitment to begin preparations for the voyage; I would sit bolt upright in a world of my imagination, alone at sea, not connected to others by space or time, and exhausted, always, by the losing battle to keep a boat afloat. Those nightmares shocked me for four months. Do you know what the hell you're doing? they demanded.

In those days, I had no allies in the real world, either, not even in my family. Manny chose then to agree with her motherly instincts, which told her my voyage was simply an elaborate scheme for me to abandon the family. And so, all by myself in that Marblehead apartment, I began to make myself comfortable at sea by working out the details of the preparations. And as I got ready, so did others, and as they did, so my load began to lighten.

My reveries are blown away, and I am yanked wide awake into my real world by an explosion of noise and motion. *Promise* has lain down in the sea and is plowing her way up into the wind out of control. The force throws me headfirst out of the pilothouse race car seat and into the cove, where my knee is punctured by the corner of the ham radio and my face is pressed hard against the lexan window. Solid water and foam spin by my eyes. The autopilot has failed again and I had dropped into a sleep too deep to notice. Alert now and running on adrenaline, I am able to steer the boat back to her broad reach and settle her down long enough to look for broken gear. There is none. The wind is forty knots and the seas eighteen feet.

Promise and I are hell-bent for Bermuda, sailing under reefed main and reefed, poled-out forestaysail. When Murphy begins operating again, even for a minute, the fatigue rushes back on me. I feel as if my mind and body are drifting in and out of any connection with each other. I observe myself with a detached fascination, one moment fighting to stay awake, the next mechanically turning the wheel to keep Promise on course. But I can't help myself do better. At times, I become confused about where I am and how much time has passed. But always circling above me are the cruel and ugly vultures of the failure I am acting out. The emotional pain I give myself is powerful, as if I want to be certain that my punishment fits my crime.

Lightning flashes, and I am shocked awake and startled by my own shadow cast crisply on the side of the cockpit. Steering in the rain and spray from the helm helps keep me from falling into too deep a sleep. My whole awareness is consumed by the constant anticipation of Murphy's next collapse. It seems a soft, slow awareness. My state allows me to sense the autopilot losses almost as easily as my own heartbeat. And then another dose of adrenaline is injected by a noise or a motion that stands out from the scream of the storm. A three-quarter-inch block on the main boom preventer blows up under the pressure of a solid wave, as Promise heels and falls off a sea as she runs. One black rubber cheek of the block caroms off the antenna tower aft of me and settles like a spent hockey puck on the tangle of lines at my feet. I do not know how long it takes me to replace the preventer. When it is completed, I do not reset the mainsail but instead pole out a lapel-size hundred square feet of jib. We are closing on Bermuda fast and the storm grows angrier.

It is only twelve feet from the cockpit helm to the helm inside the pilothouse, but I am afraid Promise will break off toward a broach again during the time it takes me to cover the distance. She is surfing along downwind in a corkscrew motion at ten knots under little wisps of jib and forestaysail, both hung out on their poles. I am suffering more and more from lack of sleep, three days' worth, and my reactions are dreamlike. Both autopilots are virtually useless to me, operating no more than one minute out of fifteen now. The rain pelts, obliterating visibility. I know I am getting close to Bermuda, but I cannot remember how long since my last fix. I make my dash to the pilothouse, to the log and the charts. With one hand on the wheel, I plot a dead-reckoned position and then the satellite navigator position. We have been out of loran range for days. Even though the two positions are not that close on a north-south axis, they both give me a few more hours of sailing east before I must decide whether I can make St. George's Harbour before darkness.

Darkness beats me to Bermuda. I have never sailed into St. George's before and I do not trust myself to find and thread the narrow channel in the dark. The seas are boiling in this easterly storm and my mind and will are not up to the challenge. *Promise* is seven miles from the island when I decide to bring her into the weather and heave to until morning. It is eight P.M on my tenth day out of Portland. I should have made my decision when I had more sea room. By the time I bring the poles in and lash them down in preparation for coming about, St. David's Light bears to my south, not west, an ominous indication that I am much too close to the shallow bank extending several miles north of Bermuda. And that drives me into another adrenaline rush as I work to bring the boat into the wind to beat off what has abruptly become a nearby lee shore. The boat does not come about easily, and after she does, we spend six hours beating into the wind and sea with no measurable progress. *Promise* does not like beating into heavy weather with shortened sail. St. David's Light remains frozen on my starboard side. It is not until early morning that the storm eases and *Promise* and I are able to claw a reasonable distance offshore. My need for sleep has become overpowering. With safe searoom, I set an alarm clock and collapse like a corpse for three hours.

The sleep and the light of dawn and the eased weather and the thoughts of shore combine to give me a second wind. *Promise* slides back downwind with obvious relief and accelerates to eight knots under deeply reefed main and jib. I want very much to be back onshore. I want very much to wallow in long sleep and to warm myself someplace out of harm's way. I want very, very much to rescue my pride.

As I barrel up the St. George's channel, I see two familiar forms waving from the harbor quay. Grant Robinson and Michael Porter are the rescue team for *Promise*. Then I see that Manny and Hoyt and Kim are there, my own rescue team. Almost before the docklines are secured, Grant and Michael and I are making plans to solve the problems that drove us to Bermuda.

Of all those who were intimates in the *American Promise* project, I thought, these people still believe. Not once does Manny ask me if I will start again.

3

When Manny finally signed up with the project in the summer of 1984, the planning was nearly complete, but the actual preparations had barely begun. No notable event signaled her change of mind. One day she was aloof, martyred by her husband's selfish concerns, and the next she was making appointments with nutritionists and listing medical supplies with the speed and determination that were, to her friends, her trademark. But even though I couldn't figure out exactly what caused her turnaround, I could certainly see its impact. Most important, the children immediately began smiling at me again, and we talked openly and positively about *Promise* and the journey. Family friends also heeded Manny's green light. My list of allies was growing. Even my mother-in-law, Allie, enthusiastically pitched in.

Manny and I differ in more ways than our ages, I being eleven years her senior, and after twelve years of marriage I was still learning the ways of our differences and how to live with them. She often fills her entire world with the present. I seem to believe that unless the present is aiming me somewhere else, the time is being wasted. A project has room for both of our attitudes and forms of action, but we definitely work better when we divide and conquer than when we try to do the same job at the same time. This was not necessarily the way Manny wanted it, but it was the way I knew it was going to be, especially on this project.

The inherent risks of such a voyage do dictate a major responsibility to one's family. I wanted to be certain that whatever happened to me, my family would be cared for, at least financially, for life. This was possible, but it would take a mountain of paper to do it. This paper mountain would make me legally disappear just in case I literally disappeared.

Three trusted friends, professionals in the three critical business disciplines — legal and estate planning, accounting and taxes, and general investment and business matters — formed a triumvirate to wave the magic wand over me. Per Hoel presided. Trusts were set up, enough of them so that a schematic was required to relate and explain them. Assets were transferred to the trusts. Wills and trusts were matched to each other. Business commitments that had been made in the past were protected for the future. Slowly, my three friends became the paperwork "me" and made me superfluous. My presence, even in the form of a signature, became unnecessary. About the only terminating action not carried out was the purchase of a burial plot. I specified burial at sea.

During this act of making myself legally invisible, the hard business questions of the voyage surfaced. My triumvirate asked me the crass question "What are the chances for making some money from this venture?" This was something I hadn't thought about and, frankly, did not want to consider.

"Start looking for a guy with more money and less sense than I have to buy the boat when I finish with her" was my answer. It mattered not one bit to me that I had to invoke the "greater fool" theory as a business objective or that there was probably no greater fool in the future for *American Promise*.

But we formed a subchapter S corporation anyway, Promise, Inc., and I actually wrote a very credible mission statement. The wheels of enterprise began to churn quietly in the background of the project.

By the end of that summer, enough checks had been written to the Little Harbor design office to legitimate Promise, Inc., as a business, at least on the debit side of the ledger. Fontaine had produced more than fifty design drawings for *Promise*.

Still Bill Peterson was struggling for a lighter boat. His battle with Little Harbor, however, was insignificant compared to his other battles. His sister, an experienced sailor, navigator, and astronomer, was one of nineteen crew members lost when the barque *Marques* sank just north of Bermuda in a "tall ship" race to Nova Scotia on June 3 of that year. The survivors recounted a knockdown and sinking in less than a minute, trapping crew belowdecks or entangling them in her web of rigging as she plummeted into twenty-six hundred fathoms of water. Bill's shock at the loss had turned, after detailed research, to rage at what he was convinced was a vessel whose design modifications over the years had rendered her blatantly unseaworthy, unstable. His rage had evolved into a holy war, fought mostly in England before the British Department of Transport against the owners and architects of the *Marques*. Bill seemed the battered hero in those days. And one could almost sense that tragedy was not yet ready to release him.

It was on a day after a late night of drinking at Michael's Place in Marblehead, playing sounding board to Bill, that I met Paul Wolter. Paul's intense energy was apparent from a distance of a hundred yards as I walked past the chaos of condos and high-rent fishing shacks and boat hulls into the Little Harbor Boat Yard. He leaned into wiry Lee Van Gemert with his chin thrust out, his fist punching Lee, then air, and his frame pumping up and down on the balls of his feet. He looked like a coiled spring on the edge of release. And the closer I got, the more bombastic Wolter became. He was like an animated, double-speed cartoon — jolly, red face fringed all around with white hair, hot blue eyes, lips permanently pursed as if to whistle. His voice was very loud. His words, in a sharp German accent, rang with absolute authority.

Wolter built the mock-up of the pilothouse and cockpit from wood scraps and cardboard, exactly as designed and dimensionally correct. I would roam about the mock-up, precisely placing sailing instruments, navigation equipment, communications gear, winches, and hardware, and coming up with little design improvements. I could also, in Paul's precise pile of junk, dream of the *American Promise* that was now becoming mine. The pilothouse came alive for me in the mock-up as it never had in Fontaine's drawings. I sat at the inside helm and imagined a chart of the Southern Oceans spread on the wide table. The mainsail was directly above, clearly visible through a skylight overhead, and I could see the horizon full circle through generous windows. A bunk was low on the port side, and a gimballed one-burner stove swung in an alcove on the starboard side. Yes, I thought, I could live here in this space.

The cockpit had the feel of a cocoon, waist high all around

with sides sloped outward from the top to give me toeroom when cranking on the dozen winches that populated the perimeter. I liked the cozy security, its enclosed feeling. But Paul had added a singular touch to his mock-up that made me catch my breath. He had placed a white stake at the point where the bow of the boat would be. It was a very long way from me as I stood at the helm, and for the first time it hit me just how big this boat was. The mock-up was built in what had only recently been the loft for Hood Sails, and it seemed to dominate the huge open space. I could sense overhead the enormous rig needed to drive such a huge boat. Could I manage this vessel in heavy weather when things were going wrong?

In mid-August of 1984, Grant Robinson and his wife, Patty, were in that same big building on their knees with wooden laths, hammers, nails, measuring tapes, and pencils, lofting *American Promise* on a seventy-by-twenty-five-foot floor of white painted plywood. Lofting is the first step in boat construction, the translation of the three-dimensional hull design into a full-size, two-dimensional floor drawing. The boat, it had been decided, would be built right there at Hood's yard. It was not an easy decision, and it had more skeptics than believers. The May 1985 target launch date was a laughing matter to yachting insiders, who like to make book on such projects. The last major building project at Little Harbor, after all, had been the rebuilding of the America's Cup defender *Courageous* seven years earlier. Little Harbor was a repair yard. The closest the Little Harbor crews had been to new boat construction in recent years was dusting off and touching up the new yachts shipped in from Hood's yard in Taiwan.

One reason to build in Marblehead was that we could not find another qualified yard willing to take on the challenge. Another reason was the advantage, perceived only by some, of having the designers and the builders within easy reach of each other. I was wary of this arrangement, for I worried that fewer finished, detailed, design drawings would be done because it would be so easy to walk across the yard with a sketch on the back of an envelope. I also worried about losing the checks and balances achieved when an experienced builder operates independently from the designer. I extracted an agreement from Ted that drawings were to be as detailed as if construction were taking place in Taiwan, for example, and that Grant Robinson, as project director, would be given as much independence as any outside builder. Still, I realized that the first point was pulling against the current of human nature in yacht design and that the second point was practically impossible under a Ted Hood dictatorship. But Bill and I had become very wary and began planning accordingly.

The initial schedule estimated that it would take 17,488 hours to build the boat. I didn't wonder if this number was conservative, only how conservative. Bill's attention swung very quickly from the Hood design team to Grant and his little band of boatbuilders. Bill had recently been yard foreman for the construction of the ninety-two-foot ketch *Whitehawk* in Rockport, Maine, and knew his way around timeline scheduling. Appalled by the lack of these skills in the design office and in Grant, he immediately began working. Grant, meanwhile, was busy using his long-standing membership in the dirty-hands contingent of the sailboat and boatyard fraternity to muster a building crew — carpenters first, then fiberglass lay-up guys. His very first team member, however, was his wife, Patty, who knew what to do and was instantly at work, quiet and unassuming when she worked alone, but later, as others joined her, quite notable by her foghorn voice, salty lingo, and decisiveness. It did not encourage me at all to watch the rest of this crew assemble. They looked a ragtag bunch, a collection of skinny, surly-looking drifters; big, hairy, bellowing wharf rats; and dewy-eyed, pink-fingered boys. And there was continual trouble keeping the force at September's planned twelve-man strength; one of Grant's daily surprises was who would actually show up for work in the morning. To make matters worse, the regulars at the Little Harbor Boat Yard, highly competent men who in some cases had worked there for a generation, treated this raunchy band of newcomers like a leper colony in their midst. Grant himself had the multiple jeopardy of being new working at the yard level, of being in charge of a major project that was outside the established political structure of the yard, and of having worked before with the "little boys" at the Ted Hood White House.

Bill immediately became Grant's aide and confidant. I began showing up as often as I could without getting in the way to spread my brand of positive enthusiasm and humor. The crew, I felt, needed its morale boosted regularly.

The first physical evidence of *American Promise* was an enormous platform, called a strongback, constructed and then very carefully leveled in the same bay where *Courageous* had been rebuilt in the winter of 1976. Hood had sailed the original *Courageous* to an America's Cup victory over the Aussies in 1974 and then had redesigned her for another victory with Ted Turner in 1977. There was no sense of this rich sailing history then, however. The place was dirty, damp, dark, and cluttered in all corners with boatyard debris.

Over in the old sail loft, the drawn lines of the boat were laid down and edited by Ted's eye. Patty and Grant worked from very early to very late at both ends of the bay, building jigs for the mold setups, then building the molds and patterns themselves. They would be the ribs and the stem and transom of a full-scale wooden model of *American Promise*, to be built upside down on the strongback. These precise skeletal sections were positioned together on the strongback with the rib boards running longitudinally. The form was then given muscular structure by stringers, also longitudinal, placed every six inches from the shear to the keel. It was, in fact, a boat built of wood in just under a thousand man-hours, sixty hours fewer than the estimate for that stage. Grant and Bill had finally written a working timeline control report to segment, forecast, and track the construction of the boat according to forty-nine specific job categories. This report projected that *American Promise* would consume a total of 22,010 man-hours of labor, a number 25 percent higher than the more general projection that had come down from the White House. I was encouraged that the first two items on the timeline had come in slightly under forecast, but I realized that this was more because of the individual efforts of Grant and Patty than the output of Grant's black sheep.

More often than not, when I spoke with members of the crew, I found them ignorant of either the art or the science of boatbuilding. The major concern was the size of the paycheck, the most common problem, car trouble. Marblehead had long since become too expensive for wage-earning laborers, and so most of these guys commuted from the mill towns to the west. It was quite common, in those early fall days, for me to learn a new name just in time for it to disappear from the payroll. Not until the end of October did Grant's band begin to harden into a team of familiar faces. They remained, however, a sullen group, overworked and resolutely seg-regated, almost quarantined, by the Little Harbor regulars to the one big gray dungeon where *American Promise* was materializing.

I watched an attitude of quiet defiance, a rising sense of pride, grow within the group. The boat was ahead of schedule. She lay like a half-afloat, sleeping whale once the dull gray, inch-thick, Airex core had been fastened and faired onto the wooden form; this core was a light, tough, closed-cell foam that would be sand-wiched between skins of fiberglass and resin. The men by that time knew the boat's purpose and began to feel special because of their involvement. There were no specialists; all of them moved from one job to another, from carpentry to cutting and bending foam core to fiberglassing. The stinking job of laying up the outer skin of fiberglass onto the core was made worse by the crisp fall weather, which forced the bay doors to be closed and necessitated huge, oil-fired space heaters that spat out equal amounts of warm air and diesel pollution.

Three layers of triaxial, three-stranded, fiberglass material and two layers of nine-ounce Kevlar cloth were individually laid up to form the exterior skin. For additional strength on critical structural areas — such as the centerline, or keel area; the chainplates, where the standing rigging attaches to the hull; and the hull flange, to which the deck is bolted — layers of knitted unidirectional cloth were added. It was a painstaking as well as a painful job, as though a fine tailor were being forced to work in a glue factory.

Grant was particular and demanding, and he taught by doing. And there were many critics who came down from the White House, with Ted leading the intense scrutiny of each day's work. Through it all, I watched my boat evolve with a growing confi-dence. The crew was showing the punishment of their dirty, resin-filled world, with red-rimmed eyes and swollen, blistered skin (most of the men insisted on working without protective clothing, in defiance of Grant's orders), but they were surely motivated.

It was, however, impossible to overlook the emergence of a major strategic problem. Bill's timeline report and forecast were proving to be much closer than the early projection from Hood's office, and this would spell trouble later that winter. The boat would not be completed on time unless some changes were made.

The Wednesday morning progress meetings began to take on

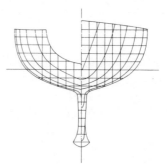

LINES PLAN

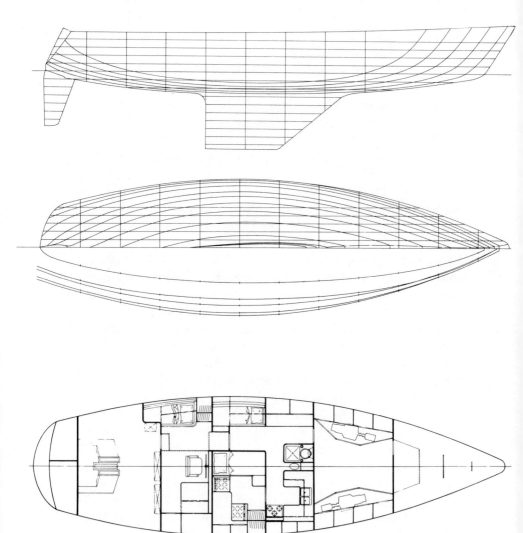

ARRANGEMENT PLAN

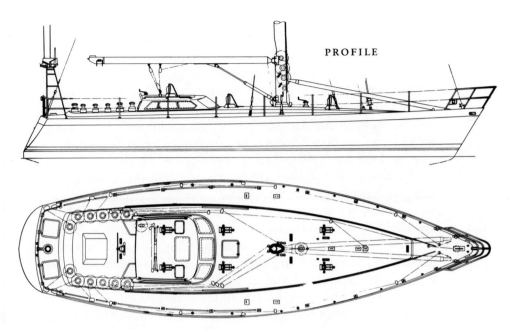

PROFILE

DECK LAYOUT

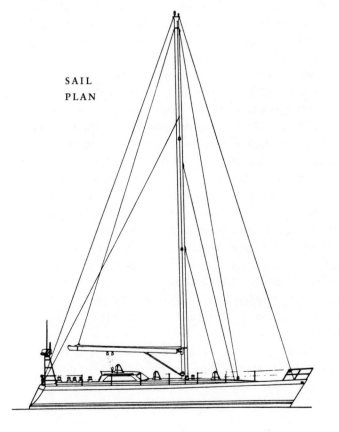

SAIL
PLAN

the character of Chinese fire drills. Some agendas were too long, the topics too broad and varied, and the discussions too detailed. Other meetings were held without an agenda. We addressed the specifics of hydrostatic reports on the projected flotation of *Promise* with various of her five watertight compartments flooded. We staggered through reams of calculations on her stability and trim, on the structural stress characteristics for her hull, on her sail areas under different wind conditions, and on her rudder configuration under a number of forces and angles of attack. Grant came late and left early and didn't much want to be there in between. Why, he reasoned, spend hours at a meeting, being singularly second-guessed and reminded of the limits of his authority, when the boat desperately needed his hands at work? The news at one meeting was that Patty was to be fired from the otherwise all-male crew. Grant would not do that job; Ted would have to do it himself. At another meeting, the news was that *Promise*'s deck, pilothouse, cockpit, structural bulkheads, and rudderpost were to be built beyond Little Harbor and, therefore, beyond Grant's direct influence.

Over the course of several meetings in the fall, it became clear that the Little Harbor regulars must be called into direct involvement with the project very soon. I wondered if this would mean a major challenge to Grant's authority from Art Fraser, the gruff and hard-bitten manager of the Little Harbor Boat Yard.

The first of his men to work on *American Promise* was the yard's premier carpenter, Joe Baier, who had been with Hood for so long and knew the yard politics so well that he seemed to report to no one. Joe's first job was to build the keel. He worked alone and in his own domain. He began by building the wooden form for the keel, upside down and sixteen feet long, seven feet high, with a distinctly phallic bulb that would later hold the lead ballast to keep *Promise* stiff and upright under sail. Joe was actually designing the subtle details of this erotic-looking sculpture as he proceeded. It was a job demanding a high level of skill and the wisdom that comes only from experience. Joe worked fast but without apparent supervision. Who really is in charge on this project? I wondered.

I proposed to fund a cash bonus for those working on *Promise*, and Ted told me, "You can give them a bonus if you want, but I can't because then they'll expect it to happen again sometime."

Ted also thought it was strange to pay extra for something that wasn't yet finished, somehow not grasping the notion that although the bonus was for extra effort made yesterday, it almost always succeeded in getting more effort tomorrow.

Fourteen people received a little more than $7,000 on December 7 in checks ranging from $100 to $550; larger checks went to Grant, Fontaine, and Bill. The bonus amounted to seventy-five hours' worth of pay for men who worked for $5 to $8 an hour. The reactions were instantaneous, but they were not all I had expected. Grant's black sheep were, of course, happy as hell. Art Fraser, however, was bullshit.

He said to Grant, who handed out the checks, "Don't you *ever* pay money to my men. I'm the one who does that. I'm the only one who does that. And if there is any bonus around here, all of my guys will share in it, not just a few." Joe Baier had been included in the bonus group because of his keel sculpture.

The field of the tension that was coiled around *American Promise* that December spread like the pull of a magnet from the construction crew and the boatyard to Hood Sailmakers, where fourteen special sails were on order, and to Hood Yacht Systems (two separate companies), where the spars, rigging, and critical sail-handling gear were to be designed or specified. It fed the whole Marblehead sailing community, fueling barroom gossip and providing great opportunities for the pundits and oddsmakers. *Promise* and I were not the favorites on the Marblehead betting line.

At the time, I thought that I had probably bought and paid for the majority of the bets on my side of the line with the bonus to Grant's black sheep. Per had become less visible to the project because of other business matters. Bill, who was working smoothly and positively with Grant on short-term concerns, was becoming increasingly negative about the longer-range goals, telling me over and over that the boat might well not be finished in time to depart in 1985 and would be dangerous to sail if it was.

But I felt my most confident after a discussion or an argument with Ted Hood, and it was then I knew *Promise* and I had the one vote that really counted. There was only one man in charge at Little Harbor, I finally understood, one king who shared responsibility, perhaps, but never shared any real authority. Around this ultimate ruler ranged a confusion of doers, some in continual collision with one another and others, the old-timers, in fiercely guarded seclusion. Ted's management style might be called autocratic anarchy with the survival of the fittest. With this revelation came a better understanding for me of many of the puzzling ways in which Little Harbor worked.

Ted Hood was, in fact, a lousy manager, particularly of people. Per and Bill and I would have to compensate for that if *American Promise* was to be completed on time. Per would use his unique ability to tell Ted off, thereby getting him to note new evidence and listen to other people's opinions. Bill would continue to test the design process, albeit negatively, with alternatives and to supervise Grant, almost as a de facto project foreman. I would be the motivating force and would rally the group around the cause of *American Promise*.

It is to me a strange and unseemly irony that people are drawn together more positively by the adversities of one of them than by the victories. Alas, once again, Bill suffered those adversities. His three-year-old daughter had been diagnosed with lymphoma, a debilitating disease that requires all the hideous and violent treatment that can be prescribed for cancer victims. The burdens of *Promise* on Bill became light indeed by comparison — and also lighter on the rest of us. The effect was subtle but sobering. Grant and Fontaine were fathers of little girls themselves. So was I. And I thought of what it would be like if my Kim were so diagnosed and I knew that I would abandon *American Promise*.

The number of people involved in the project exploded in December, as it became evident that we were falling further and further behind schedule. Even Ted overcame his tendency to ignore troubling news, and he agreed to involve more people both inside and outside Little Harbor. It certainly helped that the project had become well known in the sailing fraternity and marine industry and that Grant's gang had the boat far enough along so that it was an impressive presence.

Art Fraser blasted into the project and brought with him the full force of the Little Harbor regulars, the "old guard" of carpenters and machinists and electricians and painters and mechanics and plumbers. To my surprise, there was not the violent conflict between Art's old guard and Grant's black sheep that I had expected. The former were finishing and systems installation experts, perhaps the best on the East Coast, trained and ready to outfit *Promise* just as they had been doing with Hood's luxury Taiwanese hulls for years. Grant's gang filled the role normally assumed by the Chinese.

The sense of urgency spread, and the progress by both teams was just short of astounding. By the end of December, *Promise* had been hauled out of her shed and turned over, upright at last and, I prayed, for always. The strongback was torn off and the wooden hull form ripped from her insides. She was pushed back into the shed, and her keel, Joe's erotic shape, was dropped into a six-foot trench dug in the earth floor so that there would be room for workers on the deck under the roof. The inside skin was applied. Web frames and interior buildups for bulkheads were installed. The integral tanks, enough to hold eight hundred gallons of fuel, were built in, and the girders and floors were glassed. Fifteen thousand pounds of hot lead, melted in pots on gas burners inside the hull, were poured into the keel, a cavity big enough to swallow four men. Grant's gang had finally become a cohesive operating unit, reliably peopled.

Outside the gray shed in the various shops of Art's Little Harbor regulars, evidence of *Promise* was pervasive. The machine shop was littered with her special hardware, lifeline stanchions, bow pulpit, engine mounts, tangs, aft antenna tower, and the massive plates that would spread loads from the standing rigging. The galley cabinets, lockers, chart drawers, and workbench, even the stall to enclose the head and shower, turned Joe Baier's carpentry shop into a warehouse of oddly shaped furniture. More than a ton of copper wire and cable snaked around the electrical shop amid terminals and insulators and metal bars and panels. The stockroom and hallways were choked with boxes of winches (seventeen of them), diesel engines (three), reverse osmosis watermakers (two), pumps, lights, shackles, thimbles, valves, hoses, anchors, bales of line, reels of rope, blocks, tracks, cars, and enough gear in breadbox-size cartons marked *Promise* to make me wonder if, after all, the boat would be big enough.

Meanwhile, in Yarmouth, Maine, Walter Greene and a crew of five were building *Promise*'s deck, cockpit, and pilothouse. Walter is known for the multihull racing sailboats he designs and builds and for being one of the best single-handed sailors in the world. (It is a comment on the popularity of solo sailing in the United States that his name is probably better known in France.) Walter's boatyard, Greene Marine, looks as though they didn't clean up after the last war. It is a graveyard of parts of boats and derelicts of boats, with at least as many French fatalities as American because much of the usually front-running French fleet limps right to Greene Marine for surgery or burial after each OSTAR (Observer Solo Trans-Atlantic Race).

But for those with the courage to enter, there is always something interesting to be found inside the single sixty-by-forty-foot shed. When I first visited, work was under way on four twenty-foot hulls that, I learned, were to be used to tank-test designs for a new maxiboat (the largest class of ocean-racing sailboats). I was pleased to feel like a piker with what I had spent on *American Promise* when I learned that the customer for these models, twenty-eight in all, would be spending about half a million dollars before he even started design work on the final boat.

By mid-January, however, all the work in Walter's shed was destined for *Promise*. The deck and cockpit were being built of wood by a method called cold-molding, a process that used West epoxy glue to fasten and form the wooden structure into a tough, rot-resistant unit able to take the tremendous stress imposed by the rig and by loads on deck-mounted hardware.

When Walter and his deck arrived at Little Harbor in early February, it was snowing. Negotiating the narrow streets of Marblehead with the sixty-by-seventeen-foot platform cocked up on a flatbed truck was itself a serious project. At the yard, all the men stopped work and gathered together to watch. The huge doors of the gray shed yawned open to reveal *Promise,* waiting like a life-size dollhouse, roofless but fully appointed.

Art was in charge of the maneuvers to lift and place the deck on the hull. He had a crane, a tractor, a forklift, and twenty men, and he used them all with the direct authority and urgency of a battle commander. The men literally picked up and carried away two Japanese cars from the path of the truck. Before the driver could protest, his truck was hoisted and hauled through a narrows by the tractor and forklift. (People around Art often find themselves a step and a half behind the action.) Art's crane had the deck aloft in the wind, sailing some but heading as resolutely as Art's will toward *Promise*. Grant was aboard the boat, scurrying to stay even. Worse yet for the black sheep was that when the deck did get into position, it did not come close to a fit-down on the hull. They were in charge of trimming the bulkheads and cabinets, and several were inches too high. The question of who had screwed up, those who made the drawings or those who followed them, was not debated openly, but Art left, taking with him his machines, his regulars, and a smirk. The next day, however, Grant had the deck glued down and fastened with 816 three-eighth-inch stainless steel bolts. *Promise* was a boat.

My preparations for operating the immense machine that was evolving within *Promise* became intense and earnest when Buddy Duncan, a first engineer on an Exxon tanker, began giving me exams. Buddy's regular leave, which he normally spent working for Hood, had coincided fortuitously with our need for the critical engineering analysis and design to make the boat work. Also a world-class one-design racing sailor, Buddy managed to look and act like a caricature of a nerd — he was tall and skinny, boyish, with pencils protruding from pockets and behind ears, a roguish grin, and an Olympian stutter. It was easy for me to respect and care for this man. Buddy had learned his engineering well, and may even have perfected his stuttering, at MIT. He was also afflicted with an incurable need to tinker, to get his hands dirty. It was he who gave *Promise* what is probably the best-conceived and best-implemented electrical, plumbing, and hydraulic systems ever installed on a sixty-foot sailboat.

The exams Buddy created for me were an expression of his deep commitment to the project as well as his wisdom in recognizing me as the weak link in the performance of his creations. I had the same thought. My reaction was to complain that the Duncan engineering was "not simple enough . . . too complex for one man with enough already to do like wrestling 285-pound headsails and navigating." Buddy responded by building in redundancy, by stocking up on spare parts and manuals (writing some himself), by forcefeeding me theory, by enrolling me in diesel engine courses, and by flunking me on his tests when I deserved it.

Duncan's analysis of *Promise*'s electrical power requirements and the system he designed to satisfy them were typical of him. He summarized his projection in a conclusive, decisive fifteen-page report. He estimated that I would use between 53.51 and 143.63 ampere-hours of electricity per day, depending on which of four load descriptions — ranging from "light weather with energy conservation" to "rough weather with normal energy consumption" — I was operating under. These data were built from the details of power needed daily for lighting, navigation, and communications gear, for motors, pumps, and autopilots.

The system he conceived to match these needs, safely and redundantly, was barely short of awesome. *Promise* had 3,000 pounds of heavy-duty, lead-acid batteries in four 24-volt, 485-ampere-hour banks. She had two additional 12-volt banks for engine and generator starting only. She had two 11-kilowatt, 120-volt AC diesel generators, three independent 160-amp alternators, four 60-amp, constant-voltage chargers, and a water generator that hung from the transom (stern) to produce power from the boat's forward motion. Duncan specified 800 gallons of diesel to fuel the generators, even though he calculated that only 480 would be required for a 240-day voyage. And he was a formidable miser on the other half of the power equation, even demanding that a selection of the more efficient fluorescent lights be tested for power use as well as for any high-frequency noise generation that might interfere with communications gear. This boat, I thought, could serve as the power plant for a small community.

Duncan's hydraulic steering system was also designed and specified to be bulletproof. Complicating matters were two helms (steering stations), one in the pilothouse and one in the cockpit, and two rudders, the main, balanced rudder aft and the other an intermediate centerboard, halfway between the keel and the main rudder, which could be made into a rudder when lowered all the way. All the hydraulic piping was stainless steel, and all couplings and equipment could be isolated by quarter-turn valves. Either of two electrically driven pumps could be controlled by either of two autopilots. Buddy had assembled a textbook of data and analysis to support his decisions on this most critical of systems, and hydraulics was my best subject. It is, then, a brutal irony that it was this system that very nearly defeated the voyage.

With the deck in place, progress was dramatically evident each day. I could feel the momentum building in those late winter days of March and April. But there was a strange turn in my awareness: the closer to completion the boat came, the less I thought of its actual voyage. Events became more intellectual than actual. It seemed that I was managing the growing list of details from a distance, almost as if the whole project were a classroom exercise. The items on my lists lacked priority; each one simply had to be checked off. The fourteen sails were built: check. The spare parts and tools were received: check and check. The bill for four suits of foul weather gear was paid: check. Twenty-two more bonus checks were distributed: check. My thrice-weekly Nautilus workouts were extended to two hours each: check. And more checks as I sorted eighty-three nautical charts, five volumes of the *Sailing Directions,* and my navigator's library, as I followed Manny's routine for taste-testing freeze-dried and pouched foods, as I catalogued three file drawers of service and repair manuals for *Promise*'s equipment, and as I binged on a shopping marathon for everything from pencils to handybillies.

The launching of *American Promise* on May 7, 1985, actually caught me by surprise. Suddenly I was driving this shiny, red, white, and blue monster high in the water and rigless across Marblehead Harbor. The crowd around me — Ted, Grant, Bill, Manny, Hoyt, and Kim — were all happy as hell and therefore so was I.

The sight of *Promise* under way stunned much of Marblehead. She was launched just six days after the target date, having been completed in less than nine months, and many noisy mouths were shut. What was not generally known, of course, was that it had taken 26,335 Little Harbor man-hours to build her and that the total hours, when contracted labor was added, would certainly exceed thirty thousand. The Little Harbor labor bill was $658,375.77. The bill for materials was $576,212.75.

$\sim\!\!\sim\; 4 \;\sim\!\!\sim$

or my first sail on *American Promise*, I was one in the crowd. It was a typical late spring afternoon in New England, bright and warm and windy, and it was three and a half months before the boat and I were scheduled to begin our voyage. Ted, Grant, Fontaine, Bill, Buddy, and I stood jammed in the cockpit as we motored out of Marblehead Harbor into a southwest wind. Then the mainsail and big jib were reeled out and, together, we felt her first responses as a sailboat. It was not much fun. Sailing hard on the wind, she flopped right over to a heel of more than thirty degrees. It was an unexpected angle for me and decidedly uncomfortable.

"She sure as hell is tender, isn't she," I said when it became obvious that no one else was going to. I couldn't keep from thinking of how it would be to spend six months living with that kind of bias.

"Ted," I bellowed politely through the wind, "doesn't she seem a bit too tender to you?" Our heel had increased to thirty-five degrees, and it was very difficult to find an easy perch anywhere, particularly belowdecks.

"New boats always seem too tender," Ted answered.

Bill whispered into my ear, "This boat is far too tender. She is bordering on being unstable. You can't take this boat around the world like this. They only put fifteen thousand of the eighteen thousand pounds of keel ballast in her, but even adding the rest may not correct the problem."

Right then and there I lost some of my confidence in Ted Hood and ceased being polite.

"Why the hell is this boat so goddamned tender?" I demanded, staring directly into Ted's face. "No boat should take this angle of heel in this kind of wind," I yelled at everyone.

Fontaine shrugged, but nobody answered. Ted simply continued to sail the boat enigmatically, lightly gliding about, touching the helm and trimming the sheets with those huge paws of his. Although he is a large man, he moved with the grace of a dancer. The boat was sailing at better than nine knots on the meter. We didn't try to shorten sail with a reef. When we wore off the wind to a reach, *Promise* stood up somewhat but not enough for me.

That night I drank too much and concentrated on worrying. "Look," I told myself, "I know tender when I feel it. I have sailed a helluva lot of miles, more than anyone else who was on that boat today except Ted, probably more offshore miles, even, than he has and certainly more single-handed offshore miles than he. Boats are not meant to sail that way, certainly not in that small a wind."

The next morning I was fired up for my visit to Little Harbor, and everyone within earshot on the way to Ted's office knew my mission was a crisis of tenderness — and not the romantic kind.

As I spoke, Ted began to show his frustration and pointed out some obvious variables in *Promise*'s tenderness-stiffness equation: no stores on board, tanks not yet filled, space for several thousand pounds more lead ballast deep in the keel, and much more space for trim ballast. I became exasperated and demanded to know which of the variables we should try first. Then he left me with one of those conclusive remarks of his that invites no comment, begs no answer.

"I have been on hundreds of first-time sails in new boats, and the owners always think that the boat is too tender," he said with finality.

During the next two weeks, sure enough, *Promise* did stiffen as her tanks were filled and gear was stowed and trim ballast was added. And I got more familiar with her sailing motions. Bill also did his part in a covert midnight action by shoving a thousand more pounds of lead into her keel. The tenderness problem became less and less important until it was no longer an issue. It seemed that Ted was right again.

My boat may have been launched, but she did not yet belong to me. From very early to very late each day, *Promise* was a battlefield of workers, with their tools and parts. Her wiring was still being installed, her bulkheads being painted, her engines being tuned and lined up, and her communications and navigation gear and instruments hooked up. When we wanted to take her out on a sailing trial, it was often on the spur of the moment. We simply threw our lines onto the dock and departed as soon as we had the right people on board. Often, for these impromptu sails, we inadvertently impressed workmen below into sea duty, forcing them to scurry to corral their tools or cover their cans of paint. On one trial sail, I found a wide-eyed worker clutching his gear, propped below in a cranny behind a generator.

Colin MacDougall, an electronics expert, and his small band of technicians were among the most competent and efficient of the visiting hordes. They installed, connected, and calibrated an awe-inspiring array of electronics in five days: two satellite navigation receivers, a loran receiver, a weather facsimile receiver, fourteen pieces of sailing instrumentation, a depth recorder, a VHF marine radio, a single-side band radio, a ham radio, radar, an ARGOS satellite position transmitter, a stereo sound system, and a computerized alarm system. The tower that bridged the stern of the boat six feet off the deck bristled with nine antennas and six wind sensors. MacDougall left a stack of instruction manuals more than a foot high to teach me how to use all this gear.

The electronics wasn't all that awaited my study and practical understanding. *Promise* was filling up with complex machinery that I had no hands-on experience with, and as I walked around the boat, my Buddy Duncan seminars seemed like just so much theory. A case could be made that much of the equipment was really just so much theory, too; the main battery-charging system could not be made to work, and the hydraulic steering system remained full of bugs.

The first time I stayed aboard for the night, *Promise* was hanging on a mooring at the outer edge of Marblehead Harbor. I spent a couple of hours touring the boat to study all that equipment but not working up the courage to experiment with much of it. So I was most pleased to find that her marine toilet failed to operate because there, I knew, was one piece of gear I did understand. Though not always willingly, I had fixed many a marine head in my time, and I set about fixing *Promise*'s with a happy indulgence that was bound to be therapeutic and confidence-building for me. A marine toilet has a through-hull fitting to an intake hose, a pedal valve to let seawater in, a simple hand pump to empty it out, a ceramic bowl with a flap valve on the bottom, and an exhaust hose to another through-hull fitting. This was going to be easy.

An hour later, I urinated from the deck into the harbor. I later learned that a hose to feed seawater into the galley had been T'd into the head intake line at, to me, an unseen, inaccessible point; this prevented the pump from pulling anything but galley air into the bowl, even though water would spout several feet up from the through-hull fitting when I removed the hose. That night, very discouraged, I had to clear a narrow space on the pilothouse bunk in the piles of parts and work in progress in order to lie down.

Several days after my unsuccessful confrontation with the head, on a Sunday with no workers on hand, I decided to take my first sail alone. The wind was fresh and the day bright, and I badly needed a personal victory with this boat. As soon as I had her free of the harbor under engine power, I began to reel out the Hood Stoway mainsail. The sail is rolled up inside the mast around a rod, which can be turned by an electric motor, a manual crank, or a hand-operated line and reel. Reeling it out through the slot in the mast is much like pulling down a windowshade. There is no hoisting of halyards with this sail, no tying in of reefs. Two buttons to push and — presto! — the sailor has whatever size mainsail he wants in seconds. This was the key sail-handling system that would allow one man to operate such a large boat reliably.

When I had the sail a third of the way out, it jammed in the slot. Carefully I worked the furling controls one way and then the other, but somehow I had allowed the rod, with most of the sail wrapped around it, to wind its way clear out of the mast slot for about half its length. I felt panic trying to take hold of me; it was not the short-term crisis of a jammed sail off Marblehead that hit me but the long-term problem of a system critical to the whole project being suddenly distrusted. And my spirit, in real need of nourishment, had again been denied.

My decision was to sail, rod wound out of the mast and all. It was truly an act of defiance when *Promise* and I sailed straight seaward, away from the Sunday Marblehead fleet, without looking back. And we found a tentative kind of rhythm together. Her helm was still sloppy and spongy from a hydraulic system not purged of air and rife with small leaks. The autopilots did not steer her well. But we sailed. Together we sailed, just the two of us, she with her big broken wing and me with my battered confidence, hesitantly beginning to heal each other.

Back at Little Harbor, the design office was mounting a campaign to put *Promise* to the test with a strong crew in an ocean race. The cruising boat race from Marion, Massachusetts, to Bermuda is held in the alternate years of the Newport–Bermuda Race, and this was its year. Bermuda fever at the White House was high. But I was more interested in solving the problems with the mainsail furling system and the steering and charging systems, and I chose a race planning session to make my point. I don't generally lose my temper, but I do know how to use it.

"If it's Bermuda you guys want, then for all I give a shit you can swim there," I bellowed, solidly commanding center stage in the design office. "I do not want to go on a group tour to Bermuda . . . I want to sail by myself around the world. And in order to do that, I will need a boat, for chrissake, that I can set sails on and steer." I had their attention. "There is no damned way I will let three weeks of yachting to and from Bermuda stop work on this boat . . . If we go to Bermuda it will be on a boat that is ready to go around the world." I brought my fist down on Fontaine's drafting table for a crashing ending — the table splintered for me. The mood in the room turned sour. That was the way I wanted it.

Bill had another reason not to go. Earlier, when it seemed possible we might race and I asked him to clear his schedule for the trip, his face had drained white. Somehow, I understood that he would not sail to Bermuda because he was not yet ready to visit his sister's grave. Bill's emotional maelstrom would again work positively for *American Promise*. This time, he intensified his efforts to broadcast the boat's current weaknesses, even commissioning a team of outside experts for an independent survey of the boat. Though his efforts were poorly received by Ted, his points were being made.

During this critical period of shaking out, I became aware that Hood and Fontaine were emotionally pulling away from the project, distancing themselves from what they were learning might not be an easy success and could be a failure after all. I sensed, too,

on his words and actions while aboard *Promise,* particularly during one overnight sail in the Gulf of Maine with relatively heavy weather, ten-to-twelve-foot seas, and twenty-five-to-thirty-five-knot winds. It bothered me not at all when he tended to treat me as inexperienced, for I got the full range of his advice in very simple terms.

"Don't trust these snapshackles," he cautioned. "Trust knots. Trust regular shackles. Lead the headsail sheets down to stiffen the leeches. Never take less than three turns around a self-tailing winch. Throw away those insulated jackets. Get pile. Mark all the sheets at the winches when they are trimmed in hard. Mark all the halyards with the sails up. Mark the deck for the right running block positions on the tracks. Tie off the sheets on the self-tailers when you sleep. Get rid of these jamcleats. Put on regular cleats. Load lots of crackers aboard. You never have enough crackers. Practice breaking down and reassembling the autopilots."

Walter tried both bunks and pronounced them luxurious. He tested *Promise* downwind under poled-out jib and forestaysail and gave her passing grades. He beat her on the wind hard, under too much sail, and agreed she took it well.

Promise had accumulated just two thousand miles by the first of September, a little more than a month before departure. When not sailing, she was still occupied by people busily trying to finish building and equipping her. In Marblehead, the work by then was mostly electrical, devoted to clearing up charging system problems. On her Chebeague Island mooring in Maine, she had been adopted by Michael Porter, a friend, island neighbor, and boatbuilder. Michael was finishing her off for sea as if he were going to take her there himself, stowing and lashing gear and supplies, building spice racks and footrests, plumbing and wiring her, assembling kits of hardware, writing stowage lists, and labeling lockers and drawers. He became as intimate with *Promise* as anyone had, and his care showed.

In mid-September, I banned all workers from the boat except Michael. It was time to claim the boat as mine. I would make do with what I had.

Then, on the morning of Friday, September 27, I made a decision that very nearly cost me the voyage. I decided to let *American Promise* ride out Hurricane Gloria on her Chebeague Island mooring. The storm had ripped up the New Jersey and southern New England coasts like an enormous circular saw passing just offshore and was headed our way. But I opted for warmth and comfort ashore with my family in our island cottage.

Promise swung on a four-thousand-pound mooring with half-inch chain. I added a yoke, two lengths of three-eighth-inch chain, to the one-inch nylon pennant holding the boat onto the mooring. I lashed the equipment in place and stowed the sails below. All was battened down when I went ashore.

By early afternoon, the wind was gusting to fifty knots out of the southeast, boiling waves through the mooring area and breaking them up the beach in front of the house. It was impossible, then, to launch a small boat from that shore to reach *Promise*. There was nothing to do but watch and wait. The pelting rain blurred our view of the boat, but it became clear over time that she was moving slowly but resolutely downwind. She heaved like a shying stallion in slow motion. Each heave backed her down more, brought her closer to a ledge. Unbelievably, she was jerking her two-ton weight across the mooring area without apparent effort. I was stunned and couldn't watch. I sat in the kitchen staring at a cold cup of coffee and willing myself aboard her, sailing safely offshore.

Then I heard Michael's voice: "*Promise* has gone."

She had parted from her mooring and fetched up on a bed of bucket-size, loose rocks about a hundred yards from the shore. Her stern pointed offshore directly into the wind and seas broke over her. Still, her motion was slow and rocking and she heeled no more than fifteen degrees.

Michael and I stood on the beach in the storm and watched her. She was no longer shifting position.

"Soon we'll be able to get to her, Dodge," he said.

Sure enough, I saw that the wind was abating and veering and that soon we would be on the lee (protected) side of the island with the tide rising.

There was hope. In an explosion of energy, Mike and I launched the inflatable boat and beat our way to *Promise*. She seemed almost unaware of her troubles, appearing to overlook the sea that surged around her and the waves that broke over her. We could see no hull damage. Below, it was as if nothing had happened. The pencils hadn't even been tossed off the chart table. Her motion defied the storm.

Her savior was Joe Baier's keel. Eleven feet down, that lead-filled bulb had taken all the punishment and kept the rest of her completely unscathed.

We set two anchors from her stern out into deep water and manned the big, primary winches to kedge her off on the rising tide. Fate played its part in the rescue by putting her in the lee of the island at just the right time. Three hours after we boarded her, she was back afloat.

That night, my ten-year-old son, Hoyt, wrote a poem about Gloria. His final stanza reads:

> I wonder if our boat will make it.
> I walk gloomily down on the beach
> like a man walking to a friend's grave.
> I look out on the water —
> my DAD is on *Promise*!
> All of the lights are on;
> it looks like a hotel on water.
> the storm is over —
> this storm called Gloria.

Gloria ripped a week and a half out of the schedule. Walter Greene and his crew repaired *Promise*'s damage, which was confined to the keel and rudder, and finished just one week before my Columbus Day departure. Gloria's biggest toll, then, became her theft from me of precious sailing time.

The boat became a beehive of last-minute activity, mostly by Michael and Walter and Manny. This was a time when I was not of much use to them. I was busy distancing myself from their world and concentrating on what I felt my new world would be. Much of their work was logistical. Sixteen hundred and nine pounds of food, filling 31.4 cubic feet, were stowed. A ton of spare sails were packed below. A complete set of spare running rigging, sheets, halyards, furling lines, topping lifts, pole guys, outhauls, were labeled and hung in the forepeak. Enough tools, spare parts, and repair materials to stock a boatyard were organized in lockers. The labeler became hot as a pistol as the team tried hard to make it possible for me to find the gear later. Into the locker under the chart table, nestled in with my two sextants, went three file drawers of service manuals.

Two weeks later, under the Bermuda sun, several of those manuals were spread out on top of the chart table before Michael and Grant and me. We were agonizing over the installation and service instructions for *Promise*'s Wagner autopilots, Murphy and Carlos. I had no options. They would have to be fixed. And it had to be done quickly because the unscheduled Bermuda pit stop had to be short.

When it became clear that the manuals were not enough, we realized we needed help from two sources: someone who knew the Wagner equipment like a mother and someone who knew the Bermuda bureaucracy and business world well enough to get things done in a hurry. We got the latter first when Michael had the presence of mind to accept a friendly offer of help from a pert little Bermuda native named Barbara Gringley. Her offer came as something of a surprise to the rest of us, since it was made by a pretty young woman to the wildly bearded Michael, who at the time was dressed in long johns and draped in ripe fruit. For once, screwing off from work was rewarded. It was Halloween, and on the insistence of Grant's wife, Patty, who had come to join him and help with the boat, our repair crew attended a yacht club costume ball dressed as the Fruit of the Loom guys.

Barbara, like most longtime Bermudians, understood the problems sailors have with their boats. She knew not only where to go and who to see to get things done but she was given respect when she got there. Quickly, she connected us with a sailmaker to repair *Promise*'s torn main and jib. She introduced us to the owner of a machine shop, to an electrician, a hydraulics technician, a rigger, a customs official, and the freight manager for Air Canada. She acted as our purchasing agent, social director, public relations manager, cheerleader, and chauffeur.

But we weren't making as good progress with the autopilot. My conversations with the technical people at the Wagner plant in Vancouver had established, incredibly, that the autopilots had been performing exactly as they had been designed. Some engineer, obviously not a solo sailor, had designed a thermal overload circuit to protect the electric motor of the hydraulic pump. His thermal switch totally shut down, completely turned off, the autopilot when it became stressed by heavy work. And thermal switches being what they are, the more they work, the hotter they become, and the hotter they become, the more they work, making shut-downs longer and more frequent over time. This logic exactly described my problem at sea and explained why I had been unable to correct it. There was a right way to protect the electric motor, and that was simply to limit the power going to it. This would allow the autopilot to operate, even if it had too little power to turn the rudder against a wave in a heavy sea, rather than shut the system down. Long telephone calls with Tony Munoz, the senior technician at Wagner, also determined that the two hydraulic rams pushing on *Promise*'s rudder post should be enlarged and that the back-up autopilot should have a larger pump for very heavy weather. One reason for the need for these changes, it became apparent, was that an error had been made in calculating the balance on the forward edge of the rudder; thus, more force was required to turn it than had been specified originally. The information from Wagner was encouraging, but we needed hands-on help. We needed Tony Munoz. He was clearly our "autopilot mother," and we had to bring him to Bermuda, and fast. It took more than money to do that. It took pleas. It took threats. It took convincing Wagner that we would not go away until we got their Tony.

He arrived on the eighth of November, as the window of opportunity for my departure was beginning to close. Bob Rice was warning me that I had to reach Cape Horn before the onset of the southern winter, and that meant leaving Bermuda by mid-November at the latest. Michael and Grant had, with Barbara's constant help, completed the other high-priority repairs. It had all come down to those autopilots.

Tony was a confident, hard worker. He said there was no doubt that he could complete the autopilot resurrection just as soon as Air Canada airbill 01436937751 from Vancouver, via Toronto, arrived with the critical parts. The package had been due for nearly a week, but all we received, twice a day after each incoming flight, was a comedy of shipping errors. It was Barbara who persisted, pushing through the bureaucratic tangle until the shipment was found. The rest was easy for Tony, whose most difficult time was during the sea trial, when he was seasick. Even though it was only a two-hour sail, I was ready to bet on Tony and christened my new heavy weather autopilot Joe, his middle name.

The little band of people who had saved the voyage left Bermuda on November 11 — except for Barbara, of course. Alone on board that night, I set about again lining and labeling my logbooks and dating my journal and plotting my new waypoints for a journey alone and with no stops around the world.

$\sim\sim$ 5 $\sim\sim$

I know I am going to sail and that I am prepared to sail and that for seasonal weather reasons I need to sail right away, but I am not positive I am ready. Excerpts from my log (unedited and unexpurgated) tell the story:

DAY 1 ≈

1111 hours, November 12, 1985, Tuesday, to noon, November 13, 1985, Wednesday
32°22′ north/64°41′ west

We depart. Again. This time from a line one nautical mile true east from St. David's Light, St. George's, Bermuda.

The Bermuda departure is in stark contrast to the Portland departure. The circus clown becomes a real tramp. I leave from the St. George's Harbour fuel dock after borrowing $20 from the Deckers, a cruising couple, to pay my bill for topping off the fuel tanks and for forty gallons of fresh water. A few sailors from yachts heading to the West Indies watch me with mild interest. The most enthusiastic sendoff comes from the customs officer, shaking his head at the wonder of my voyage as it translates onto his forms: "From Bermuda to the high seas destined for Bermuda." We both have the thought that maybe this doesn't require any customs clearances at all.

The boat is not really readied for sea, much gear not properly stowed, some equipment not prepared for quick use, pre-sail checklist not completed. But I am going! I am sure as hell going!

Passing slowly out of the narrow channel of St. George's Harbour, I feel very much alone. I think it is good to have no one from home, no one at all, to wave a good-bye to me. This is the proper departure for such a voyage, alone and without the folderol and fanfare. Out there, for months, there will be no one but myself. It is fitting to get on with it that way.

Wind blows from the southeast at fifteen to twenty knots and the seas are five to eight feet in height. Autopilot Murphy performs flawlessly, but I sleep fitfully in the pilothouse bunk. Yet I am in the bunk twelve hours today, getting up only five times to trim or reef or shake out sail. The morning of my first day of my new beginning breaks bright and sunny.

DAY 2 ≈

We register 175 miles for our first day. Wind remains southeast at sixteen to twenty knots, seas ten to twelve feet. Sight container ship about six miles upwind and a ketch with mizzen furled directly east and bound south.

I sleep and nap a great deal, read some and then snooze some more. What is this? Sleeping sickness? A natural collapse from the hectic days before departure? A subconscious way to prove to Murphy he is needed? Perhaps just a reaction to the sea motion, a mild kind of seasickness the first day out? Maybe a nervous system pushed too far by an awareness that we are off again on this amazing quest?

I am very tentative. It is very close that I am, in fact, back under way on this voyage, and I am not certain yet that I should be, only that I must be. The reality of it all is thrust at me and I am intimidated, somewhat afraid. And so I am sleepy all the time and it takes a major effort for me to attack the chores I must accomplish. I spend my time on deck or in the pilothouse. The dry cabin and galley are too far away from it all, down in the darkness of *Promise*'s belly. I find it hard to live one hour at a time as I know I must because I cannot avoid the debilitating awareness that five thousand of those hours here at sea await me. If I succeed. One hour is such a helpless little thing in that monstrous crowd of time.

DAY 3 ≈

Miserable sailing. Beat into thirty-to-thirty-five-knot wind and sixteen-to-eighteen-foot seas. We struggle, really struggle. The boat slams and pounds and seas roll aboard regularly. I feel lousy. Mild form of seasickness, I guess. But I eat when I should and thank the Lord for autopilot Murphy, who allows me enough sleep.

A loud, constant wailing sound of the wind, part scream and part whistle, hypnotizes me into a mood of threat. I choose to exclude all else while I find the source of this siren. It is the slots in the backstay turnbuckle resonating. I close them with duct tape and it becomes quieter and my tension eases.

My log for these first days is brief and almost illegible. I am slightly seasick. I am apprehensive. I am lonely. I am asking myself the question so many asked me over the past months, "Why are you doing this?," and my clever and glib answers are painful in my memory now. I am in a depression, and that is a state with which I have very little experience. I don't want to speak with anybody on the radio, not when I feel as disconsolate as I do now.

DAY 4 ≈

Weather remains hard and mean from the east and we make poor progress into it. Squalls punch us. Very uncomfortable. I come about to starboard tack for easting and away from tropical depression to the south. I do not cook and eat, munch granola bars instead. And when not serving the demands of the boat, my time is spent on the pilothouse bunk, staring straight up and willing by the minutes one at a time.

The tropical depression becomes Hurricane Kate. Our day gets us no progress in the right direction. The cockpit is heavy with water from breaking seas and the mainsail leech line [a line running inside the back edge of the sail, used to keep it from shaking or motorboating, critical on this battenless, roller-furling sail] will not stay made up, threatening to let the sail self-destruct.

DAY 5 ≈

Hurricane Kate, ranging the Greater Antilles a hundred and
fifty miles south of us with one-hundred-knot winds, fits right
in with my paranoia these early days at sea. But I find a reason
here to be thankful because I know there are sailors in small
boats fighting that storm now while I am well away. Yet I fall
off farther east to give Kate an even bigger berth.

The fact that I have something tactical and measurable to be
thankful for is good tonic for me. I begin to pull out of my
slump. Will avoid an affair with Kate. The goal energizes me. I
make a number of small running rigging adjustments to avoid
chafing damage, move the jibsheet running blocks forward for
a better reefed-down trim, finish stowing and lashing down
loose gear. The work is great therapy, and for the first time I
hear myself bellow an involuntary cheer. The seas drop some
and some blue sky shows and I begin to rebound. I take a hot
shower. I nap in the dry cabin for the first time and have sexual
fantasies.

There is a more powerful human drive than self-preservation
and it is pride. And pride is much of why I am under way
again after the brutal failure of my first attempt from Portland.
The mechanical failures are repaired or the faulty equipment
replaced — sails, rigging, hardware, winches, autopilots — but
the cold reality of six months alone at sea hits me again with
puzzling suddenness. I am amazed I can prepare so intensely
and be so acutely aware of this challenge and then be so abruptly shocked when I actually get under way.

To cope, I try to live life as short term as possible and to ex-
aggerate and overcelebrate anything positive. I am cheered by
missing Kate, by successfully warding off chafing problems, by
a drop in the sea height, by a show of blue sky, by a good nap
and an erotic dream.

I feel good enough to use the radio for a call home. Hoyt's
voice springs from the speaker and I feel a rush of affection,
then Kim speaks up and has me grinning happily. After the
call, though, I am very sad and feel incredibly alone. It takes
me a couple of hours to get my mind back on *Promise* and attack the many jobs at hand. It seems I cope better with the
loneliness when I do not remind myself of the delicious alternatives. People. Home.

DAY 7 ≈

More of the same weather and sailing. Life sure is a beat. Pound, slam, spray, heel, bounce, jerk, spill. Never anywhere without firm hand grips or braced stance. But still the satisfaction of progress. Making a hundred and sixty miles a day beating into this onslaught of wind and water is no mean accomplishment. *Promise* surely is strong and capable. We sail cracked off ten degrees from hard on the wind. The wind is thirty-five to forty-five knots, seas sixteen to eighteen feet.

Fierce rain squalls keep punctuating the day. One spawns an incredible rainbow, horizon to horizon, a fat, brilliant, prismatic dome. During the night a half moon sheds enough light for me to play shadow animals with my hands, using the side of the cockpit as a screen. I get a perfect turtle but can't decide which voice should go with it, a falsetto or dumb growl. I find I can sound just like Kermit, but realize he's a frog.

I reluctantly finish *Growing Up* by Russell Baker. I cry uncontrollably as Baker tells of the warmth and love shared by family and friends. His final meeting with his dying mother, who has lost her memory and awareness, is sad and disheartening for me. I vow never to let myself dawdle in the gray ground between life and death. I will leave the living with a conscious leap or, if too late, by pure force of will. Promise.

I feel myself getting used to this life aboard *Promise*. I find it much easier to be cheerful if I do not allow myself to dwell on matters outside those right here on the boat. Sometimes, though, I catch myself with fantasies about finishing the voyage.

DAY 8 ≈

Seas abate to eight feet and wind to high teens. More sail gets *Promise* boiling herself along at eight and a half knots. I sleep the sleep of a baby, solid and short. Weather fax shows Kate over Cuba, well away, and strong easterly trades right down to seven north. Below that is the ITCZ, the doldrums to sailors.

Gravitywhaps is what I call a Newtonian category of spills, drops, slips, fumbles, and drunken-like behavior aboard *Promise*. They are the practical joker side of the law of gravity and

I'm sure Newton's ghost is watching. How utterly gleeful he is when a cup of soup arrays itself horizontally — well, vertically, but it looks horizontal — across the cabin, or when water flows straight from the faucet into a cove where the crackers are kept, not a drop hitting the sink, or when I pull off a tight somersault into a lee crevice with my pants wound round my knees.

I've begun to sing to myself in the evenings, making up the most bizarre songs. The singing is so awful and the tunes so ridiculous, they break me up into fits of laughter. I know I should be singing sea chanties or folk tunes, songs more fitting for a gentleman at sea with himself. But, no, I scream out, "Give my regards to Broadway, Remember me to Harold the Bare." I am also getting quite accomplished at bellowing noises that sound to me like real words but from an as-yet-undiscovered language.

I do find that one of my worst fears has not materialized. I do not have a boat that doesn't leak. I have always said that one should not trust a boat that doesn't leak, a maxim, perhaps, more often quoted by wooden boat owners. Sure enough, though, I find water in bilge compartment four, a few gallons with no trace of entry point. And I find a foot of water with much diesel oil in the main bilge, compartment three, and I pump. The diesel oil is what worries me.

I am just into my first ocean with *American Promise*. Nobby Clarke, Guinness's recordkeeper, has said, "Ninety-five percent of those who say they are going to sail around the world do not get their boats in the water, ninety-five percent of those who get their boats, do not get under way, and ninety-five percent of those who depart do not complete a circumnavigation." Lousy odds.

It is a historical fact that most sailors hoping to circumnavigate from departure ports in the North Atlantic never get out of their first ocean. Collection bins for lost-hope boats are all over the West Indies and in the ports of Panama. First-ocean dropouts not only prevail among cruising romantics, but are also frequent in serious races where one would expect well-found boats and experienced and prepared sailors. Just three of the seven contenders in the Golden Globe race, the 1968–69 solo, nonstop race around the world, made it out of the Atlantic.

It is the first ocean that kills the ill prepared and the weaker willed, not because it is the toughest ocean but because all oceans are tough. Any serious flaw in a man or his boat can and probably will be smoked out by any ocean, whichever one comes first. It is not the specific brutality of the weather in midocean but the ultimate persistence of time itself that takes the toll. And to cross any ocean takes time — the bigger the ocean, the more time, and the more time, the steeper the odds for failure. As time wears away at the boat and sailor during a long voyage, just the contemplation of time can sometimes be enough to kill the sailor's will.

One can, however, make a case that the first passage of the first leg in an easterly circumnavigation from a North Atlantic port should be the easiest. The sailor and his boat are fresh and, if hurricanes are avoided, the Atlantic Ocean weather is relatively non-threatening in the midyear months in the tropic, subtropic, and middle latitudes.

The proper sailing routes are defined and described with details of weather in the volume *Ocean Passages for the World*, published by the British Hydrographic Department and available wherever nautical charts are sold for about fifty bucks. No deep-water sailor's library should be without this volume. These routes have been honed down by many generations of experience and should be observed; sailors who plan long voyages without the benefit of *Ocean Passages* are not placing the odds in their favor. There is also some route planning advice in the U.S. Government's *Sailing Directions,* a series of volumes primarily describing meteorological statistics in great detail. In spite of the title, the routes described are for engine-powered rather than wind-powered vessels.

Selected routes should then be plotted on the Pilot Chart for the appropriate ocean and month of the year. These large-scale charts are published by the U.S. Defense Mapping Agency. They present a cornucopia of historical weather information, winds, currents, air and sea temperature, barometric pressures, wave heights, storm tracks, and percentages of gales and calms, all in geographically relevant and easy-to-read form. Plot a course on a Pilot Chart and you have a graphic presentation of all the major climatological variables for an ocean passage as well as the information to determine the optimal season and times for a passage.

These publications have some biases that are worth noting.

The *Ocean Passages* sailing routes were refined for square-rigged ships and therefore do not anticipate that the vessel will sail well into the wind. Modern sailboats like *American Promise* allow one to cut the corners significantly on the upwind passages. The Pilot Chart data have been collected over time largely from ship reports and, since ships tend to avoid nasty weather, the information tends to be biased toward fair weather. For instance, if an area of the chart shows 15 percent gale-force winds or stronger for a given month, you may well in fact experience a gale one day out of three.

DAY 9 ≈

Short rain squalls cool off an otherwise brilliantly sunny day. Wind is the low twenties and seas are down to ten feet. We are passing through 20° north latitude.

After working the twenty-meter ham band at sunset with limited success, I walk the deck and become captivated by the vastness of the night sky and endless sea. So many shooting stars — one every ten minutes at least. I make a wish on each in the name of a friend. These wishes are certain to come true, made, as they are, in such a godlike place. I certainly hope my choice of wishes is acceptable.

The world is round. I know that! But it seems more likely shaped like a platter than a ball, and every single fraction of a degree on the horizon is exactly like every other.

During my rounds, I still note the purple of the diesel oil slowly but continually rising in the bilges and it worries me. I search everywhere for any evidence of leaks — the tops and sides of the tanks, the hoses and fittings, the engine fuel lines, all the hoses. I sound the bilge with a dry line, trying to determine how much fuel and how much seawater we are getting. I pump the bilge dry, then open and check the pump filter bowl for levels of fuel and water. My hopes fade that we have a little bit of oil looking like a lot. I tighten every fuel line connection from and to each of the four tanks — and a helluva lot of connections there are. Twenty-one valves, for example. The job takes me more than three hours, but all I find are many small weepings. I do not find the real problem.

The continued loss of diesel oil could extend or end this voyage. I need to generate power each day to replace what I've used to keep *Promise* under way. I don't need the electric lights; I've got oil lamps as backup. I don't need the sailing instruments or the radios to keep going. The satnav displays can stay black because I can depend totally on my old friend the sextant. All the winches can be cranked by hand, as can the mainsail furling system. The loss of all these devices would most certainly slow us down, but won't stop us from our goal. But I can't keep going for long without a significant amount of autopilot operation. I have simply got to have steering help from Murphy or Joe for about eight hours a day, and that means forty ampere-hours of power, which takes thirty minutes of generator time to replenish. A third of a gallon of diesel fuel per day. I left Bermuda with eight hundred gallons and have lost an estimated one hundred of those gallons through leaks in the first ten days. The leaks must be stopped. I start carrying wrenches and a wiping cloth with me full time and spend my leisure looking for leaks.

Other mechanical problems begin to surface. The portside wind instrument is giving me readings of ninety knots. (There are two wind speed and direction sensors, one on each outboard side of the antenna tower aft; the tower location makes this gear accessible, and having two units allows me to choose one out of a turbulent windstream.) And ARGOS stops transmitting, making it more difficult for those on land to determine my location.

ARGOS is a global position tracking system. A small, battery-powered global transmitter on *American Promise* continually sends a coded signal that is picked up by orbiting satellites and sent on to a computer center in France. Manny — and anybody else with a personal computer and the proper password — can dial the local number of a computer network at any time and get my precise position and the time it was taken. These positions, available to the rest of the world but not to me, are recorded an average of ten times daily. When Manny heard of this amazing device, she told me, "Dodge, this sailing voyage may be the very first time in all the years I've known you that I will actually know where you are most of the time." For her I will try to repair ARGOS.

For some reason, I choose this time to reread *Around the*

World Alone by Alain Colas, about his solo, one-stop circumnavigation aboard the sixty-seven-foot trimaran *Manureva*. His descriptions of Indian Ocean sailing frighten me. I decide I'd better get my reading time in while still sailing the lower latitudes. The questions keep homing in on me. If he, a younger and very experienced solo sailor, also with a boat specifically made for the job, was driven to the edge of fear and physical punishment by that ocean, how will I fare? How much am I depending on good luck to get me by that place? And then again, the big question: Why did I ever think I wanted to do this in the first place? Right now, the alternatives look real good. I could be comfortable, tightly held in a safe world surrounded by friends, pampering myself. I am here instead, alone and heading like a solitary lemming for the roaring forties of the Southern Indian Ocean. Is it simply because I am afraid of becoming an overcivilized, pink-fingered dilettante, a soft and puffy comfort creature? Or is it simply that I have developed an overblown sense of my own capacities? Why? Oh hell, I know why. I know.

Fate chooses this time to surprise me with a momentary touch of humanity.

DAY 11 ≈

We are crossing the sixteenth parallel with a southeast breeze up and down from fifteen knots to zero. Suddenly I sight a sail on the horizon, a ketch, hull down and sailing west. On VHF radio, a voice answers my call. He is Francis Beniste, a Frenchman from St.-Molie, near Toulant. His boat is *Krolos,* and he is sailing her on a delivery. She is a "shit boat" in his words. I am reminded that the oceans of the world are populated with these guys, sailing bums, unheralded, competent, willing and purposeful dropouts from society. And there is Beniste from a place near Toulant sailing a rich man's shit boat to the Cape Verde Islands to Guadeloupe Island in the West Indies, then through the Panama Canal to the South Pacific, Bora Bora in French Polynesia. All in a day's work. And then the rich man will fly to Bora Bora to sit on his shit boat and consume tropical drinks. It does my soul good to see and hear another human spirit in this wilderness.

At noon, we are 1,560.4 miles from Bermuda for an average

of 141.9 miles per day of progress on the great circle route. We have sailed 1,748 miles, noon fix to noon fix, for a daily average of 158.9 miles over the bottom. This, I know, is not an example of precise navigation. We have sailed 188 miles, or 12 percent farther, than we should have had we kept on the great circle. If we perform this poorly for the entire circumnavigation, it will take us 30,744 miles to get around the world instead of the planned 27,450. That would mean 10 percent more time, another twenty days or so.

My daily routine in these easy sailing conditions is predictable and quite laid back:

0700   Up to shake all sleep from whiskers, topsides to view the new day, check weather, tour deck, adjust sail trim, write in log, drink two cups black coffee, outline day's chores.

1000   Navigating exercises. Review progress and heading to next waypoint, chart current positions of known weather elements — fronts, highs, lows — try for some weather charts of the facsimile receiver, take sun sight with sextant if ambitious.

1100   Breakfast, pretty big one. Clean up body afterward.

Noon   Daily position taken and recorded and calculations for the daily progress averages are made. Sextant meridian transit of the sun.

1300   Record weather and navigation information in log and thoughts in journal.

1400   Chores. Walk the rounds to check for chafing and wear of lines and sails and fittings topsides and for engine oil levels, diesel leaks, hydraulic leaks belowdecks.

1600   Radio communications schedule on specified days. Read. Bake bread every few days.

1900   Charge batteries with generator for about two hours. Make fresh water if needed. Prepare dinner.

2030   Eat dinner straight from cooking pot. Sit on deck if good weather, in pilothouse if not. Contemplate state of world. Maybe more reading or writing.

2345   Time for science and a few laughs; take psychological tests.

2400   In sack to daydream, let imagination run riot, laugh at how ridiculous life can be, then sleep. Up at least every two hours to trim or change sails, adjust heading, fix broken things.

·   ·   ·

Promise's computer alarm system doesn't work well enough for me to depend on it. But as *Promise* and I become friends, we don't need the alarm; it actually gets in the way of our feel for each other. I am able to sense the changes in her performance, even while I'm sleeping, earlier and better, more accurately, than the computer or the instruments can. I find myself using the sailing instrumentation less and less and for confirmation rather than information when I do.

It begins to look as though we will carry our luck through the ITCZ, or doldrums. Bob Rice reports that the zone of calms is narrow, between three and four degrees of latitude, or just a couple hundred miles of light-to-no-air sailing.

DAY 13 ≈

I am fascinated by a short visit by some birds, wave skimmers. They may be shearwaters, but they're not close enough for me to describe and investigate in my Peterson's bird guide. So much of my life has been spent on or near the sea and I really know so little about the names of her birds.

I try to read *Sea of Slaughter* by Farley Mowat but cannot. It is devastatingly discouraging, how man has wreaked havoc on nature. I want the Mowat of *The Boat Who Wouldn't Float,* his humor and imagery, now. I pick up *The Magus.*

After a dinner of gummy macaroni and cheese (it's supposed to be gummy, right?), I stay on deck to watch the rise of a full moon through a parade of muffin clouds and have some deep, deep philosophical thoughts that translate into words as childish rhetorical questions. Can a human mind measure the sky? Or time? The hardest is time. If I knew the true measure of time, I think I could measure life. But what are we all here for, anyway? Is there a grand plan? Are we the major factor? Or is all existence a happenstance, a cosmic joke? I end up being horny.

The night passes as easily as if I were in bed at home. I trek out to trim the sails just once. I am supremely comfortable in my little dry cabin listening to the hiss of the sea sliding by. It makes me a bit nervous because solo sailing is not supposed to be this easy. But now we ride the rails of the trade winds and soon enough it won't be this easy. I'll take the good times while I can.

What I'm having trouble with are those damned movie cameras all over this boat, mounted everywhere I want to sit or lean, staring at me and then whirring at me. Hey, you friggin' cameras, there's nothing to whir about here. Every day is much, very, very much, like its predecessor. This is not a big action deal going on here, with crisis following crisis. What it is is one small step after another, forever these small steps, so small that progress does not show. But you don't understand that, do you, just blinking your eyes at whatever world is in front of you when the switch is closed by some mindless circuit. You don't know there probably is no film in this venture. And besides that, you piss me off, eavesdropping, peering at me from only God knows where.

At midnight I am awakened abruptly when about ten gallons of seawater shoot through my dry cabin hatch to land on me. This is proof that "dry" and "hatch" do not belong in the same sentence. I swab up the wave below and retire to the cockpit, where waves are supposed to be. As I am steering and star-gazing, a flying fish hits me a glancing blow on the back of my head. I see phony stars among the real ones for a moment but am left with nothing more serious than a small bald spot. I wonder what the lesson is when I am hit by wet waves when below and hard waves when topside.

DAY 15 ≈

I am suspended in space and time. It is like reliving the same day over and over. Even though the encircled crosses of the noon positions march across the chart, it is an intellectual struggle to understand that progress is taking place, that the voyage is proceeding. It is obvious, however, that the spiritual goal is yielding, that those discoveries are under way. The mysteries of solitude are unfolding.

DAY 16 ≈

The barograph draws a straight line around its recording drum at 30.00 inches of mercury. It is the temperature of siesta land, eighty-eight degrees, and humid. I feel as though I'm learning how to sleep like the real sleep pros. You don't have to earn your sleep, you take it simply because it's there. This motion has something to do with my sleep education, I'm sure. Soft and hypnotic undulations endlessly.

I do the routine chores and replenish the hydraulic oil reservoir and look some more for a leak and maybe find it around some valve stems. Then I wash myself and shave and make myself feel so good I take a nap.

Intense squalls are flying by me as my afternoon radio schedule puts me in contact with home on Hoyt's birthday. He thanks me for my present, a small gold pocket knife, the kind that careful men keep at the ready for a lifetime, the kind I've never been able to hang on to for six months. The boy is twelve today. In some cultures, he'd now be a man. Manny reports all is fine at home except that the heating system is acting up. I am sitting in the pilothouse seat, naked and perspiring, six degrees north of the equator.

Lo and behold! At 0345 the jib is aback. I sail by hand and learn a wind shift to the south leaves us on the starboard tack! After sixteen days of east wind, we have south. The boat, myself, the whole world, seem very strange on this foreign tack. This may be the edge of the ITCZ and time to say good-bye to lazy days of one wind, one heading, and Murphy. Another signature of the doldrums is the squalls descending on us. They are magnificent. Downpours I cannot see through and winds of thirty-five knots, requiring much reefing and shaking out of sails. Between the squalls, light rain and light wind.

DAY 17 ≈

During my rounds on deck, I find the gooseneck pin holding the hydraulic boom vang to the mast has dropped out. This sets the boom adrift, held only by the clew of the sail. Replacing the pin is one sonofabitch of a job. The boom must weigh several hundred pounds. I must capture it and tie it down and up before working on the vang. I rig a rope cradle to hold the vang in place [it is a big hydraulic ram, seven feet long and sixty pounds, used to hold the boom up in place of a rope-topping lift and to bring the boom down for trim while sailing hard on the wind]. I use a spare halyard to rig a rope-topping lift to the end of the boom and guy the boom to both sides of the boat to hold it steady, or almost steady, since we find ourselves in a squall, thirty-five knots of wind and ten feet of seas. Fiddling and diddling the half-inch-by-six-inch pin up through the series of holes is like performing delicate surgery on a non-tranquilized spastic outside during a thunderstorm. The cause for this failure is again one of those frigging roll pins, a little, coiled piece of stainless steel stuffed through a hole. The only good that comes from this is that we didn't lose the boom itself and I get a feeling of accomplishment after the successful repair.

How many times must I be taught the same lesson before learning it: never handle a live sheet unless it is on a winch or a cleat around something that is between me and the sail. The jibsheet snags around a fitting. I reach out to flip it off and the sail flicks a luff. And blood erupts and flies from a couple of fingers. Just one little snap. Lots of blood. More blood than trouble. No breaks. A bandage wrap is enough. And once again Manny's trauma kit remains unopened. But the immense power of a luff in thirty-five knots of wind on sixteen hundred square feet of sail is again demonstrated.

We hit the empty hole of the doldrums in the night. Hand steering to get every inch. Family of small, bottle-nose dolphins light up our stage at daybreak. I clown with them from the bow pulpit and consider jumping in to join their frolic. I make them grin at me.

DAY 18 ≈

We make history! We punch through the doldrums already. My Bob Rice report confirms that we have passed the ITCZ and are now sailing into Southern Hemisphere weather; on his satellite weather picture, he sees the signature squalls of the doldrums to our north. In our slowest day through this infamous band of calms, we make a hundred and thirty miles. That's a 5.4-knot average. Incredible performance. The blue ribbon goes to Bob Rice at his Weather Services International desk in Bedford, Mass. The red ribbon goes to Ted Hood for being right when he said, "Heavier displacement is not a detriment to performance in light air." Rice wove us through the windless barrier at its weakest point and *American Promise* has shown herself to be one helluva light-air performer just when she needed to be. We rode the momentum of those squalls.

We slide by the tiny offshore islands of Penedos de São Pedro e São Paulo, just fifty miles north of the equator, and sail into Shangri-La. The wind is a rock-solid fifteen knots over long, low swells under a sky of bright blue busy with puffy cumulus. *Promise* settles into an eight-knot speed on a gentleman's beat, the big 150 percent jib and main trimmed hard, heeling us at twenty-five degrees as steady as if we were permanently ballasted that way. The dominant sound all around us is that of rushing water. Miles slip by us effortlessly.

We cross the equator on day 19 at 0410, at longitude 25° 45.6' west. From Bermuda we have sailed noon fix to noon fix 3,014 miles; this is 2,780 miles of great circle distance. Our planned waypoints show a distance of 2,961 miles. Thus we have sailed 53 miles more than the planned waypoint course, just 1.8 percent more. This is one hell of an improvement over our earlier sailing job. Although we had sailed in the wrong direction to avoid Hurricane Kate, we get the lost distance back by cutting the eastern corner off the dogleg of the traditional sailing route down the North Atlantic.

DAY 20 ≈

Have my equator-crossing celebration today, but not in the traditional way of screwy costume and champagne. I dedicate our crossing to science!

It is known that a low-pressure point causes a counterclockwise circulation in the Northern Hemisphere and a clockwise circulation in the Southern Hemisphere. This is often demonstrated to schoolchildren by watching a sink full of water drain. North of the equator, where most of the world's school-children are, the water obediently circulates counterclockwise around the low-pressure center of the drain.

The tool for my experiment is a plastic bucket with a hole punched in the bottom which is filled with seawater and suspended in the cockpit by strings. The scientist is not helped in this experiment by his rolling and pitching laboratory and swinging and squirting tool. I find myself plastered to the top of the pilothouse, hanging on for dear life and intently studying the swinging bucket for signs of Coriolis. Sure enough, I see the seawater circulation switch to clockwise when we enter the Southern Hemisphere. I'm quite sure I see this. Really, I am.

But science imitates life and my experiment is flawed. I am unable to prove my major hypothesis, which is to find that magical zone between north and south where the water flows straight down the drain. I am unable to locate the ITCZ of Coriolis.

$$\sim\!\!\sim 6 \sim\!\!\sim$$

*T*he initial leg of this voyage, the first rite of passage, is now behind us. *American Promise* and I are friends as we cross the equator together, and I feel that as I have become more sure of her, she has become more sure of me. She has become a kind of living thing to me now, the only living thing I have, and I begin to relate to her that way. She knows the job we must do together. She wants the progress out of each day just as much as I do. We are beginning to make a good pair. And although she is the stronger and the bigger and the more durable of the two of us, she is still hopelessly dependent on me. In spite of her great strengths, I must constantly coddle and care for her because she is, in some places, shockingly fragile and sensitive. As I get to know those vulnerable places more intimately, I get better and better at doing what she needs me to do. And she, in turn, takes care of me.

My daily rounds of *American Promise* have now become like a religious ritual. I examine every surface with my eyes and much of her also with my touch. I gather my small set of tools, coil of stainless steel wire, roll of duct tape, stick of grease, ball of marlin, and can of oil and slowly walk the sixty feet on deck from stern to bow. My detailed study then begins with my moving back aft. I work and lubricate the furling drums for the jib and forestaysail and study the sails for rips or chafing and examine and feel all fittings within reach. I am always astonished by how much wear has occurred in just one day. A jibsheet is badly frayed and I turn it end for end. The line on the jib furling drum is chafed from being in one place too long, and my temporary fix is to serve it with waxed line. I operate all the winches. I swing on the standing rigging and sight up the mast to see that it is still straight. I search the rigging aloft very carefully with the binoculars. I have come to know the view well.

The round below takes longer, but I don't need to be quite as meticulous as I am on deck, because down here she is shielded from her two greatest enemies, chafing and exposure. If I discover a job that will take time, I jot it down on a pad for later attention. Walking below to the bow, I enter the forward watertight compartment through a heavy metal door that wouldn't look out of place on a submarine. *Promise* has four such doors to close off her five watertight compartments. Up here, there is a large deck hatch overhead for moving sails to and from the deck.

This compartment is always wet. It is festooned with sails and lines — hanging from hooks, lashed to the hull, and filling the bow of the boat. The nine sails here weigh more than a thousand pounds, and the line would stretch a half mile. Anchors and ground tackle are stowed here.

I move back aft into the generator room, a compartment roughly ten by fifteen feet, taking the full width of the boat. The only natural light enters through two small, thick, glass deadlights embedded in the deck. Two bright red diesel generators squat on either side, each caged in a web of pipe and netting and covered by cloth tents stretched to shed the water that makes its way through the dorade vents overhead. I keep these vents open to supply air to the diesels. There are banks of lockers tucked under the deck over the generators on either side, each with thirty square feet of space. Engine parts and rig fittings and spare equipment and food are stowed in these lockers. Two more sails and coils of wire halyards are lashed to the hull beneath the lockers. I check the engine fluid levels and belt tensions and feel for fuel leaks. The after bulkhead in the generator room is a living schematic of *Promise*'s fuel system, red and blue hoses, stainless steel manifolds, ball valves with bright yellow handles, pumps, and the golden glass globes of fuel filters. I feel for leaks and drain the filters of water. Beneath the cabin sole there are batteries, fuel and water tanks, and more plumbing. The sole, here as throughout the boat, is covered with thick rubber and cork matting and has removable panels with big chrome lifting rings.

Before I leave, I start the port generator to charge the batteries.

I move aft from the generator room though another watertight door into a long, narrow passageway on the port side. All the passageways are narrow so that I won't be thrown far by any sudden motion. To my left in a closet-size room are the head and shower and to my right the workbench and tool lockers. Aft beyond the bench is a bunk, now used only for bulk stowage. Beyond the head, a passageway extends across the boat to the starboard side, where the little galley and my dry cabin are located. *Promise* is her widest, seventeen feet, at this point, and her deepest bilge is beneath this passageway. I get into this cavernous bilge by lifting the center of three large floor panels. The bilgewater is visible by flashlight through a maze of hoses and filters radiating from five bilge pumps — two electric, two hand-operated, and one engine-driven. I pump the bilge by hand to learn better how much diesel oil continues to leak into the ever-rising seawater. I clean the strainers. One by one, I open the big valves to drain the bilges of each of the other compartments. Clean water gushes from the forwardmost and aftermost compartments; they are the ones with deck hatches.

I resume my trek aft. One step up and I am in the pilothouse, out of the dungeon and into the light. Here my inspection turns to matters electrical, electronic, and hydraulic. I belt myself into the race car seat and have the inside helm directly before me, the radios and depth recorder stacked to my right, the autopilot control heads to my left, the satellite navigators in front of me, and the sailing instruments and clocks filling the dash forward. I can see the electrical panel in the entryway to my left, a four-by-two-foot display of breakers and switches and gauges and red diodes that now tell me the generator is doing its job. This is where I live so much of my life now, and the ocean view is fantastic. I can see all around, and there is no distortion in the big, half-inch-thick Lexan windows. I can see the mainsail overhead right up to the top of the mast.

Beneath the pilothouse floor, I examine more tanks, more batteries, and the main engine.

I move farther aft into compartment five, which is under the cockpit and has crouching room only. It is crammed full of equipment to check: four huge, sixty-amp chargers, the two reverse-osmosis watermakers, hydraulic tanks and plumbing, the trunks and mechanisms for the three retractable boards, and heavy weather autopilot Joe. Two more sails are stowed here, strapped up against the bottom ends of the twelve winches poking through the cockpit combing above me. This cave of a place is always coated with a film of oil because it is where the engine and hydraulic oil are stored in bulk. My stop here is as short as I can make it.

In compartment six, my last stop, I check the rudderpost bearings and my old and dear friend, autopilot Murphy. The only entrance to this area is from the deck through a hatch that leaks, mixing enough salt water with the hydraulic oil from Murphy to create a unique environment in which corrosion rampages in a place as slippery as fish guts.

My ever-looming awareness of the Southern Indian Ocean is a major reason for these careful inspection rounds. This ocean has dominated my thoughts about the voyage ever since I started to plan it two and a half years ago. Now it is the next passage, and I am continually in a low fever of preparation, getting both of us ready in every way I can, consciously and subconsciously.

The passage from the equator to the Southern Ocean takes three weeks. We cross the South Atlantic trade winds, solid dependable easterlies, then tend west around the South Atlantic high-pressure zone, and, finally, slug through the windless horse latitudes, thirty to thirty-five degrees south, into the latitudes of the big west winds. These are easy weather conditions, and I have the time to intellectualize about solitude. I have discovered that it is not a condition like pain or love or hate or pleasure that lets its secrets go in big, abrupt, emotional events. In fact, it is not much at all when you're going through it. Loneliness is not solitude, or even representative of it. I've been lonelier in a crowd in a strange city than I have ever been at sea by myself. Perhaps solitude is more the absence of everything than it is the presence of anything. I still don't understand it. But I think its most crucial element is time.

DAY 21 ≈
Noon, December 2, 1985, Monday, to noon, December 3, 1985,
     Tuesday
3°59.53' south/29°33.98' west
     This day is identical to yesterday — same wind, same sky, same sea, *Promise* locked into a twenty-five-degree heel nod-

ding monotonously. The lack of evidence of civilization is absolute. And the evidence of living nature is also scarce, a few flying fish and perhaps a bird a day. I have an eerie feeling that this may be much like a world struggling to recover from a nuclear holocaust.

I'm entering another phase in my forced study of solitude and this may be the most persistent one. I am bent on moving the time behind me without much concern for how I do it or for what happens in the course of using that time. A prisoner with a known, definite sentence must feel this way. One with a life sentence, of course, would have to see time differently. He would have no choice but to get into the world he was living in and participate with time as it passed. And he would plan on participating. Somehow I've got to find the use-time-as-it-comes attitude of the lifer. Somehow I've got to fight this tendency to lolligag around in limbo simply wearing time away. This time just might be all the time I have.

Another night of stupefying sleep. *Promise* sails herself dutifully, needing little or no help. Sometimes I feel guilty. Sometimes I know I will pay for this easy living later.

I have to keep careful track of the days of the week. My memory doesn't associate events with names of days at all. The recent past seems just like, well, the past in one amorphous, timeless lump. When was it we slid past the unseen islands Penedos de São Pedro y São Paulo? What day was the equator crossing? Let's see, I finished *The Adventures of Huckleberry Finn* when? Today?

The only significance to the names of the days is my radio communications schedule. On Wednesday and Saturday I try to reach home by way of my ham buddies. Tuesday and Friday I must speak with Bob Rice.

Bob Rice is my big brother. The steady, dependable drum of his voice proffers weather wisdom to all from Bedford, Massachusetts, and I know I am but one of his needy waifs, that kings and presidents also wait in line for him. But when I can get my plug in on a Tuesday or Friday, he is always there and ready for me, and I am always so proud and humble and thankful he is.

I made fresh water last night while charging, perhaps twenty-

five to thirty gallons in two hours. The generator-powered watermaker has developed a leak in a high-pressure line, an eight-
hundred-pound-per-square-inch spurt. Now I will have to go to
the backup watermaker, which operates from a power takeoff
on the main engine. Boy, that setup had better keep working
because I am just not ready to give up my weekly shower. We
have about ninety gallons of usable hard tank water storage;
our two rubber bladder water tanks have already chafed themselves full of holes from the constant motion.

The environmental movement would be proud of me. I am
doing extremely well on conserving electrical power on board.
We are consuming 180-240 ampere-hours daily, depending on
how much time the radios are in use, and that is replenished by
a charging cycle of less than two hours in twenty-four. Two
more items of good news are the superb, trouble-free performance so far of autopilot Murphy and the fact that diesel oil is
less evident in the bilges.

I keep digging deeper into a belief that my epiphany for solitude lies somewhere in the equation of time. I am certain that time
aboard is not truly measured by clocks and calendars except for
navigation calculations. I force time by in very short increments,
and sometimes each tiny bit passes like an eternity. I have not yet
reached the point where I know enough to be deeply comfortable
out here alone with *Promise*.

DAY 31 ≈

Another daybreak, and I am again struck by the lack of any
visible signs of life — no ship or plane or bird or even a flying
fish in these calm seas. My remaining link to the world of the
living is my radio, but even the conversation seems very remote. Even though I look forward to my radio contacts, it
doesn't bother me that much when I have days without them.
Life is very monotonous aboard, so there is no real news for
me to report anyway.

But it is also true that the news I hear from those ashore —
plenty of news, too — often doesn't seem that important or
meaningful. I hear about ball games and dinner parties and fi-

nancial statements and flu bugs and stock market moves and weather statistics. Manny tells me that the New England Patriots are tied for the lead in their division of the NFL. The information seems so puny, like one tiny point in the path of a huge, perpetual pendulum as it swings through an arc ordained by fixed and eternal law. I couldn't care less about the Pats this year. It is of such small consequence, I wonder why anyone would care.

Tell me instead if Hoyt has begun to learn how to live with that deep and dense will to succeed of his, the will that causes him sometimes to have stomach aches before ball games and to stay aloof from a challenge until he knows how to best it. Even as he makes a success of virtually all he does in his life, will he know how to ignore risk, to abandon himself to a challenge for its own sake? Has Kim begun to see out from the shadow of her brother's will how beautiful she is and how talented? Does she still need to seek her self-esteem in a play world by the light of her imagination? Will she learn she can believe in herself as deeply as she should?

Also, please let me know if the world has found out how to wage furious war without death as a scorekeeping device. Or if scientists have confirmed that incurable diseases can be cured by Marx Brothers movies. Or if anyone has written an explanation that I can understand for where and how space and time do or do not end. Or if proof has been found that existence itself is only a state of mind and that consciousness is but a series of quick animal acts.

My life out here is certainly a series of quick animal acts, and there can be great practical satisfaction in living this way. Cook. Navigate. Trim sails. Eat. Clean up. Get over next wave. Tighten bolt. Shit. Sleep. Add oil. Brush teeth. Sleep. Masturbate. Check cave. Sharpen tool. Make fire. Find club. Kill deer. Get woman. Woof!

On our forty-first day, three days before Christmas and just below the 41st parallel, my struggle with solitude takes a different tack.

DAY 41 ≈

Promise lopes along at five knots. There is a nip in the air. The sky is gray, overcast. I am melancholy, a sign that the solitude is digging a hole in my mind, that I'm wandering off the path of self-control.

It's okay, Dodge, just don't wander too far. Too far and it's not a pleasant trip, you know. You begin to dwell on those absent emotions and the human interactions that feed them, and then, painfully, painfully, you see the interminable time and distance you must go before you can taste those beautifully chaotic human juices again. And then you realize you may never. Oh, so sad a thought. Fight back then. Keep yourself on the path of self-control. Keep yourself from danger.

Sleep comes to me easily. My dream is an animal dream, the same one remembered and rejoined involuntarily after each drowsy awakening to see that *Promise* continues on her way, properly synchronized with what little breeze she has. My mind keeps having sex. Round, juicy sex that smells like brown earth and tastes like a sweet tidal flat. She is huge. I dominate at her will. Now she wants me to. Now she says, "Stay down and look up and relax and I will take care of you," and takes control. She drives me close, so close but not over. Hers is an endless orgasm.

I am up and feeling very alive, very rested, very content. I know I can take the world one day at a time and one hour at a time and that puts me back on the path of self-discipline.

I begin to sense a powerful egotism emerging during this passage from the equator around South Africa's Cape of Storms into the Southern Oceans. It is the egotism of a human brain functioning with none of the human senses in place. It is always looking inward because that is the only direction there is. Solitude does that to you over time.

The journal is part of my daily regimen, but, unlike the three working navigation logs I also keep, writing it is pure recreation. Having no specifications, it evolves into a verbal grapeshot blast of practical concerns and emotional flights of fancy written in a stream-of-consciousness form. The practical concerns I write about are like a droning mantra of little problems and threats and small solutions and victories, as unadorned as one would expect them, since they essentially describe one very long chore accomplished one short step at a time. In the more personal, emotional entries, however, I write with abandon and with a candidness, and a self-centeredness, that is childlike.

If the journal is confusing and repetitious, so is the voyage. If the journal makes light of problems, then that's what's necessary to maintain a positive attitude, without which we'll never make it. If the journal celebrates victories that seem too small, then those are the only victories I win. In the calms of the horse latitudes:

≈Oh, I am frustrated by this. No wind. This is the most nerve-racking of assignments, to keep the boat moving in light and variable air. The boat continually rolls in the seas, and the terrible slatting of the sails and slamming about of gear below is tougher on the boat and gear, particularly on sails and lines and fittings, than a gale of constant pressure. I cannot relax. I am on edge, using every muscle and all of my senses in attempts to create, to influence anything that might steady *Promise* and move her forward. I search the sea surface for wrinkles, signs of breeze, and physically and emotionally will them up into her sails. I suppress the waves with downward motions of my hands so that the boat won't roll and jerk the precious air out of the sails. None of this does much good and is exhausting as well, but I can't stop.

I must make peace with the immediate present somehow and, at all costs, avoid projecting our long-term progress for the whole voyage by our current performance . . . or I begin to calculate that at one and a half knots it will take me 136 days to reach Australia and, and . . . No. No. Let's get over this next hump. One more day. The next low-pressure cell will come to us, will be here, and then we will have the other problem of wondering how deep the storm will be and how rough a time it will hand us. And (hooray!) how many two-hundred-mile days we will take from it.

We go thirteen miles in four hours. The hard way.

But I forget my woes for a while as this day's ham radio meeting is a busy one. In spite of very noisy airways, my land commander and social manager, Dick Morse, W1GR, plugs me

Above: Promise is reefed down to a small sail area in heavy weather but still makes eight knots speed.
Below: American Promise beats on a lively breeze. About 20 percent of the nearly 27,500-nautical-mile circumnavigation was sailed into the wind.

Above Left: Ted Hood's no-compromise, single-hander, nonstop-circumnavigator slides out of her Little Harbor shed in Marblehead. Carefully specified, she is a controversial design with no precedent.
Above Right: Promise's designer, F. E. "Ted" Hood.
Below: Promise is fitted with an intermediate centerboard and two daggerboards that are lowered to keep her tracking straight when running down the huge Southern Ocean seas. When lowered all the way, the centerboard becomes an emergency rudder.

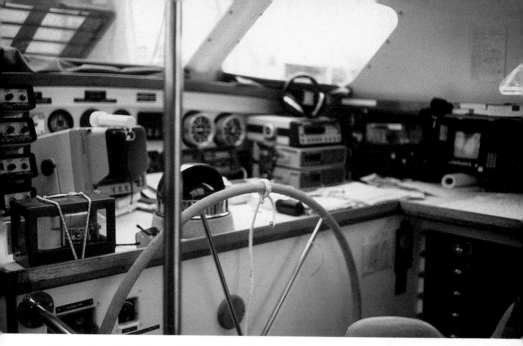

Above: Looking forward from the pilothouse helm across the array of navigation equipment, radios, and sailing instruments. I spent most of my time at sea in the pilothouse.

Below Left: The "black sheep" crew and Little Harbor regulars proudly pose together beside their creation. Relations between the two groups were not always rosy.

Below Right: The snug bunk in *Promise*'s "dry cabin" was placed low in the very center of the hull, where motion was easiest, but I slept no more than two hours at a time.

Opposite: Ted Hood was right. Although she had a relatively heavy displacement, *Promise* performed extremely well in light airs.
Above: *Promise* sailed at a steady ten knots on a close reach in twenty-five knots of wind.
Below: Midocean calms were much more stressful than the fierce "roaring forties" storms. Alone and becalmed on an endless ocean, I felt helpless and depressed. Here I photograph my reflection.

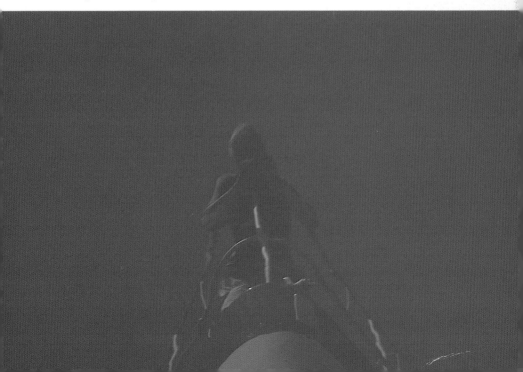

Above: The lofty cutter rig on *American Promise* made her a powerful sailer over a wide range of wind conditions. Two twenty-three-foot poles were used for downwind work.

Below: Promise sailed much of the 11,000 Southern Ocean miles under her poled-out headsails.

After five months of solitude, I sail *American Promise* into Bermuda scrubbed and polished. The wear and tear and broken gear are not obvious to the welcoming crowd.

Above: I pat my friend while the spectator fleet celebrates our Bermuda arrival.
Left: The sailor has returned. My wife, Manny, and my children, Kim and Hoyt, look on.

into the network, a conference of strong, deep voices that threads me for a time back into the human race. It is a spiritually nourishing event. These voices from so many thousands of miles away break into my solitude and give me evidence that the clock of humanity still ticks.

I devote myself to avoiding work as the thirty-fifth day begins. Again, I feel down and empty, solemn. Even a couple of swooping albatrosses fail to cheer me up. I bury myself in reading Bill Manchester's *Goodbye Darkness,* about the Pacific war. I like the book because it gives me courage.

≈I love it when a man in the story deserves a victory and he wins a victory, a victory justified by sweat and guts and perseverance and courage and hard work, and the best ones, of course, won against the odds and not against any specific enemy. The just victory leaves me in tears, with a stiffened back, a tensed jaw, and my right fist involuntarily jerking short punches into the air. I feel reassured, then, that there is no real victory without real challenge and real risk. I know I have placed myself in jeopardy for the chance at the sweet, golden, pure emotion of one of those victories. I am the proud victor I read about in the book. And then I tell myself how much easier it would be if I could be satisfied by reading about it instead of by doing it, and this makes me feel special, like one of those good guys in Manchester's book, because I really do not want it to be easy, do I?

This night is glorious. Father Fate decided I needed a lift. The wind comes out of the east at fifteen knots, with five-foot seas, and *Promise* settles into a lightly bouncing, effortless close reach at better than nine knots and keeps it up for hours.

Then a sudden confrontation with the world of people shocks me and has a surprising effect.

≈At daybreak, we come about to tack south after beating all night, slamming really, slowly into the east. The autopilot does not handle this sailing into a wind that wavers twenty degrees and so I steer. We are nearing the Southern Ocean latitudes. I am very drowsy as I crank the winches to bring her sails back in hard.

Once on the new heading, I am confused and taken aback by a large but almost subliminal image looming in the corner of my eye. Then I am wide awake with the shock of a ship, a huge container ship, and quite close by. She has an Arabic name and is bound westward. This is my first visible evidence of humanity for several weeks and I am mesmerized by the sight. The ship silently slides by, puffing up bow waves in the swells and stinking up my air. I think about the people on board together and become melancholy. The morning passes in a somber mood. I think that solitude is easier when I am not directly reminded of the company of others. It takes me hours to rid myself of the lonely feeling the great ship left me with.

Just as the sun goes down I have more visitors. A roving band of dolphins encircles *Promise* and gives us a show, some leaping five to six feet out of the sea and traveling in twenty-to-twenty-five-foot arcs through the air. If only I knew how, I know I would hear them singing to me. A magnificent albatross gives me a swooping aerobatics demonstration. And a lone greater shearwater glides by. I wonder if the shearwater chooses to be alone. I wonder if the bird sees me and feels any kinship.

One of the great inner joys of sailing alone is how carefully and completely I can observe the world around me, totally free of the presence of others. Another person on a boat, even if out of sight and asleep, always fills much of my awareness. I cannot help but wonder if the other sees what I see, if the other will be awakened when I tack, if the other is hungry or wet, is afraid and needs reassuring, or is worried about me. So I can't overlook another person's presence and sometimes I resent it. When sailing alone, I have no interruption in my view of the act at hand and, most important, of nature in her act. My view of the nature of things, I feel, is direct, clean, and pure. I feel that I am closer to some universal truth. It is a transcendental, spiritual feeling that brings the humbling recognition of how immense is nature, how incredibly insignificant is each of us in the realm of nature, and how enormous is our ignorance of nature.

Another inner joy of sailing alone is the feeling I have of absolute independence, of knowing that every act belongs exclusively to me — I am totally responsible for every bit of progress, every mistake. There is something very alluring about knowing that no one else will be there to help when there is a challenge or to share a success when it is earned. There is something very satisfying in dealing with the quick and certain victories and defeats of sailing a small boat alone.

There is also the danger and fear of sailing alone.

DAY 24 ≈

This afternoon at 1620 hours Zulu [Greenwich Mean Time] we sail right by a bright red and brand-new-looking buoy, ball float with a staff and triangle flag maybe eight feet high. It is at 12°44.75' south latitude, 28°11.41' west longitude and looks like it is meant to be here. Yet we are in the middle of an ocean where little or no ship traffic passes. Who put it here? What's it for? I don't know.

But I wonder what other manner of objects *Promise* and I have grazed by that I have not seen because most of the time, a clear majority of the day, we are sailing blind. Sailing blind is a necessary part of sailing alone. Collision at sea is the solo sailor's most common nightmare. Although I have generally scoffed at this danger, maintaining that most sailboats in mid-ocean do not travel the shipping lanes so that the odds of not being even within sight of a ship are much better than those of being run down by one, the buoy leads me to some doubt now. I do know that after days of seeing nothing but a circle of barren water surrounding us, I worry so little about it that I choose to save power and leave the running lights off at night. Tonight, though, I will use the running lights while I sleep. All it took is the pure chance of sighting a red buoy in the middle of the ocean.

Anticipating a challenge is often more intimidating than meeting it. And so it certainly is for me and the Southern Ocean. The farther south *Promise* and I sail and the more I reread my pile of literature, the greater the challenge becomes. All the books on the

Southern Ocean are threatening, Bob Rice's report is not encouraging at all, and my own research from *Ocean Passages, Sailing Directions,* and the Pilot Charts confirms that *Promise* and I are headed for a test. A very big test. Every day I either make some effort to prepare for my test or I feel guilty because I don't make an effort.

DAY 27 ≈

Smooth seas and moderate easterlies give us ideal old man's sailing conditions and me time to think more about the Indian Ocean. I add to my trepidations by rereading Alain Colas' *Around the World Alone,* in which he calls the chapter on this ocean "Sea of Troubles." The book on the BOC single-handed around-the-world race, *Ultimate Challenge,* describes the fleet's passage east from the Cape of Good Hope as the most devastating of the entire trip, with numerous knockdowns, several dropouts, and one sinking. Right now I don't look forward that much to having the experiences I'm reading about.

DAY 28 ≈

I'm unable to find any encouraging evidence from these books about the Indian Ocean weather. I sure as hell hope that part of the problem is that the publishers are demanding foul weather from their authors. I am certainly jerking myself up to readiness for some really nasty business, but I'm beginning to count on getting some good luck for that ocean and the thirty-five to forty days it will take to cross it, from the Cape of Good Hope to New Zealand, and good luck means getting there.

Today I've scurried over *Promise,* preparing, double-lashing heavy objects in place, rearranging and tying down gear in lockers, lashing halyard coils in place, pumping silicon rubber into crannies and crevices in and around the mast, replacing the air vent scoops with solid deckplates.

Gratefully, my Indian Ocean preparations are interrupted by a western horizon sunset explosion of pastel pink and blue, hard gold and sooty gray. The wind drops to a couple of knots, but we are on a close reach and can maintain a couple in boat speed. The morning is clear, depthless blue, and carries a breeze of five knots, evidence we have not slipped into the dead calms of the South Atlantic's dominating high-pressure zone. The sailing now is so gentle. Long, slow swells move the horizon hypnotically up and down. *Promise* sways and nods, pops and creaks. There is the soft, bubbling sound of moving water and the contented, steady growl of Murphy. Again, I have the feeling of being suspended in time, flowing with it rather than watching it pass. I can procrastinate on my preparations. It doesn't make much sense to put this kind of time to use because I'd have to give up my ride. Soon enough I'll have to step off my time machine. Soon enough.

Promise has delivered me from the underlying fear that I lived with constantly at sea with the old *Coaster,* that the boat could very well come apart at any time. I know that *Promise* will not come apart. She might lose her rig. She might lose her electrical power. But I truly believe that if there is a risk of a fatal break somewhere, it is in me and not in the boat. The potential problem, then, could come from my having too much confidence in her strength, pushing her too hard, giving her too much punishment because she tells me she can take a lot. There is no boat strong enough for the sea; all are vulnerable, all can be broken. The weak link surely is me and I have ample reminders of that.

≈I am looking into the deep, sooty line of a front moving at us as fast as a double-speed film. The wind edges north and I decide to pole out the jib and staysail to get some practice downwind in heavy air, a kind of practice run for Southern Ocean conditions. My first fuckup is off the top of my "please don't" list. The starboard pole lift [a line from the end of the pole to a point high on the mast for holding the pole up] comes adrift and drops the twenty-two-foot pole on my forearm. The failure is that a snapshackle opens up, probably not completely closed by me in the first place. My forearm becomes instantly larger and turns blue. But the bigger problem is that the lift line slowly rises up the mast out of reach, taunting me, "Okay sucker, come on up and fetch me if you can." It knows I don't want to climb the damned mast. I lose my temper. In minutes and in a rage, I am climbing and cursing and waving the fifteen-foot boat hook, the hook end of which I have wrapped with duct tape, sticky side out, to help snatch the line. The line whips around in the wind as I fish up for it with the pole held in my one free hand. I smack myself in the nose with the pole, trying to guide it through the wind, then drop it once and have to lower myself to fetch it, then scream the curse of the permanently damned when my right nut seriously hangs up on the pole track while climbing again. After what is probably a half hour of painful almosts, I get the sticky tape to grip the wayward line long enough to wrap it around the hook, then lower it slowly and carefully back home to the deck and, at the very top of my lungs, bellow a victory oath in defiance to the bastard fate that caused the problem in the first place. I get the poles out with the sails on them like wings just in time for the damnable wind to switch off north and switch on east inside the squall line. The poles have to come back in. Shit. And then, while I am crawling forward through white spray and green water to stow the poles away, another instant wind shift backed by a gust jibes the mainsail. The boom preventer [a three-eighth-inch line rigged from the boom end to the front of the boat] parts with a shot and belts me as it sizzles past. This blow knocks me flat. But it hits me only on the triceps of my right arm, tearing the rim of my ear on the carom.

What a day. I am beat up some. When I think about what could have happened, though, acting as I did in a rage and overlooking my wounds along the way, it makes me shiver. The problem isn't an arm badly bruised in two places, a split ear, or a crushed gonad, but the kind of abandoned behavior that makes widows. Unless I'm more careful, the boat may make it to the Southern Ocean but maybe on autopilot and without me.

I keep my Wednesday ham and home radio dates in spite of my battered body and am engaged in a real social whirl, W1GR-Dick in Massachusetts, W2IBN-George in New York, W1DEO-Herb in Maine, and finally Manny and the family. The Cape Elizabeth home is decorated for Christmas, which for Manny means not a single surface, vertical or horizontal, will go unfestooned. The Hoyt clan, I learn, will be nineteen strong in Maine this holiday. Even though I don't normally like crowds, even family ones at home, particularly if they are around the next morning, I'm thinking that right about now I would make an exception. But — wow! — that Hoyt family. I certainly did marry into a classic, textbook, pure New England WASP family, I did. Polite and proper and conservative and honest and hard-working and proud and self-congratulatory and certain, just certain, that they are blessed with a basic superiority assured by genes.

My Christmas decorating efforts this year consist of changing some four thousand square feet of headsails on *American Promise*. I am following a script that was written by Lee Van Gemert of Hood Sails. For the first two Atlantic Ocean passages, we could expect light to moderate winds, forward of the beam a high percentage of the time. This calls for the big 150 percent jib and, for heavy weather, the 85 percent forestaysail. In extreme light air, I use one of two weights of light headsails called MPSs, similar to a spinnaker but with the luff of the sail tacked down on the bow of the boat. These light sails are twenty-two hundred square feet in size and they are furled in a nylon tube or sleeve that I can lift to set the sail or pull down over the sail to furl it. For our Southern Ocean crossings, with heavy winds expected behind us, I put on a 90 percent jib and 110 percent forestaysail, a quarter less total sail area balanced more equally between the two headsails, because much of the time I will wing these sails out on poles, making us look like a square-rigger. This poling out of the headsails makes it unnecessary to use a spinnaker, a difficult sail to set and control single-handedly. (These percentages describe the sail's size, with 100 percent being the area of the foretriangle of the rig, that space enclosed by the mast, deck, and headstay.)

Changing each headsail on *American Promise* takes me several hours, and it's best to do it in light conditions. The sails are enormous and, for one man, handling them is hard work in the best of conditions and very dangerous in less than ideal conditions. Most of the physical effort is in muscling the huge bulks of Dacron in and out of storage below, up and down through the one available hatch, and in and out of the turtles, or sailbags, on deck. The situation that must be avoided is a sail going out of control in the wind while it is being changed. The potential of this danger is evident in the dimensions of the 150 percent jib, some thirteen hundred square feet in area, 275 pounds in weight, and stowed in a turtle that is forty-five feet long. I have borrowed Sir Francis Chichester's invention, the spider, to help me keep a sail from flying out of control during the changing process. A spider consists of a number of short lines with large snap hooks; the lines are held on a common loop. With the loop made fast to the bow pulpit, I can snap the hooks, one by one, into grommets in the sail's luff as it comes out of the slotted headstay while being dropped. The sails are stowed with spiders attached so that I can reverse the procedure when putting a sail on. This system neatly holds loose sail on deck by the luff. I had the grommets put in the luffs of all the headsails for another purpose as well, so if a slotted headfoil failed, I could set a sail around the stay with cloth or rope hanks.

I bring the boat up on the wind and reef down to slow her way, get the new sail on deck in its turtle, and lash it to the windward rail. I lash an empty turtle to the leeward rail to take the sail that is coming down. I lead the halyard through snatch blocks to my position at the headstay and lower the sail out of the headfoil slot as quickly as possible, snapping in the spider hooks as I do. I flake this sail into its bag. Then I bring the boat about to put the new sail on the leeward (downwind) side and move the sheets over to it. I tie down the spider and attach the halyard to the sail peak, which is easy to identify because of color coding, and make the hauling end up on the self-tailing electric winch on the foredeck. I operate the winch by a remote foot switch while feeding the sail's luff tape into the headfoil slot, removing the spider clips as the sail goes up. Then I fold and bag and shove and haul and bully the old sail below into its stowage space.

I choose some mild weather for changing into our Southern Ocean sails, days 34 and 35, when we are still north of the roaring forties. The forestaysail change takes me three hours, and the jib, four hours. And I screw up the staysail change.

≈The wind is freshening, and so I hurry to get the sail up. When I go to the winch on the mast for the final turns on the halyard, I see the bad news. My mark on the halyard is ten inches past its companion mark on the mast. Damn! I've hoisted the sail too far. The upper swivel of the roller furler has been carried off the headfoil. The problem is seventy feet straight up, and my overriding fear is that I will have to climb the mast again. I curse myself for not remembering that this exact problem happened to me at the dock in Marblehead because some sailmaker didn't bother to use his measuring tape. The luff of the sail is not the correct length. I tell myself that I raised every sail on the boat back in Marblehead Harbor. But not this sail I didn't. When the sail does come back down without my going up the mast, I thank the fates. I do have spares for the plastic sleeves that were shattered in the mishap, and the sail does go back up and it sets well. *Promise* and I will never again assume a new sail is cut the way it should be cut.

We are now ready to take on the roaring forties. I am beginning to repeat myself preparing for them. Best of all, I am beginning to believe that my Christmas present for this year could be a sail in record time for the Bermuda to Cape of Good Hope passage.

$$\approx 7 \approx$$

Promise and I celebrate Christmas by sailing through our first Southern Ocean storm. The forties roar for us on Christmas Day, our forty-fourth day at sea, as we sail into the east on the 42nd parallel, 420 nautical miles south of the tip of Africa.

DAY 44 — December 25 $\approx$

Christmas Day matches my Southern Ocean expectations. At daybreak, the barograph pen draws a cliff, a sure signal that a storm approaches and is moving fast. The sky is smoke gray and turns the sea to slate. The air is heavy with haze. The wind picks up first from the northeast, but soon backs to the north, then west, intensifying all the time. I can see the storm clearly, a night-black line on the western horizon that moves with astonishing speed to obscure the western sky and then to close down over *Promise*. The west wind is thirty-five to forty knots with gusts to fifty. The seas build quickly to eighteen to twenty feet, tops breaking. *Promise* lopes along under her winged-out headsails, seven knots up the seas and fourteen knots down. She rolls thirty degrees either side of straight up and does a quick corkscrew that whips her heading through some thirty degrees. The motion is amusement park caliber and the racket of gear caroming around in lockers is deafening. Nothing stays in one place, including me, but I hang on. I find I can calm her down some by cranking the two daggerboards and intermediate centerboard way down. We sail forty miles in four hours.

Sonofabitch — she loves it, she loves it! The gray sky opens and pours gray rain over the gray sea. I could be color-blind and the view would be just the same. Going forward on deck for my inspection rounds or to set or reset the headsails on the poles for this downwind work is a moving experience. *Promise* shoves her nose out into midair when she comes off the top of a sea, and sometimes the forward third of her hull is levered out. Then she pitches forward and accelerates down the back-side of the sea like a train down a mountain, nose stuck out and water flying. When she hits the wall of the next wave, her nose buries in and throws a curtain of solid water straight up. The wind over the deck is less when she is down in the trough of the seas. Then she struggles up the next mountain to do it all over again. When I'm forward in these conditions, the ride is wild and I keep my lifeline attached to a runner on one of the two tracks that run from the cockpit up to the foredeck.

I notice the western sky brighten just before sunset and check the barograph to see that its line has turned up. The wind backs farther to the south. It is a cold wind but has less strength. This storm has passed by us in twelve hours. After-ward, we endure six hours of light southerly winds over a bas-ketweave of sea, waves every which way.

My presents, opened on Christmas Eve and left on my bunk for more appreciation, are now strewn all over the little dry cabin. I have books and tools and tape cassettes and things to eat. But I do not have any Christmas spirit. And so the day will pass as just one more day. One more day. Just one day at a time.

The classic Southern Ocean storm begins and ends much as this one did, although most of them last longer. They pass us, on the average, every four days in these high latitudes. Their intensity varies, and the ones that stay around longer bring the heavier winds and larger seas. Big seas are far more dangerous than high winds. The confused Indian Ocean seas will teach a sailor a new definition of discomfort, because they are big in all weather and so the chaotic motion never really stops. Yet the good news for us is that *Promise* appears to perform just as she was designed to in these conditions.

My inspection rounds become even more important in the Indian Ocean, but they are also much more difficult to do well. The gear failures increase and almost always occur during the heavy weather. We have the Southern Ocean just as we expected it.

DAY 48 ≈

The wind increases during the afternoon to forty-five to fifty knots and comes at us from the northeast; this puts us on a damned beat. The seas come at us from abeam and lay *Promise* down on her ends often. (The movie cameras keep whirring in response to these knockdowns. A tilt switch turns two cameras on automatically when the boat heels past forty-five degrees for three seconds. But the system is too slow, and the cameras start up just as the boat comes back upright. Screw the cameras, anyway. I turn them off.) All night I beg the wind to back to the north to put us on a reach, but it won't go there. We are reefed down to just a lapel-size mainsail and are being driven south. By daybreak we are 120 miles south of our rhumbline course, below the 44th parallel. Seas are forty feet and steep with tops breaking.

DAY 49 ≈

Finally, the wind creeps north and then northwest. Good thing, too, because it pipes up well past fifty knots. The seas are enormous and look like combers breaking up a beach. Somehow we manage six knots in this mess. And then the block on the main outhaul, at the very end of the boom, comes adrift. A half-inch-diameter, six-inch-long steel rod holding the block on its car throws a cotter pin and nut and is within an eyelash of casting the clew of the mainsail free from the boom. But I catch it. I furl the main and we sail under small bits of jib and staysail winged out. The rod is bent like a boomerang. I make the repair with a new bolt and use a hammer to bugger the threads so that the nut will not wind off. It's not pretty, but it's not carried out in pretty conditions. Breaking waves are washing over the deck and often I stand in solid water to mid-calf. The cockpit is awash. The seas are mountainous, their own best metaphor. *Promise* rolls more than forty-five degrees to each side. Nothing loose is found where it is left. The gunwales dip solid water up from both sides, and the poles, even carried high, occasionally kiss the waves.

DAY 51 ≈

The relentlessness of the violent rolling motion demands a tough constitution. There is no respite, no haven, except in the sturdiness of the mind in its goal to ignore the ceaseless motion. It is not unlike the torture that achieves its end by repeating over and over again a starkly uncomfortable act. It is easy to see a man losing his mind if he loses his ability to see and understand that it will end. It will end. It will end.

I am eating granola bars and pouched food cold and right out of the pouches. The noise from the lockers throughout the boat is deafening as food and hardware and supplies slam forcibly. The seas from the north are forty feet and from the west are twenty feet. They meet to erupt into pyramids with no linear form, no directional or positional logic. They are quite accurately described as chaotic. Only the boat in its form and weight and forward motion translates this chaos into a rhythm, but a painful rhythm.

Sanity is exploding chaos with a rationale, any rationale, valid or fake, but something the mind can deal with one facet at a time. At the least, that rationale can be rising above the chaos with the knowledge that time will alter the state of the matter. So it's you and I, chaos, one on one, and I am going to make an alliance with time and outlast you, you sonofabitch. Indian Ocean, you may stay here and harass sailors forever, but we are not going to hang around here with you but for a few more weeks.

We are surfing down these obscene bucking seas at speeds of more than twenty knots. Surfing. A seventy-thousand-pound surfboard. The big autopilot Joe is steering *Promise* like a champ and the water generator is churning away to replace the extra power Joe soaks up. For a while, anyway. In an awesome display of grinding vibrations loud enough to be heard clearly over the roar of the wind and waves, the generator gives up.

DAY 57 ≈

The day wears on painfully. The seas are up and very steep again and *Promise* slams into them like a tank into a trench. Solid water covers the decks, and spray shoots high over the pilothouse and the antenna tower aft. We are, damnit, in for another night of hard work for *Promise* and extreme discomfort for me. We are sailing hard on an east wind, forty-five knots of shrieking, creaks and groans below. I chicken out of this hell. I heave to until the wind gets behind us, where it belongs, or until the gale abates. The night is spent hove to under a mainsail reefed down to maybe fifty square feet, but we do make some slow progress through the water, four knots except when we are knocked down and beaten back by a sea. These are conditions one must simply survive, brutal, I know, on poor *Promise* and on me. We've had two days of this beating. And so I do not feel guilty for giving up for a few hours. We have another twenty-three-hour day as we cross into another time zone, now five hours east of Greenwich.

DAY 58 ≈

The first six hours of our fifty-eighth day continue the misery of the past two days. I can't help but think that anyone who willingly submits to this kind of awful punishment is either crazy or masochistic. Which, I wonder, am I? I do not eat well during these episodes of painful foul weather. The beating into it is the worst of it, and we have been beating damned near a third of the time in these latitudes. A crock of shit, it is, that winds out of the east are very rare here.

Seas are forty feet and prevail on the beam. The tops are breaking and sharp. The wind is a northeast gale. *Promise* takes a seventy-degree knockdown maybe once every five minutes and the gray-green water rolls by the pilothouse windows as if we were a submarine. The sounds of wood on wood, her bulkheads below creaking and groaning and popping, are not encouraging. The poor girl is really complaining. Yet we make over five knots. I would ease us off the wind some, but we are being forced too far south and I know the wind will finally back to the west. It must. And I must survive until it does.

·   ·   ·

Of course, the wind in the Southern Indian Ocean always does eventually back into the west and the storms always do pass. But life aboard *Promise* is largely a matter of getting through one storm to get ready for another. Getting ready for the next front involves a number of activities, some planned, like replacing running rigging that looks chafed and ragged, repairing small, recurring sail tears, performing long-term navigational planning and strategy, and plotting as well as simply taking sextant sights. I also catch up on my food intake and sleep. I read. I repair, rebuild, and ready my stock of hardware from the surviving parts, particularly blocks, which have many pieces and a tendency to fail. Snatch blocks quite often just blow apart and disappear as if into thin air. My supply is running low, and I find myself assembling them from scratch, using my box of spare parts. It is the big Harken snatch blocks that prove to be best for the challenge, so they soon come to occupy all the critical positions on *Promise*.

Each noon — reviewing my navigation, making entries in my logs, reexamining my projected waypoints ahead, recomputing daily miles run and speed averages and miles to go — I am, in fact, indulging in a kind of therapy. It is when I am intimately aware of how well the voyage is progressing.

My Christmas turned into a celebration after all because of these calculations. Upon entering the Indian Ocean, I had completed about 25 percent of the circumnavigation, 7,014 miles from Bermuda to a point 420 miles directly south of the Cape of Good Hope, in 44 days — an average of 159.4 miles per day, or 6.6 knots. I have actually beaten the record time of Philippe Jeantot, who sailed *Crédit Agricole* from Newport to Cape Town in 47 days in the 1982–83 BOC race, the three-stop, solo circumnavigation. (Jeantot had sailed some 280 miles more for this passage than I. One must add his 700 miles from Newport to Bermuda, then subtract the 420 miles I have sailed south of the cape. He took three more days to sail the added 280 miles.) *Promise*'s time is certainly a ringing endorsement of Ted Hood's convictions about sailboat performance and displacement weight. The fifty-six-foot *Crédit* weighed twenty-two thousand pounds without water ballast; *Promise* weighs sixty-eight thousand pounds. Both experienced similarly good weather through the calms of the doldrums and horse latitudes, yet the heavier boat won.

Again, the calculations yielded good news for me in an even more important category after I crossed the Indian Ocean. Having sailed more than twelve thousand miles across the North Atlantic, South Atlantic, and Indian oceans without a major mishap, *Promise* was also winning the battle of endurance. Hardware failures, equipment breakdowns, and chronic problems are rampant, of course. Some are a nuisance, whereas others are important but not critical because of adequate backups. A few have the very real potential to end the voyage. In the nuisance category are busted locker latches, a broken propane shutoff switch, furling line fairleads pulled out of the deck, the loss of the wind instruments and the computer alarm system, the many lost snatch blocks and snap shackles and lines, no electric power on some winches, an intermittently operating pump for fresh water pressure, a jammed pump to empty the sink and shower sump, running lights that never work, drawers under the workbench with their bottoms fallen out, the zipper on my heavy foul weather gear with 20 percent too few teeth, my one and only 35mm camera seizing up, and my favorite set of dividers entering the world of the irreparable.

The failures in the important-but-not-critical category make me deeply thankful for all the redundancy on *Promise*. In addition to one water generator, we have lost both 160-amp charging alternators on the generator diesel engines. But the eleven-kilowatt generators themselves continue to churn out amps, and our batteries stay charged. One fresh water maker fails, but the second keeps producing like a well. I fill jugs as a backup in case it decides to give us a drought. One of two ham radios malfunctions. (I am out of communication totally for several weeks in the Indian Ocean.) One of two heavy weather forestaysails blows apart. A couple of lifeline stanchions break off at the base, and several are bent inboard by the storm seas. Chronic problems like diesel oil leaks, recurring and unexplained bilges suddenly filling with sea water, hydraulic leaks that ebb and flow, chafing damage on lines, are treated with constant care. The most threatening problems are real or perceived ones with the autopilots or the rigging aloft. These are the two areas where I feel most vulnerable. And then there are those times when I am reminded of just how close we always are to ultimate failure.

DAY 47 ≈

While eating a cold pot roast lunch right out of the pouch in the pilothouse today, I have one of those shocks of subliminal awareness that I am looking at something new and ominous. I am staring at the mast and, now comprehending, see that three feet above the deck the black line of a crack is clearly visible in the gray paint. It runs around the afterside of the mast and disappears under the baseplates of the winches mounted on both sides. A one-act tragedy shoots through my mind. Is this the way it ends — dismasted in the Indian Ocean? Panic propels me on deck for a close look. The paint is definitely cracked all around the mast's aftersection; it is not simply scratched. Then I note more cracks higher up, six inches above the boom gooseneck. I sight up the mast; it is straight. It is not twisting or working unusually. The cracks are not opening and closing with the rig's motion.

I shave the paint from around the crack with my knife. Blessed relief. The metal beneath is not cracked. Why just the paint? Why would the paint part in such a neat but obviously not man-made crack clear across the metal? And then I realize that I am looking at the results of a last-minute paint job; the paint was probably sprayed on quickly without proper sanding when the new gooseneck fitting and main furling motor were installed months ago in Marblehead.

I feel immense relief and even a kind of invulnerability. I feel as if I am protected against disaster by a moat of good luck. And if my feelings of relief after such a scare are ephemeral, my assumption of good luck actually grows over time. I define luck as the good things that happen to me that I have not specifically planned on. Many times those good things were simply threatening situations that just turned out all right.

DAY 52 ≈

I am in and out of the sack constantly this night with a fickle wind — to set out the poles for downwind work, then to stow the poles for upwind work, and to set and then stow again. I am now doing this job mindlessly, like a mother picking her

kid's clothes from the floor. While I work, I practice self-depre-
cating humor. Afterward, I return to my dry cabin and a bunk
warm and dry as a barn swallow's nest. Up to down, wet to
dry, cold to comfy. And then the Southern Ocean storm cycle
ends again with a light south breeze, and *Promise* slows to four
knots. It is daybreak.

With reluctance, I decide to replace the broken water generator instead of crawling back into my nest. It takes me four
hours to complete the job — I am pleased I don't have to pay
myself by the hour. The old generator rattles like a coffee can
full of random parts and I save it just for that reason, a can of
spare parts. While I'm over the transom drilling holes and bolting the new generator onto its track, I notice a colony of gooseneck barnacles hanging down under the counter, dipping in
and out of the sea as *Promise* undulates along in the swells.
Uh-oh, I think. Growth on her bottom will slow her down. So I
busy myself chipping the barnacles away with a putty knife,
reaching farther and farther under the stern as I go.

My arm and face dip in and out of the freezing water as I
chip and scrape. Then the boat takes a lurch, my boots slip on
the ladder rung, and my feet fly. Suddenly I am looking up at
Promise's stern — it is five feet away and departing, a stupefying sight. The forty-degree water seems to take a long time to
soak through my foul weather gear and pile pants and jacket
and long underwear to my skin. When it does, I can't breathe. I
am eight feet behind *Promise* when I begin to follow along
obediently in her wake. My personal lifeline is clipped to
the boarding ladder and it straightens out and holds. Then,
almost as if *Promise* understands my predicament, her sails
luff and she stands straight up in front of me. Then I can
haul myself back to her and climb the boarding ladder. It
is not easy because of the weight of my sodden clothes. And
I remember being told how even a strong man cannot pull
himself upstream on his lifeline through a six-knot wake fully
dressed.

I am back in the cockpit, breathing hard. My clothing is
glued to me like skin and does not shed easily. I am naked in
the cold air but have no sensation of it. I am numb. I have
goosebumps almost as big as the gooseneck barnacles. I feel a

lot of things, but most of all I feel again like the luckiest man alive.

There are so many times like this that I form a theory about luck and myself. I believe it is a partnership we have formed, in which I agree to do my very best all the time — or as much of the time as I reasonably can — and not to count on any outside help, like luck, and luck in turn agrees to help anyway when I really need her. When I think of it, we've had this agreement all my life.

DAY 45 ≈

Luck! No other word for it. I am without question the luckiest sonofabitch I know. What I have managed to do all my life is to parlay average capabilities, intellectually and physically, into one helluva winning streak, big successes and small ones time and time again. I choose an objective and with time almost always reach it. How is this? Why me? I remember winning a race over a faster runner; it was as if I knew the other guy was faster and still knew I would win. I succeeded in a business venture when much brighter people did not. There has to be an element of luck here. What I add is determination and enthusiasm. And a born-again optimism.

If the up side of happy single-mindedness is having good luck, then the down side may be a natural tendency to put the blinders on to the needs and concerns of other people. And to discount those who do not share my optimism, actually, those who simply don't agree with me. It's interesting that I think of these things out here alone and have the uneasy feeling that more important than winning may be compassion. And I find myself now making promises to try harder with others if I am again given the chance.

But the luck side of the formula? Even though I don't know how all my luck comes about, I do know that I've gotten used to it and would have a hard time getting by without it. I even know how to stop it from running out. Whenever my mind's eye sees the hourglass of luck running down, I just flip it over.

· · ·

When *Promise* and I passed our fiftieth day out of Bermuda, just into the Indian Ocean, I set a new personal record for consecutive days at sea. I was not alone in 1964 when I sailed my old, gaff-headed schooner, *Coaster,* from Balboa, Panama, to Honolulu in forty-nine days. Aboard was my first wife, Lael Warren Morgan, and our Swiss friend and crew, Roland Paul Ernst. For the year and a half before that passage, I had sailed with Lael through the Bahamas, the Greater Antilles, and, after a seven-month stop in the Virgin Islands to make some money, down the West Indies to South America and Panama.

We set out on that 4,776-mile Pacific crossing without any of the frills — no electronic navigation equipment, no life raft, no self-steering system, no big inventory of sails, spare parts, and gear. *Coaster* was thirty-two years old and I was thirty-one. She was old for a boat and very hard work to keep up and, often, hard work to sail (gaff-headed rigs can be double-hernia rigs), but I was young and strong and impatient. We had sixty gallons of diesel fuel and one old alternator on the main engine to charge two car batteries, yet we didn't run out of electricity because we just didn't use much. We carried a hundred gallons of water and had plenty left over when we got to Hawaii. We used a kerosene stove, baked a lot of bread, ate a lot of rice, and didn't go hungry.

Just a week into the Pacific, we spent six days becalmed or making less than fifty miles. We were almost blown under by one of those wild windstorms off Mexico and had to hand-pump one hour of two to keep the old girl afloat. We navigated by sextant and dead reckoning and several times went days without knowing exactly where we were. We talked to no one on the radio and, because of the demands of the watch system, had very little conversation with each other. We sailed about fifty-five hundred miles, averaging just over a hundred miles per day. Afterward, I was — we all were — damned ready to trade the simple pleasures of sailing for the smelly confusion of land.

DAY 50 ≈

Fifty days is now my record. This time, however, I have just barely begun. Four more oceans to cross. I tell myself I can't afford even to think of the smells of land and civilization now. But fate has something else in mind.

In the violence of the boat's motion, a small sack of pine
needles from Maine, a scent of the Pine Tree State, is tossed
into my bunk during the night. It nestles down between my
cheek and the pillow. I sleep my usual half sleep, drifting down
for twenty to thirty minutes and then getting up just enough to
check the feel of the boat — her sounds and the sounds of the
wind, her speed and heading on the instruments at my feet. I
find myself rising to an awareness of soil and musk and sweat.
I can sense the presence of armpits and loins and the forest on
a hot day and lobster bait. I have an erection. It is the bag of
pine needles.

And Happy New Year to 1986. Leaving my pine needles behind, I turn out for a round of chores on deck and then settle
into my pilothouse seat to record some New Year's resolutions
on movie film: I will not covet my neighbor's wife . . . I will
not argue with the boss . . . I will not stray far from home.
These resolutions will certainly be easy to keep, at least for the
next few months.

My waypoints across the Indian Ocean are along the parallel
of the mid-forties, south far enough to keep the heavy westerly
winds and to significantly shorten the distance we sail (a degree of
longitude, which at the equator is 60 miles, is only 46.5 miles at
latitude 40), but not so far south as to invite problems with ice.
My course meanders to avoid the clearly charted seamounts, peaks
four hundred meters below us on a sea floor three thousand meters
deep. It is there on these benign-seeming peaks that the seas can
build to enormous heights and that the rogue waves play their
havoc. It is there that the knockdowns, broachings, and pitchpol-
ings most often occur. I also remain well north of the Kerguelen
Islands, to avoid the foul currents and the huge magnetic disturbances reported there. With these large, rapidly changing disturbances added to the charted magnetic variation in this part of the
world of 50 degrees west, the compass becomes almost useless.
Both the air and sea temperatures along this route average in the
forties. Gales blow almost half the time and the waves are seldom
under ten feet. The skies are nearly always overcast and a light,
cold rain often falls. Yet I do find in this place a kind of peace with
myself.

DAY 59 ≈

Today is washday for me and my long underwear. I have never ever enjoyed a hot shower as I have aboard *Promise* in this dark, cold, gray ocean.

I don clean underwear and a pair of new white socks from my supply of two hundred pairs, all a gift from Allie and all with *American Promise* name tags neatly sewed in as if I were a child at summer camp. Allie instructed me to toss my soiled socks overboard, leaving a trail of labels across the oceans and, perhaps, a souvenir for a beachcomber on some island to identify. For me, Allie has stuffed surprises into many of the toes. This time I find the 107th Psalm, to "they who go down to the sea in ships." I read the psalm several times, marveling at how appropriate this two-thousand-year-old poem is and thinking of dear Allie, who placed it there for me to find.

> For He commandeth,
> And raiseth the stormy wind
> Which lifteth up the waves thereof.
> They mount up to the heaven,
> They go down again to the depths:
> Their soul is melted because of trouble.
> They reel to and fro,
> And stagger like a drunken man,
> And are at their wits' end.
> Then they cry unto the Lord in their trouble,
> And He bringeth them out of their distresses,
> He maketh the storm a calm,
> So that the waves thereof are still!

And they become more still for me as the two and a half days of beating into a gale and huge seas have passed.

The wind is fifteen knots from the south. The seas are kindly lumps and holes. *Promise* is giving us a ride to remember. If there is ever a sailor's utopia, the past day on *Promise* describes it. She heels fifteen degrees, rolls slowly five degrees either side of that, bobs like a galloping racehorse. Spray dusts her off like a soft brush. And she parts the sea like a parable, nine miles of it every hour. I haven't touched a line or altered our heading in twenty-four hours. *Promise* has taken nature's gift of a favorable wind and wrapped it up for me. Oh, Lord, this feels as good as the other felt bad.

By noon, the south wind drops and the barometer shows a slow rise to signal some slower progress ahead. But this day produces our second best day to date, 216 miles, an average speed of nine knots noon to noon.

DAY 60 ≈
Noon, January 10, 1986, Friday, to noon, January 11, 1986,
    Saturday
40°00.27' south/78°24.12' east

We have, by almost any measurement, completed one third of the circumnavigation. We've logged 9,660 of the total of some 26,000 miles. We've been at sea 59 of the currently esti- mated 170 days for the voyage. My latest list of estimates has *Promise* just south of New Zealand on February 4, after 86 days and 13,511 miles. I should round the Horn by the first of March, on day 108, with 18,900 miles logged. Bermuda should be reached the last of April after 170 days at sea and 26,675 miles of sailing. At 59 days, *Promise* has a daily average of 163.7 miles, noon to noon. Not all of these miles have been sailed on the direct routes between great circle waypoints. We have also, because of meanderings between noon fixes, sailed considerably more distance through the water.

This day has another thrill for me. I am back in communica- tion with the world. After a couple of weeks of no contact, a surprisingly strong single-side band radio signal from Lyngby, Denmark, puts me back in touch with civilization in the form of Bob Rice, and I learn that another low-pressure trough is due in three days and my wind should harden and move west soon.

Rice is right. We have Southern Ocean winds twenty-five knots from the west. *Promise* spreads her wings and glides with them. Day breaks with a spiritually fulfilling surprise, sunshine bursting through bright blue holes in the cloud cover. Oh, how I love the sight of the light in this sky, and I salute it aloud with a cheer. It does feel so damned good, reassuring, to see the open sky through those windows of blue infinity. It cures the claustrophobia of being closeted in the fog and mist and thick overcast that is the standard Southern Ocean fare. I feel suddenly cleaner and freer. The ocean swells, forty feet high, have soft corners and the hard blue color of new steel. Wavetop spills and *Promise*'s wake scratch bright white wounds on this endless, sunlit canvas.

Our constant company now is the smaller, dark brown albatross, with wingspans of three feet, and I can often spot one of the larger, white and light brown species, who span four feet or more. The larger are my favorites. Their flight is grace without effort.

This is a world of direct and absolute simplicity. It is ultimately honest. Values are obvious. Nature is at her base where she is best, purest. The truth is easy to see in the constancy of time on the wavetops and wingtips and flying skies. My world is naturally obvious and simple and direct, lived as it should be lived. Existence belongs to creatures and elements with quick honesty, snap action, and interminable patience. Nothing else counts in this realm. Not intrigue or duplicity, rationalizations or negative wisdom, or life that needs change or senses that need constant stimulation.

An individual human being belongs in this world. Humans' institutions do not. Institutions have lives of their own, burdened by symbols and rites and castes that obscure any view of the truth. And the truth is beauty and beauty is God and God is the fixed and eternal laws of nature. Fuck them all, these institutions, from religions to college fraternities, organizations dedicated to dividing people and blurring the image of truth. We all must stand in our own space and see with our own mind the farthest horizon, and perhaps there we will see the source of our nature. Each of us has but one moment to devote to the search and the moment is but a lifetime. We cannot squander our moment on the busywork of social definitions, intellectually complex and precise formulas for the relationships of ideas that spin sophistic conclusions that are as meaningless as a picture of the image reflected around many flawed mirrors.

$\sim\!\!\sim 8 \sim\!\!\sim$

I celebrate my fifty-fourth birthday with some extraordinary weather two thirds of the way across the Indian Ocean. *Promise* delivers three days of more than two hundred miles a day. My spirit bounces way up. These wild mood changes I've been having are something new for me — from happy to glum, joyful to gloomy, way up to way down and back in short cycles and for small reasons. I am normally quite even in my moods, not letting either the tough times or the good times really get to me. But the longer I am at sea alone, the further these moods seem to swing. I can be utterly joyful at nothing more than a brief sight of the moon and utterly dejected just minutes into a Southern Ocean fog. Something breaks — it could be a fitting on the boat or a filling in my tooth — and I am paranoid; then, after a couple of hours of good sleep, I am invincible. But one constant is directly related to all my moods. It is our physical progress, by the hour and by the mile, back to Bermuda. So even though it may not be that common for a man to greet his birthday with pure inner joy, I do, because on this day *Promise* and I sail for home as if we were powered by angels. And our sailing speed works its marvelous magic on me. I am on such a high that, even when something frightening happens — in this case an accident at sea that is the one most universally feared by solo sailors — my spirit is not dampened.

DAY 64 ≈

Darkness falls on a day much like one would find sailing the coast of Maine in September. Cool, crisp, clear, bright, the

III

kind of weather that makes one live forever. The sailing is simply exquisite. *Promise* has twelve to fifteen knots on the beam, a north breeze, and lays down more than sixty-two miles in the first eight hours of our sixty-fourth day, just as easy as a pearl rolling downhill.

But at 1640 local time the reverie is shattered. *Promise* hits something and stops. Sails still pulling, hull still heeled over, she halts dead, a stop in the middle of one of the deepest oceans in the world. When the blow comes, I am reading in my dry bunk, keeping an eye on my baking bread. The force of it rolls me into a bundle on the bulkhead forward of the bunk. But it takes me very little time to recover and get on deck, even if bootless and wearing only my long johns. By the time I do, however, *Promise* is already beginning to accelerate back to speed. With a flashlight, I frantically examine all the hull I can see by leaning over the side but find nothing amiss. I crank the daggerboards and the intermediate centerboard up and down and rack the helm back and forth, looking for damage to her underwater appendages. She is now back to full speed and sailing well. I check the bilges and the rudderpost. Nothing seems to be wrong anywhere. A whale. I must have hit a whale. Hard enough to stop us, soft enough to stop us easy. Maybe *Promise* and the whale were traveling in the same general direction and the blow was pillowed. Maybe the whale was just showing some affection for a fellow creature in this lonely ocean, and he simply slowed *Promise* down for a better look.

After my investigations prove *Promise* is all right, I remain on deck in a reflective mood. The crescent moon is pure white. The Southern Cross is high in the sky and bowing to the east. A lone shooter spins across the northern sky. I wonder where Halley's Comet is writing her signature tonight. The boat smells of fresh bread. I decide to take a hot shower, to greet my birthday with a clean slate. In a very short time, I almost forget our collision, concluding that it is just one more element of proof that the luck sure rides with us and that *Promise* sure can take it when she has to. Her motion through this ethereal night has the feel of constant tension and relentless power, and she boils up a bone in her teeth three feet high. Ten knots of power. It feels almost as if we really do belong here in this ocean wilderness.

I end my visit in this magical world to go below and open my birthday presents and see that the sixth sense has struck again. From my earlier thoughts of Halley's Comet, I get absolutely no excuse for not paying my personal respects to it. Not only do I have a telescope, fifteen to sixty zoom power with adjustable field of view, but I also have a pillow that automatically heats up when sat on. What more can this aspiring astronomer ask than a once-in-a-lifetime comet, fancy new gear to view it with, and a warm butt while doing so. I also unwrap a magnificent tripod that can be leveled on any slanting surface. It doesn't matter at all that the telescope is useless aboard the boat, because it demands an absolutely stable and still platform in order to view anything. Even a tremor obliterates any intelligible picture through the high-powered, narrow field of view. *Promise* has not been and will not be anything close to a stable platform for months before and after this birthday. But it is gift-wrapped and for me and in its concept defers to the heavens; I treasure it and fondle it like a piece of art.

Promise's birthday present for me, however, is her best daily run of the voyage, 225.3 nautical miles in the noon-to-noon twenty-three-hour day — twenty-three instead of twenty-four hours because we cross another time zone. We are crossing these time zones and losing another hour on the clock now every fourth day. For the record, I take a satnav fix to get a full twenty-four-hour day's run: it shows we sailed 236 miles. It is interesting to note that, although we are well short of the official world record for a solo, twenty-four-hour run — 257 miles, recorded in the Southern Pacific Ocean by Richard Konkolski in the 1982–83 BOC race — we are way, way ahead of Konkolski's daily average so far for the whole circumnavigation. World record or not, however, *Promise*'s great run surely is my birthday present of the year!

DAY 65 ≈
Noon, January 15, 1986, Wednesday, to noon, January 16, 1986, Thursday
42°11.67' *south*/99°20.64' *east*

My birthday euphoria doesn't last. It's almost as if I have to compensate for it with some foul spirits just a day later. I decide that my solution is that today I must solve a problem, any problem, at least one of the many problems. The new water generator I recently installed on the transom doesn't produce a charge. It vibrates. It growls. But no electricity comes from it. I choose this problem. So I go over the stern of the boat again to troubleshoot, tighten bolts, and check wiring. I keep my lifeline short and move very carefully because of the memory of my chilly trip overboard a couple of weeks ago. While I work, some wind pipes up from the northeast and a rooster tail spurts up from the spinning propeller of the rattling machine, but there's still no power. Something electrical is happening, though, because I can give myself lively shocks. Further crude work with two wet fingers shows that the shocks are sporadic, not continuous. Damned French machine is intermittent, the worst kind of problem to have; when you hunt for the malfunction there isn't one, and when you think you've found one the infernal machine is really working. I am hugging the machine as I work on it and can hear its throbs better than my own heartbeat. When we pick up some speed sliding down the seas, the machine complains loudly. And so it goes for today's problem-solving promise.

It's interesting that the sunsets and sunrises here appear to occur south of us rather than to the north, where, of course, the sun's path really is. That strange effect is caused by our being so far south, so near the polar axis, that we see the day's first and last sun by peeking at it from under the bottom of the world. By midday, of course, the sun is behaving as it should, showing right out there to our north, and my sextant sights for the noon fix answer the "Where are we?" question just as they should. Just as our satellite navigator does. That satellite navigator breaks all the rules of Puritanism. It makes the sailor lazy and efficient and accurate all at once. In a mystical way, this makes me nervous. I keep using my sextant just in case God is a Puritan, because I sure do want to stay on his good side while I'm out here.

By 0800 local time, the wind is up and the seas are up and our speed is up and the uncomfortable motion is up. But the barometer is going down. The western sky bubbles with cumulus and the horizon is dirty. We will have another storm soon. I want this storm very much.

DAY 66 ≈

My life has become a drudgery, and I have been dragged from a state of confidence to a state of boredom. I have trouble keeping myself involved in this job other than to repair what needs most to be repaired, to cook as little as will satisfy my stomach, to navigate as seldom as necessary to know where I am. What I do is waste much time over my charts with the same projected dates and times and waypoints and headings, trying to imagine the miles and the days behind me. I do this, I know, because my imagination has gone soft with the solitude. There is not enough natural diversity in my little world.

As I stare like a stuffed animal at the charts, I think most of getting by my next milestone, Tasmania. I must get by Tasmania. New Zealand. Stewart Island. The Horn. Oh, by the fates that guide us, get me around Cape Horn! After the Horn, only after the Horn, will I be on the downhill slide for home. I cannot and will not allow anything to happen that could possibly keep *Promise* from that rounding for home.

I miss so much the heat and joy and chills and pain of human contact, abstractly and specifically. Most of all I miss my children and find myself looking at their pictures, left aboard by Manny, and their drawings and poems and puzzles and jokes, arranged for me to discover each month in my mailbook. I cry uncontrollably when I see what they have left for me to find during the voyage.

I miss the confusion and the unpredictability of the human anthill, to walk on a street crowded by people to whom you relate only by being one among them, to sit on a barstool and happily remain a stranger, one smile away from a shallow and passing friendship. But to be with my family, oh, one day would never be enough. And with friends to talk the sun into setting and to cheer a life that is too short and passing fast. I am not afraid of death, only of missing something important by dying. Numerous times in these past months I have prepared myself not to live through the ordeal, even while knowing that I damned well *will* live through it. The prospect of not living through doesn't frighten me. I can think of many ways of living that would be far worse than dying. And most of them prove again that pride is a stronger force on the human mind than the instinct of self-preservation.

As I write I am heaved, doubled up like a fetus, onto the chart table by a knockdown. My nose is flattened against the starboard pilothouse window, and I can see solid black water roll by. Small gear follows me and collects in the leeward crevices. Too much sail. I roll in some reefs and some of the tension eases out of her. Less sail and she stands up better and without any loss of speed. The reefing job takes me maybe ten minutes to complete and, again, I bless the roller-reefing systems on *Promise*. I am surprised that outside my pilothouse cocoon in the wind it is a wild night.

DAY 67 ≈

Now blows the wind another day. Huge swells are pimpled with five-foot wind waves. Mostly they are charging up behind us, their tops ripped off in lacy sheets by thirty knots of west wind. *Promise* skids downwind at nine to eleven knots. Slowly the wind is backing south, though, telling me I will soon have to lower the poles and then gird myself for a return of the light airs. At least I may have some few hours of sailing on a reach and get rid of this rolling motion. Even after these months at sea, I'm still not used to *Promise*'s amazing downwind roll. The poles wing out the jib on one side, the forestaysail on the other, to present the following wind with perfectly flat targets and freeing the boat to roll like a barrel. I try a small amount of mainsail to steady the motion, but it is more trouble than help. We roll through ninety degrees. Belowdecks, the incredible noise of items slamming around in lockers is, by way of a defensive psychology, humorous. I think this is well over the government noise pollution limits. But then, there is one thing that this world most certainly is not, and that is quiet. Never, ever quiet.

It is natural, I guess, that when we are sailing fast as I do my noon navigation chores, I see how well we are doing in the overall voyage, and when we are sailing slowly I do not. Today I note our average daily run is 166.6 miles, a 6.9-knot average speed. And, so far, we have lost eleven hours from these averages because of passing time zones, hours we will get back in one bunch when we pass the international date line and receive a whole day free. This is a very credible performance for us and, if maintained for the rest of the trip, would take us back to Bermuda in the incredible record time of 154 days. Oh, shit, forget it, Dodge. This is just so much pie in the sky at this early point. But I have now moved our plots to one of the South Pacific Ocean charts, putting the Indian Ocean behind us. I wonder how the Pacific will treat us? More kindly than the Indian?

I try for a radio call through an Australian station on the single-side band rig. As usual, I have no luck because almost no one in the Southern Hemisphere points an antenna south to listen. No action down here, just one idiotic solo sailor. I do manage a contact with an operator in Singapore, but she won't make my call because I don't have a proper company name and account number on her register. AT&T credit cards don't pull any weight with her. Bureaucracies come in all sizes.

By dawn the wind drops under ten knots, but the seas remain, and so we barely make five knots of rolling, slamming, slatting progress.

I use the time to replace the jib furling line, which has chafed through again, again peeling fairleads off the deck as the line's outer jacket bunched up on them while furling. The chafing damage happened fast; twelve hours from no visible wear to worn out. This should be a simple job, but it is complicated by the fact that nothing stays put anywhere — not tools or parts or even I. When *Promise* rolls, I must quickly stop work and stuff the tools and parts into my pockets, under my arms, and into my mouth, so that I can just hang on with both hands. Water washes by me from one direction and then the other, filling and emptying a pantleg over and over again. Progress on the repair comes in frantic spurts between rolls. Occasionally, in the panic to complete a step in the job before we hit another roll, I get caught neither finishing nor hanging on, but skidding across the deck and fetching up hard on the lifeline. I break one stanchion clean off with this trick. I lose a screwdriver and a drill bit over the side and am forced to pack everything up to go below for replacements. Incredibly, this simple job takes five hours.

But even worse is what happens afterward. While testing out my repair by furling and unfurling the jib several times, I feel

the furling drum jam and then go limp. The realization of what
has happened shoots through my brain and then hits my gut
like a lost wallet in a strange town. The jib halyard has parted.
Will I need to go aloft again? Have I lost the roller furling on
the jib?

My only defense here is to act and act fast. I bring the jib
down to the deck and see the upper swivel assembly still attached to the sail. Relief. No immediate trip up the mast. I rig a
spare halyard, raise the jib again, and get it to furl. Relief
again. I get to keep the major advantage of our roller-furling
headsail a bit longer. Lady Luck returns.

DAY 68 ≈

When an important, vital piece of gear fails on me, I become
threatened. Afraid. Paranoid, even. Someone out there is out to
get me. This is particularly true when the failure is aloft. And
still we have more than halfway to go. I wonder why my daily
round isn't catching these problems, first the furling line and
now the halyard. How many other pieces of gear are close to
breaking? When will the next break be? How well, if at all,
will I be able to fix it? I'm so far from any help, and still so far
from the goal.

My ability to fix things is crude, so the cruder and simpler the
broken gear, the more likely I can succeed in the repair. I tend
toward half-assed repairs of fairly complex equipment, durable
and not pretty repairs of simple gear. I also tend sometimes to
make costly mistakes when screwing around with tools, tightening
nuts to the point of breaking bolts, wreaking havoc because I use
the nearest tool rather than the right one. It is not uncommon for
me to be painfully literal when I break down a piece of machinery.
This means that I often spend as much time fixing my own mistakes as I do repairing the original problem, so that repairs seem
to take me forever to accomplish with results that are at best util-
itarian. When planning this voyage, I wrote in a specification paper:

"I am competent, well, reasonably so, with the maintenance
and operation of machinery. I certainly am no expert mechanic. I
tend to the crude approach and pride myself on a level of make-do

rather than precision and skill. I am more often amazed at how well machinery works rather than disappointed that it doesn't. I'm not comfortable with bottom line dependence on electrical wizardry or internal combustion contraptions, but am quite pleased when they work because of a benign pleasure in doing things the easy way."

The cavalier attitude toward mechanical repairs doesn't rest well out here. Oh, how I yearn for the skills of the Michael Porters and Grant Robinsons and Buddy Duncans of the world now. The paranoid awaits the next mechanical failure.

DAY 69 ≈

Another colorless Southern Ocean day. Six hundred miles south of the coast of Australia. Rain or drizzle. I feel apprehensive. The lost halyard made me realize that this voyage could end anytime. Maybe will. The day passes with me forlornly staring at charts. In maybe eight days we will have completed half the voyage, 12,797 miles in 77 days. Then we begin the whole damned trip over again. Hoo boy. End not near enough to contemplate. Yet that is what I do, contemplate the end. And become morose. I wonder what I would be like if I were not so far ahead of my plan? We match the first-half performance in the second and beat my original 180-day target by 16 days. And they all said 180 was crazy. Maybe I wouldn't have it for the longer voyage. Maybe I will never reach the point when I don't think of completing the voyage. Just celebrating the sail for itself and not wanting it to end. Like Bernard Moitessier did.

That beautiful, poetic sonofabitch Moitessier. Sailed alone around the world in the Golden Globe race in 1968. Old steel ketch *Joshua*. Got back into the Atlantic on the home stretch and suddenly said friggit. Back to Europe? Trade the sail for Europe? Hell no! Fall off and sail around the world again. And that is just what he did.

DAY 70 ≈

We are now visited by a small black and white bird that flies very close to the waves, smoothly gliding, then wildly fluttering. I think it is a murrelet of some type, family of auk. Australia is the closest land in many weeks. The night is spent in light air, slatting out slow progress. The slatting is very hard for me to take because it causes more damage than the pressure of steady, heavy wind. Sails and lines crack like whips.

The new day begins on the same desultory note on which yesterday ended — almost no wind, lumpy sea, gray, sullen sky, and months to go before I rest. This is now my world. I don't like it much. I am totally alone and fumbling, grappling with an adversary that has time and fate ultimately on his side. I can never be the victor in this contest, only the survivor. And the contest is one that I cannot now avoid. I'm locked into it without escape for whatever eternity it will take. No white flags. No diplomatic backing down. I now comprehend better why this solo, nonstop sail has been so seldom accomplished.

The messenger line for an external emergency halyard becomes tightly wrapped around the jib furling gear aloft, freezing the whole assembly. But in time I free it without a trip up the mast. And then I am handed a surprise victory while pulling a new case of irradiated milk from the cove behind the navigation station. Lashed down in a sandwich between the milk cases is a case of Michelob beer! Twenty-four golden, gorgeous cans. Judiciously rationed, that will keep me a couple of months. I have one and remain up all night, fighting the light airs to keep a way on.

In the morning another halyard messenger, this one set up by Walter Greene, tangles in the gear aloft. I stow the pole and twice must lower the jib on deck in my attempts to clear the tangle. But I am overtired and fumble the job and have to cut the line away. Even more ominous, I see that the new halyard is seriously worn in just a few days of use. I bathe the upper swivel assemblies in oil and shorten the sail's luff length to change the point of wear, where the wire passes over the sheave at the masthead. This twenty-four-hour-a-day, week-after-week, month-after-month use wears the hell out of gear. No one designs for it. The sails and running rigging are really showing it now, and I have changed nearly every piece of rope on the boat at least once. I must keep up my daily vigil. I must not let this get ahead of me. It is my only hope of slowing the failures.

DAY 73 ≈

I think the second half of this voyage may be very slow at best. At the rate we are losing gear, we may have to sail much of the distance without roller-furling the jib. And I will have to go up the mast again to keep any jib working. The halyard won't last. I sift through the what-if alternatives and weigh the consequences and list the actions. It is disheartening work that imbues my whole awareness with negativism. And to a person for whom hope must spring eternal, this brings dark hours. Where I am now.

DAY 74 ≈

A bustle of wind finally covers us. Darkness falls on a twenty-five-knot south wind with thirty-foot seas, then suddenly the night lights up as if the roof had been blown off. Bolting a streak across the waves and glinting off the mast and dancing shadows on the deck is a full moon. She cheers me. And, oh, I crave the cheering.

The lively south wind is unusual, and to confound the odds further, it veers quickly in the early morning through sixty degrees to the southwest and becomes light. Damnable high-pressure zones.

While rigging the jib back out on its wing, I again have trouble furling it. The top swivel jams with the sail halfway out. I gingerly, carefully, feel out the problem, furling, unfurling, watching, testing, feeling for any tension, the slightest binding of the roller gear. As I do, my gut is tied with a please-don't-do-this-to-me knot, as if there were a direct connection between my intestines and the apprehension sensor of my brain. The jib finally furls. I add to my list of routine chores: twice a week I will lower the jib to inspect the upper swivel assembly and the halyard.

Noon ends the day with a wind suddenly piping up to forty knots and the seas jutting up like forty-foot geological faults, with sharp tops and corners. This brings back the wildly uncomfortable corkscrewing motion but gives us a good daily run of 191 miles. Some intermittent sun warms the pilothouse to sixty degrees.

.   .   .

My spirits are in a nosedive. In the past weeks I have passed through boredom and sunk into a funk. A trail of gear failures has me convinced that the boat is coming apart before my eyes and that somehow the useful life cycles of *Promise*'s accessories are all the same and near their end. Our daily progress has slowed. Here at the high latitudes, in the terrifying roaring forties of the Southern Ocean, we have our worst day of the voyage so far. Not in the doldrums or the horse latitudes do we slow to a stagger, but here, where the big winds are supposed to rage, we have our darkest hours. Here, halfway through, I can only see we still have halfway to go. Here I have my deep depression.

Days drag like a time block and my thoughts veer toward home, a frozen collage of distant memories, and it seems so very long before I can even hope to return. Hope is out of reach. I can barely get out of my own way and do not sail the boat well. Twice I let her founder in the light airs because I run out of will.

I feel a lack of space to move around in, a lack of actions to choose from, of views to look at, of sounds to listen to. Taken away, too, now is any sense of progress. I need a sense of progress. It is the only dimension I have for life. But instead of the hissing sound of water there is the horrible sound of slatting sails. Instead of looking forward each day to my noon calculations, I find myself multiplying over and over a dreary few knots of boat speed by twenty-four hours in a day by seven days in a week by forever.

We sail deeper into the Southern Oceans to below fifty degrees, and still the high-pressure light wind prevails, punctuated by short, violent gales that take their own brand of quick toll on gear. I begin to wonder if these halfway blues are fatal?

DAY 76 ≈

Tasmania means people 120 miles but centuries of time away because I am not going there. Hobart is the capital. There is a well-known yacht race from Sydney to Hobart, but I don't know when it is held. I am so far from the world of yacht racing that it is like a foreign custom ridiculously contrary to any of my learning. The idea of groups of people crowding together in sailboats and sailboats crowding together around buoys, all carefully watched by committees crowding together under flags on little powerboats with the objective of raising great social hoopla because one sailboat traveled a very short distance a minute faster than the rest is fucking ridiculous. It is overcivilized.

The people of Hobart are finishing their Sunday brunch right now. Maybe some of them look at the same gray sky I see, but not with the same meaning. Will it rain during their Sunday stroll? On their fresh paint? A wool sweater is enough to keep them plenty warm because it is maybe sixty, sixty-five degrees this time of day on Tasmania. People are planning their evening, the end to a weekend. Some will work and some will fight and some will make love and all will act out, even if they do not acknowledge, that their existence and the few people with whom they share it are all there is to their reality. They do not know that I am on the sea to their south. Or care. I am not part of their reality.

It is as if I do not exist, and in fact for them I do not. I exist for myself and my few people. Only now I cannot share myself with those people. Why do I put myself to this pain? Why am I here alone, bobbing on this endless, relentless ocean?

Even though my existence now is a painful one, edged in on all sides by threat, I do not want to go to Tasmania so close by. I want my own world back with my own discovered loves. But, God, how far yet to go. No shortcuts available. No alternative but to go the distance. None.

The shape of the distance that remains is roughly this: In just a few hours I will have gone halfway around the globe. I have about thirteen thousand miles of sea between me and Bermuda. If the second half goes like the first, I have seventy-six days of sailing left in the voyage. If the second half follows the rule of multiplying time by wear and tear, it'll take me longer, maybe much longer. Maybe forever. So the true shape of things to come is unknown. I am fighting for home every day just as hard as I can. I am lonely and tired. But I keep fighting. I am counting on a reserve of strength within me that I have never tested but that I know is there.

A flurry of radio contacts with hams and the Sydney SSB station put me back in touch with Bob Rice and Manny. They have talked to Ted Hood and the experts in Marblehead about my halyard and roller-furling problems. Ted says that I should duck into a quiet anchorage along the New Zealand coast and spend some time aloft to rig a spare halyard, make repairs, and ready the rig for the rest of the voyage. He says the second halyard won't last.

The anchoring for repairs would not disallow my nonstop circumnavigation as long as I do not touch shore or accept any help from others. I realize it is a wise suggestion, but I won't take it. I just pray that I don't regret my decision to keep going. I know there is as much gut intuition as rational logic in my choice. But if I had done the rational thing to begin with, I'd be in Maine, running a newspaper, not in the Southern Pacific Ocean on a sailboat with two and a half months of solitude behind me and the same amount or more ahead of me.

Bermuda is my destination, no matter how many thousands of miles away. It is burned into my brain as resolutely as if it were my spawning pool and I were a king salmon. We pass the halfway meridian of Hobart, 147°17' east, at 2231 hours Greenwich Mean Time, 0831 local time, on January 27, 1985.

$$\sim\!\!\sim 9 \sim\!\!\sim$$

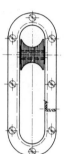

ood has turned out to be a colossal nonevent aboard *American Promise* in spite of an enormous effort in planning, in the procurement of an awesome array of foods, and in my anticipation that, with so few diversions aboard, I would become interested and maybe competent in both cooking and eating. But so far my appetite remains about as discriminating as that of a seagull, with cooking skills to match.

The food planning for the voyage began with my making a simple estimate of the amount of food needed to keep me alive for two hundred and fifty days. The weight and volume of that food were taken into consideration during the designing of the boat. I then asked Manny to plan menus with nutritional value. We had one false start. A professional nutritionist insisted on analyzing my many nutritional problems rather than planning the food for the voyage. She asked me to keep a three-day log of my food intake and, after seeing it, told me I was seriously malnourished and quite lucky to be alive. Although a doctor had examined the real me, instead of a list of the things I'd eaten, and given me a strong endorsement of health, the nutritionist would not be diverted from her goal of treating me rather than planning for the voyage. So Manny took over.

Manny's research was thorough and, as a result, we loaded aboard 1,608 pounds of healthful, good food and drink. It was about equally divided between irradiated pouched food, freeze-dried food, and canned food. I had a detailed written menu arranged on a twenty-one-day cycle. There was food for celebrating and food for rough weather. I had a book of a hundred and fifty

125

recipes Manny had collected from friends especially for the voyage. I used virtually none of them. For the most part, I simply reached into a food locker and ate what came out first. However, I did find some nice memories and some interesting reading in the recipe book, such as:

"*The H.C.L. Jackson Sandwich.* This concoction has little potential as an object of self-reward. One may, in fact, come to view it as a handy vehicle for gentle reprimand. Acclaimed by woofers, no tableware of any kind is required if eaten within hovering range of the pan: *melt btr to coat surface of lg fry pan. *fry egg sunny side up in one corner of pan & brown 2 slices brd in other corners. *when sunny-side egg just shy of done pour catsup on top & sprkle w/pepper. *with no pause break yolk & cover with one slc brnd brd & apply more catsup & cover with other brd slc. *turn once artfully & bring to highest temp psbl w/o having egg leave runny yolk state. *eat instantly or not at all.

"*Roaring Forties Gorp.* Mix all kinds nuts, M&Ms, chopped dried fruit, raisins, bran, wheat germ, raw oatmeal, etc., in a tub while still ashore. Fill pockets of all heavy foul weather gear with the gorp. Set sail."

My cooking problems began early in the voyage, after I ran out of store-bought bread. On day 22:

≈Bake bread this P.M. Well, fuck it, I really bake brick. Damned goo refuses to rise. Cook it anyway. And eat some with margarine and peanut butter. The eating part is the hardest. The loaf is brown throughout and brick-sized and would be suitable building material for the asshole of the Sphinx. I will try again.

On day 35, another experiment goes awry:

≈I must describe my "Konkolski concoction," a one-pot mélange of foods generally specified to me by single-hander Richard Konkolski. His written description of this stew — really a culinary technique rather than a dish — is precisely confusing, which is appropriate, and punctuated with the admonition to "never attempt to remove from original cook pot. Eat directly from cook pot. Otherwise you make mess." Surely I have made my mess directly inside my pot but have also made some interesting discoveries along the way.

My mélange is but five days old. Each night I add something to the pot and eat my fill from it. The pot becomes more rather than less full, even as each time it seems I have eaten more than I have added. Most additions, like tomatoes, tuna fish, dried beef, mushrooms, canned stewed clams, serve only to dull any distinction of taste. Only one addition, outside of an almost fatal early error, has succeeded in penetrating the taste desert, and that is canned sloppy joe. The entire mess, and I do mix very well, is subtly but noticeably altered by six ounces of sloppy joe. Nothing changes the color, however. It remains identical to what I produce the next day when I donate some of the same meal back to nature. The initial mistake was the asparagus. I don't like asparagus. Out of the can, it tastes like it smells, and it smells like urine. I tried to make a can of this growth disappear in the mélange. It did not disappear. Not until the sloppy joe.

I believe I have at least held my weight in spite of my culinary uninterest and ineptitude, which, if anything, grew worse as Bermuda came closer.

The state of solitude, unlike most others, does not seem to help me to understand it better. The more I sail, the more I understand sailing. But the more I am alone, the less I feel I know about solitude. I can't describe solitude, the real meaning and feeling of it, any better now than before I began this voyage months ago. Even the many shorter periods of sailing alone over my life have not added to my understanding. I can write a laundry list of what I believe are the specific effects this much time spent alone have had on me, or I can describe in vague terms a general void I feel. I can even give tips on how to cope with solitude: live one hour at a time; adopt a routine for ordering your life, down to the smallest detail; act immediately on any matter demanding attention; keep busy at all costs. But I still can't solve the riddle of solitude.

I wonder if solitude is just a matter of the mind, accessible to anybody who wants it, regardless of the presence of others. Can one will solitude on oneself then? Is remoteness from others a necessary part of the definition? And if so, is it a physical or mental remoteness? How about someone in a coma, mind still whirring in high gear but senses walled off? Do I, with all my senses in place but in isolation, now know more about the world of those without the use of their senses? Which is more isolating, not to hear or not to be heard?

You probably have to be a philosopher to understand solitude and a poet to explain it, and I am neither. But I know you also have to experience it. That I am now doing in full measure and coping rather well, I think.

For one thing, I do not allow myself to catch the hermit syndrome. I understand that its first sign is neglect of one's personal hygiene. This is followed by a general loss of interest in life, a loss of pride, and finally a loss of will. And when a human being reaches that point, there is not much significant humanity left. When we stop striving we essentially stop living. And so to save my soul I am bewitched by the ritual of brushing my teeth.

Two Boston College psychologists, Randolph Easton and William Nasby, had warned me to prepare for the effects of sensory deprivation, which include boredom, ennui, carelessness, and hallucinations. At the time, it seemed very odd to me that being slammed around in a small boat could ever be called sensory deprivation. But I understand their point now and agree with it. They defined sensory deprivation as the absence of change in one's environment rather than the lack of stimuli. That makes sense. I am constantly battling boredom and do have a tendency toward carelessness. But I have not hallucinated.

DAY 83 ≈

I am getting enough sleep in the voyage so far and have learned how to cope with the frequent awakenings at night. I get my sleep, pending weather or crisis, during the normal hours of darkness, usually hitting the sack between 2200 and 0100 hours local time and arising between 0730 and 0900 hours. My sleep is taken in short increments, averaging, perhaps, an hour and a half each. I awake at the slightest change in the sounds and motions of the boat or in precisely two hours if no changes occur. I am extremely sensitive to these sounds and motions now. And I need no alarm to tell me when two hours have passed. If I deduct the average awakenings, which can take as long as a day if all hell has broken loose or as short as minutes for a quick fix, I still average about seven hours of sleep a night, enough so that I do not take naps during the day. I am not sleep-deprived.

Perhaps it is because of this ample sleep that I have escaped hallucinating or anything approaching the tricks of the mind that so many other solo sailors report. I believe there is a direct relationship between sleep deprivation and hallucinating.

Of course I do talk to myself, even though I seldom address the words to myself (this excepts the standard mumblings and curses of the half-assed mechanic, cook, etc.). I speak in a very loud voice, a bellow, really, to make sure the someone somewhere out there hears me. Words blurt out particularly when something different happens, when there is a special occasion such as a sudden view of the moon, a hot shower, a visit by a bird or dolphin, a problem quickly solved, a good day's run. Back in civilization, I would have never thought it reasonable to speak out loud to myself, but it seems quite normal out here. Of course, I also talk to my movie cameras and radio microphones. Maybe all these letting-it-out verbal exercises are, in addition to the ample sleep, also antihallucinatory.

Still, it is amazing that there have been no strange or mystical thoughts or sights or sounds for me out here. None.

But, boy, do I dream. And, as instructed by the psychologists, I write these dreams down in detail in my journal. In spite of being alone, this is sometimes difficult and embarrassing because many of these dreams are X-rated. In these porno dreams, I have sex with all kinds of women — some I know, some who are celebrities, and some who are surreal, symbolic females, the latter more envelopes of sensation than specific forms.

I know that I am involuntarily obeying one of the predictions of Easton and Nasby by vividly recalling so many of these dreams; they said the frequent awakenings would cause this. That half these dreams are purely sexual is puzzling for a man my age. It is also interesting and very convenient that I am able to rejoin a dream in progress after a short awakening.

I dream I am wandering alone through a very large building that I sense is my home but has the look of a warehouse. As much as I look, and never in the same room twice, I cannot find anybody else. But then I see my old leather jacket, lost a long time ago, even before my air force days. It is hanging high on a wall, out of reach.

I have nightmares, too. I am completing the voyage and arriving in Bermuda. I can see Hoyt and Kim standing at the edge of the quay on St. George's Harbour, and I am desperately but unsuccessfully beating *Promise* into the wind to reach them. There is a foreboding of something terrible about to happen. They can't hear my warnings through the wind. And then the wind swings suddenly around and drives *Promise* rapidly up to the wall, and just as we get there Kim slips and falls into the water between the wall and the boat, and I jump into the narrowing space after her, and Hoyt does the same, and the three of us are there together after so long a separation, and there are our cries and the world turns black.

But this same night I compensate myself with a dream of happy return. I believe I will this dream to occur. In it I perform several feats of superhuman physical prowess. I manage to leap in two magnificent bounds from the middle of this ocean to Bermuda to the dock of DiMillo's Marina in downtown Portland. Instantly, I scoop Manny and Hoyt and Kim into my arms and, keeping them there, add more and more faces of my past within my grasp in an orgy of hugging and love until we are one great, grinning crowd of joy, safe and happy.

In another dream I become exasperated with my mother (dead seven years now) for being unconcerned, even unaware, that the roof of her house is literally disintegrating, and I spend all my time trying in desperation to close her in against the storm with plastic sheeting flimsy as gossamer.

Yet another dream combines a character from the past with one from the present. Bill is an old college friend who has been out of touch and Anna a current business associate. Bill's idea of a well-spent summer evening is to buy a two-gallon jug of fresh milk, pour the milk into the bathtub and bathe in it, refill the jug with martinis and ice, take it to a girls' softball game on the Boston Common, and get thoroughly drunk while calling obscene remarks to the players. It seems that Bill has been fired from his job as a salad chef and is despondent. Anna stays out consoling him all night. I am very pissed off that she doesn't show up for work and that she can be so concerned that such a bum lost such a crummy job.

In another dream, I find myself alone at a ballet in which Kim is performing. I have trouble appreciating Kim's dancing because somehow I have gotten into the theater and become seated bare-assed, naked below the waist. I try to ignore my condition. This is not easy to do when I get up and walk to the lobby to join the crowd for champagne at intermission. Most of the crowd are polite enough not to look directly my way, and no one seems interested in joining me. I am thankful for this because my defense is a belief that my nakedness is not a problem if not discussed. My desperate concern, though, is finding pants or some acceptable cover for my nudity before I meet Kim backstage. I awake before I do.

This is a dream that was one of my most common as a boy. It was long, long ago when I last dreamed I could fly. I mean flapping my arms and flying. The trick, of course, is willpower, not physical exertion. Intense mental concentration, a ferocious focus, is what does it. But here I am again soaring over heads and rooftops, happy and free by myself and invisible to all. As a boy, after this dream I was certain I really could fly. Now I know better. Well, maybe for a moment . . . I do wonder what this dream may prophesy, coming on the day it comes.

For this is the day I live twice. We cross the international date line and, therefore, I get to see February 3 two times and get back all the hours lost one at a time since beginning to sail into the east. Actually, February 3 the second time is almost exactly like February 3 the first time. A world of gray. Intermittent fog. The wind northeast at twenty knots heels *Promise* twenty degrees hard on the port tack.

DAY 101 ≈

The overcast burns away early this afternoon, revealing a welcome bald head of blue sky fringed by a horizon of gray. Glorious.

I install a new twenty-pound bottle of propane and note five full bottles remaining, enough to cook and heat shower water through three circumnavigations. This is the case with many of the supplies aboard *Promise,* enough for three complete voyages. Maybe I will have to go around again and again without stopping. It would be like having to clean one's plate as a child.

I am healthy enough now. Actually, I feel healthier than I have in years. My only physical complaints are the expected and constant cuts and bruises and scrapes of sailing. I know I lack enough regular aerobic exercise, but I certainly have plenty of peak loads of work — changing sails, cranking winches, hauling lines, climbing and lifting. My upper body is strong and hard and my hands tough enough to barely feel a running line burning through them or a direct spill of boiling water. My knee joints, though brutalized by old sports injuries, are for some reason limber and free of pain out here. On days that allow it, I do pushups and situps and run in place. Performing these exercises on a heaving, undulating platform has its own challenge; one second my body weighs nothing, the next it weighs four hundred pounds.

My head feels bell clear all the time. No stuffiness. No congestion. Not a hint of a migraine or any kind of headache. Actually, the only pains I feel are the clean, honest ones of surface injury and used muscle. And it is pure sensual pleasure to pull in a deep lungful of sweet sea air. Fifteen months ago I forbade myself cigarettes, and now I marvel that I could have ever, in any way, enjoyed the habit. I don't know what's happened to my weight but feel I have shed a few pounds, maybe down under 180.

If any of my equipment is suffering in a serious way, it is my intellect. There is not one helluva lot of intellectual stimulation out here, only that which is self-applied, and much of the time I seem not to have the drive to make that application, taking instead a tomorrow-maybe attitude toward mental work. I read but am tending more often to the easy, light stuff. Perhaps it is true that creative stimulation of the intellect comes only from others, a social and not a solitary act. Maybe you just can't do it to yourself. Maybe, as I spend more and more time alone, I will be less and less able to philosophize and will have to content myself mentally with memorizing multiplication tables.

The psychological tests and questionnaires I fill out each day don't interest me much because they are so irrelevant to my world now. I'm sure I complete the personality profile questionnaires much the same way each time. Do I like my parents? Would I rather be an engineer or an actor? Do I enjoy playing practical jokes? Am I the life of the party? Who really gives a shit? I am the only party here.

And the little quizzes I take hit my funnybone harder than my mind. Sitting in a corner wedged against the wild motion of forty-foot seas and searching for hidden shapes within hatchwork patterns of lines in tiny printed squares has the intellectual quality of slapstick. Surely the psychological pros will be able to learn something useful from these hundreds of strange and irrelevant pieces of paper I scribble out for them. Oh yes, surely they will.

I certainly hope they do learn something. Because a great deal of effort by a number of people has gone into this study.

It started a year before my departure. Manny wrote to Professors Easton and Nasby, describing my voyage as an opportunity to study an individual in an environment of solitude and stress for an extended period of time. Easton's special field of interest is sensory deprivation and Nasby is a clinical psychologist. They saw *Promise* as a rare research laboratory and me as an available and willing subject. They were able to overlook the bizarre elements in the plot of a fifty-three-year-old man planning to sail alone around the world supported by a wife who wanted his brain examined. Also, most important to me, they did not quickly conclude that I needed psychiatric help more than psychological study.

In the initial research stage, they found that the bulk of information on the subject of isolation was not scientific but anecdotal, such as Admiral Richard Byrd's classic and beautiful book *Alone,* about the winter he spent by himself at 80° south latitude, deep in the Antarctic. They found diaries of balloonists and mountain climbers, logs of solo sailors, journals of confined prisoners. One formal study by the English psychologist Glen Bennett of single-handed sailors in the 1972 OSTAR was not at all encouraging.

Bennett found that his subjects experienced psychotic fears, compulsiveness, severe depression, and hallucination. The sailors became careless. And their Atlantic crossing was barely one tenth the distance of my trip. This information deepened my understanding of the emotional challenge I was undertaking and altered some of my planning. I began paying more heed to those matters that would keep me rested and alert. When we were designing *Promise,* I told Ted Hood that I would trade a half knot of speed average for a better night's sleep.

The Easton-Nasby study went into high gear when I began a twenty-five-hour program of testing that included written and oral tests, reaction time tests, emotional stress tests, and inkblot tests. Some of the tests were categorized under abnormal psychology; others were chosen to satisfy rival schools of academic thought and to cover key psychological factors. My patience and sense of humor were also, if unofficially, tested by the course of these tests. I underwent whole weekends of testing with Randy and Bill, the last of them just three days before leaving. Out of all this arose my "personality and cognitive profile," which then formed the baseline of comparison for tests taken on board during the voyage and for follow-up tests afterward.

I was told little about my prevoyage test results, the psychological portrait drawn from them, or the objectives of the tests on board. My orders were to do what I was told and, of course, to carry out my plan to sail around the world so that there would be a study in the first place. This was just fine with me because I had no interest at all in somebody else's view of my own psychological condition and had more than enough other matters to worry about.

The tests on board were designed to take me an average of seven minutes a day to complete, with longer sessions scheduled every couple of months. Arranged in twenty-one-day cycles, they were stored in six fancy, waterproof boxes. Some tests simply asked in multiple-choice fashion how I felt about myself and my world; others were timed arithmetic, vocabulary, and problem-solving quizzes. Together, they were designed to track important aspects of my brain function, value system, self-esteem, and ability to concentrate. I was also asked to keep a sleep log and a dream log.

Another graphic source of data for the study was the film from the motion picture cameras. The well-known documentary film maker Chris Knight was ideally suited to the challenge of filming my voyage. He had solid experience in solving the technical problems of getting cameras and camera operating systems to work reliably at sea, having made the film *American Challenge,* which recorded the victory of solo sailor Phil Weld in the 1980 OSTAR. He was also an avid sailor himself and preferred to work alone. Chris installed six super-8mm sound cameras on *Promise:* three in the cockpit, two in the pilothouse, and one below in the dry cabin. He idiotproofed the cameras, mounted them in sealed, clear enclosures, and supervised the installation of a smart — and very durable, it turned out — electrical circuit to control their operation. Three of the cameras were programmed to expose thirty seconds of film every four hours if enough light existed and to expose film if the boat was knocked down to more than a forty-five-degree angle. He also gave me operating and maintenance manuals, spare parts, a couple of nonsound, hand-held cameras, and four hundred three-minute film cassettes.

I exposed some nine hours of film during the voyage, an average of about three minutes a day, and the two psychologists viewed every foot of it. Watching so much film of a single actor on a set that doesn't change in a scene that doesn't vary has to be stupefying work. But it was work that helped flesh out the dry bones of the study with graphic evidence. The film confirmed the extraordinarily painful impact of the early failure that forced me to Bermuda. It reinforced the test results that indicated I felt the discomfort most during the voyage when we showed little progress. And if the film did not provide new information, it did support the key features of the psychological portrait.

Bill Nasby gave me only a brief outline of the psychological profile drawn of me before I left Portland, but what he told me was enough to make me say, "I don't think I want to spend much time with the guy you are describing, and I sure as hell don't want him living with my family." In his thumbnail sketch, Nasby noted that some of my overriding personality traits are classified as antisocial and narcissistic. His good news was that these traits should bode well for a solo sailor.

By the time the full study reached print, however, the bluntly negative descriptions "antisocial and narcissistic" had magically become "thick-skinned and flamboyant." I don't know how many other aspects of my psychological portrait yielded to happier and more generous description, but, because I would not dare attempt to improve on it, the final version as published by the two doctors appears here as Appendix III.

~~~ *IO* ~~~

*T*he average wind force during our crossing of the Southern Pacific Ocean is about what *Sailing Directions* and Pilot Charts say it should be, close to twenty-five knots. But that is a little like the joke about the average human being having one tit and one ball. Here in the "roaring forties" and "ferocious fifties" it blows a storm or not at all. High-pressure zones ooze unusually far south and cover the Southern Pacific Ocean with calms, then these calms are detonated by two tropical cyclones that also drive far south this year. The official weather watchers don't pick up these strange weather patterns quickly, but *American Promise* and I sure do.

DAY 80 ≈
Noon, January 30, 1986, Thursday, to noon, January 31, 1986,
    Friday
48°56.32' south/161°01.85' east
The subject today is weather. Again. There is a plentiful supply of it around us now, and the prognosis is that we will continue to be oversupplied for a couple more days as strong westerlies associated with another low-pressure trough hit us. Tomorrow we will be passing a hundred miles south of New Zealand's Stewart Island. I don't know if having land that close has anything to do with the awesome state of the sea here.

The seas are bigger than life, like something out of Disneyland, a mouse that's ten feet tall with a three-foot grin. On by us they march, as relentless as time itself. And there are the giants among the giants, rogues that stand up from the rest breaking white frothy crowns. *Promise* is assaulted like a toy boat in a tub with a child. These rogues are bounding within my sight all the time. Most we avoid. Those we do not lift *Promise* up by the stern until we are corkscrewing down a thirty-degree grade of water, then flick the hull on its side in an almost broach.

Promise creaks and groans below, the sound of wood grinding on wood under great pressure. It is the mast twisting in the deck partners, causing bulkheads to grind against the deck.

The wind blows in cycles of speed like an orderly sine wave on a scope, forty-five knots for fifteen minutes, sixty knots for ten minutes. Then we are in and out of the wind on a shorter cycle as we drop into the trough between seas and have relative quiet, then rise up on the crest, where there is wind enough to pull my breath away. The gusts are seventy knots. They shove *Promise* on a more acute heel, but are notable mostly for the loud wailing sounds. We still sail under a tiny lapel of a reefed mainsail alone. I have much time to study these seas. They are forty to fifty feet high, one hundred to one hundred twenty feet apart, and travel at twenty-five to thirty knots. The wind waves on the top of these seas are five to six feet and breaking.

But some sailors a couple thousand miles to our north are having a lot more weather than we. Tropical cyclone Winifred is giving them hell along the north coast of Australia. The output of my weather facsimile receiver is frenzied, enough printouts piling up on my chart table to paper a path from here to New Zealand, and they show Winifred's broad track tearing southwest across the Coral Sea and colliding with Queensland, Australia. Hurricane-force winds cover the southwest Pacific Ocean. The forecasts say these hurricane winds, actually wind arrows showing seventy to eighty knots, will blow way down south in our part of the ocean within the next twenty-four hours.

It is strange how times like this alter the reach of my memory. And so it seems like forever I've been bouncing on this carnival ride. Great, foamy, gray liquid pyramids. I'm accustomed to them; the calms now seem deep in the past. They make it impossible for me to recall what it is like to stand on

solid ground, surrounded by unlimited space that is available
to me simply by placing one foot naturally in front of the other
while my hands swing a balancing rhythm by my sides. It's
called walking, I think. Oh, for a world where a drinking glass
remains upright in gravity and contains blocks of frozen water
that tinkle, where sleeping surfaces are wide and resolutely horizontal and not fenced in like baby cribs and often wrap two
warm bodies at once and . . . Well, forget it, Dodge, for a few
more months, forget it.

DAY 81 ≈
   The weather fax charts follow every corner of Winifred and
scare the shit out of me. It sure is bad going to the north, but
the gurus are forecasting even worse weather where we are sailing. Hurricane-force winds, they still say, will blanket our entire expanse of ocean, not a chance to escape them.
   This makes for a weird contrast of emotions as I stare at the
pile of wild weather charts and feel the wind drop. Drop. Unbelievably, but literally, the wind goes away. Here I sit bobbing
up and down, almost becalmed, dead in the center of the paper
rage of storms.
   I think I know what is going on here. The Aussie weather-
crats simply assume that weather is always worse down here
and so they just forecast it that way. Worse. They only care
about their little knot of civilization anyway. I'll bet there is an
Australian weather service directive: "All forecasters be advised
that Southern Ocean weather is generally terrible and always
worse than our weather. This is all anyone has to know about
Southern Ocean weather. The farther south, the worse it becomes. Even when this forecasting axiom is not specifically accurate, do not worry, because nobody is down there but idiots,
masochists, and solo circumnavigators, and all those guys love
and deserve bad weather anyway."
   I have had it with machine-made sick jokes. I turn my fax
receiver off. To have no forecast is better than to have one
that's way wrong and frightening.
   I am blessed at the close of this day with an aquatic show,
rare down here. The introductions come with a great albatross

swooping huge figure eights around us. The dolphins soon follow, coughing and pumping up to us until we are surrounded by their action. It's easy to tell the kids from the old folks. The kids splurge energy, bouncing in wasteful circles and leaping straight up to crash, more often than not, on their tails rather than their heads. These dolphins have markings like killer whales, ebony-black capes and pure white bellies, two absolute colors that meet suddenly and cleanly without any connecting shades of gray. They are, however, unmistakably dolphins. The little ones are such a joy to watch as they play with complete abandon, with no sense of discipline or economy. They even wear mischievous grins. They remind me of Hoyt and Kim celebrating their energy together in the back yard at home. I make myself a celebration now, too, whistling and screaming and clowning in return. And I spend much film on them with my hand-held movie camera.

Next comes a stately family of whales, about twenty. They have blunt, round noses, large, almond-shape eyes, are black all over, and range in length between fifteen and twenty feet. They puff and bob in an orderly formation behind us wearing saintly expressions and patient smiles.

I feel guilty this evening, uneasy that I've somehow gotten pleasure I didn't deserve. To make it worse, I take a hot shower. It is pure ecstasy and I know, as I wallow in hot water and suds, that the gods of the Puritans cluck at my excess. The guilt shames me into doing my laundry, a well-grown, gummy pile of long underwear. And into forcing myself, naked, out into the forty-degree cold to wring out the washing. Then I take a hot cup of cocoa. Oh, certainly the simplest pleasures of civilization are the surest and the dearest.

DAY 87 ≈

Still we slat. Still we bob and wallow. Still the sheets slacken and then snap taut, whipping the sails in epileptic violence. The wear and tear on gear is inexorable and violent. The wear and tear on me is even worse.

A storm, as frightening as it often is, can somehow be dealt with by actions. The calm sets my nerves right on the edge.

When *Promise* wallows, I feel each violent jerk of the lines as if they are my own sinews. I am under high tension. I hunt for any whiff of breeze, not only with my eyes but with my very soul. I hold the wheel in a death grip, inching it one way and then the other to keep any perceptible way on. I hold my breath to help me anticipate any cat's paw of a breeze and to feel the slightest change in the boat's motion. At least once per hour I let go, vent the pressure to scream curses into the west. And then I tense up again and plead, plaintively beg, for some wind.

The night passes painfully and slowly. The speed indicator registers zeros. I know we move, though, because *Promise* still responds, even if oh so slowly, to the helm, and she holds a general heading. She doesn't founder. I test my sense of this minute motion by tossing crumpled pieces of paper into the sea by the forward edge of the cockpit and watch them slowly pass aft. Often they take five minutes to drift the fifteen feet past the transom. We sail 180 feet per hour, a rate of eight tenths of a mile per day, taking us back to Bermuda thirty-eight years from now. But we do move, and when a cat's paw does come we are in position to use it to accelerate our way, which we then can keep because of the momentum of our weight. In the little puffs, the speedo registers, and we hold it through the minutes of calm that follow. We are like a precisely built and well-oiled locomotive rolling along under pure momentum. As long as I can concentrate on this awful job, we keep making progress, three knots' average on the worst of days.

At midnight I give up the struggle to brood. Alone we sit in the middle of the ocean, eleven thousand miles from our destination, powerless like a sick, old man with a broken cane abandoned in an endless desert. The big, light-air headsail, MPS, wraps itself around the headstay. Almost with relief I go to work to free it. The sail and its lines are badly tangled, fouled, locking it aloft. In the course of clearing the mess and bringing the sail down to the deck, I fall through the forward hatch, carelessly left open. This punctuates my feeling of helplessness. The fall paints my spine with bruises, but, miraculously, I am not seriously hurt. I figure my layers of clothing protected me.

By four in the morning, a two-knot breeze descends on us from the east, the wrong direction. In disgust I let the boat go and she founders and wallows around to head west. At least we drift the wrong way slowly.

It is nine days now with no more wind than ten knots and four days with no wind more than six knots. Not in the doldrums have I seen calms so pervasive. The only rival to this in my memory is when the three of us, Lael, Roland and I, were sailing *Coaster* from Panama to Honolulu and were essentially becalmed for six days. *Coaster* wouldn't move in light air like a precision, well-oiled locomotive. I remember standing on the schooner's bow screaming curses at the wind god and calling him by name. Shortly after my curses, a wind came off the Central American coast that almost did the old girl in, tearing at her sails and rigging and working her so badly, we had to pump fifteen minutes of every thirty. *American Promise* carries a memento of that storm, a pillow embroidered with the words "Don't Swear at God," especially made for me by Lael, who forever after that storm preferred calms to heavy winds.

I turn to the ham radio to relieve my pain. The Pacific mobile maritime net informs me that the abnormal high-pressure zone now swallowing our wind may stay for four more days. *Promise* is a good light-air boat but a very poor no-air boat.

Bruce from Fiji, call sign 3D2GB, informs me that a solo sailor named Frank Shirley tried three years ago what I am now trying, to be the first American to circumnavigate solo, nonstop. Shirley, he tells me, died aboard his boat in the attempt, leaving, for a while, the mystery of whether his drifting boat may have completed the voyage with his corpse and whether that would count. I tell Bruce, even while thinking that this is a helluva story to pass on to me while I'm out here, that I will invite Frank Shirley's spirit aboard *Promise* to get at least that part of him the rest of the way around with me. I post a note in the pilothouse, welcoming aboard this spirit, and I wonder about being the first posthumous solo, nonstop circumnavigator.

DAY 89 ≈

Glory be, I am healed, the spirit is whole again. All it takes is
twelve hours of sailing on a steady wind. The northeast breeze
stiffens to ten knots, and *Promise* knows exactly what to do
with it. She points up and bubbles Southern Ocean out from
under her transom at eight and a half knots. I am blessed with
a four-foot sea and skies that are broken by blue, and I am
going home.

Since we are sailing again and we are well more than halfway, it is appropriate to discuss some of the sailing characteristics of *American Promise*. I begin by stating that she has re-
written the book for me on how to sail. Before *Promise*, I
sailed a considerable number of miles, most shorthanded or
alone and almost all in gaff-headed schooners. That is itself an
aberration in these times. *Coaster* was a twelve-and-a-half-ton
schooner, thirty-six feet overall, twenty-nine and three quarters
feet on the water, eleven-foot beam, and six-foot draft. *Eagle* is
a seven-ton schooner, thirty-one feet overall, twenty-three on
the water, nine-foot beam, and drawing five feet.

The two schooners sail essentially alike. Their most significant differences are because of size; *Eagle* is so small that she
has no forestays'l and is very much wetter in a blow because of
her low freeboard. Both boats have traditional hull shapes, a
fairly sharp entry, firm mid-futtocks, and fairly flat exits. Both
have graceful counters and full sterns and sit in the water like
well-fed geese. Both are fitted with main topmasts and, with all
lowers and uppers set, carry a cloud of sail. For one who
knows them, they are marvels to sail and will perform tricks,
sailing one minute, heading up and waiting another, and always obeying a properly delivered command. These two are
among the world's most forgiving boats to their sailors, good
teachers to beginners and obedient friends to those who know
how. I can comfortably sail *Eagle* through a crowded anchorage, onto her mooring, up to and away from a dock. I enjoyed
taking *Coaster* alone under sail into a harbor while sitting aloft
at the crosstrees of the foremast.

But my, how sailing is changed by a design and rig like
American Promise's. The thought of threading her through
very confined spaces under sail raises a fast sweat on me. How-

ever, I can guarantee that one does not have to know that much to sail *Promise* on the open water. Even though Ted Hood always seems able to trim her and steer her a knot faster, almost anyone can put sail on and get her to move. I am just talking basic sailing here, not all the other critical seamanship skills, such as dead reckoning, anchoring, rules of the road, etc., that one needs to have to be proficient on a small boat. She is a deep-sea, bluewater boat, not a gunk-holer, and what she does best is to sail fast in a straight line. She does that, though, with ease.

In light wind she is surprisingly quick, preferring, of course, to go hard on the wind in these conditions. She has a powerful "in the groove" characteristic, largely because of her weight and attendant momentum. Her seventy-five-foot mast allows her to carry a large sail area and to set big light-air headsails for off-the-wind work. The roller-furling gear on all working sails, mains'l, jib, and forestays'l allows one to increase or decrease sail area in minutes. This sail handling capability, in fact, is the key to her optimal performance in all weather conditions, because it allows me to hang everything out in light airs, secure in the knowledge that I can reef quickly and safely when needed. If poles are not set out, I can rig the boat from catching cat's paws to standing up to a whole gale in the span of a minute.

Sailing into a four-knot true wind, *Promise* will deliver five knots of boat speed and do it with some sea running. She is making her own wind here and so points no better than fifty-five degrees off the true wind, but that is where the schooner goes on a heavier wind under the best of conditions. Give *Promise* ten knots of true wind and she will give you back nine knots of speed and tack easily in ninety degrees. Like any sailboat, she does not like downwind work in light air, but at least in these conditions I can spread twenty-five hundred square feet of sail area, fixed and steady on the two poles square-rigged fashion, forestays'l on one side and jib on the other.

In heavy weather, *Promise* has proved to be extraordinarily capable of sailing on points off the wind. Close reaching into a gale — which is what one does if one is on a lee shore or stupid — is a wet and noisy adventure, but *Promise* does it well enough to keep me trying to do it. Off the wind in a gale is sailing heaven itself with *Promise*. And sailing dead downwind under the poles in a gale is simple, safe, and fast. One thing I know not to attempt with the schooners is dead downwind work in heavy weather; the boat will sooner or later broach and, even with boom preventers, will jibe gaffs and something will break. *Promise*, on the other hand, just loves it. Her bad habit is that she has that annoying corkscrew motion and sometimes digs in for little broachlike moves when running in very big seas. But she always recovers quicker than the crew does and continues sailing in a straight line like a quivering arrow. Lowering her two daggerboards and intermediate centerboard greatly helps her sail a straight course. The roll that causes the corkscrewing is often eighty degrees or more and does demand a grim, physical resolve from the crew, but there is heady compensation in watching the speedo yo-yo from ten to twenty-five knots sailing in fifty-knot winds up and down forty-foot seas with no more than two hundred square feet of sail winged out on poles. She feels safe and under control in these conditions. Except for those rogue waves, green water from even the bigger breaking sea slides under her transom. When she is knocked down to more than ninety degrees, it is usually when a sea hits her broadside and she literally falls off the top of the wave. These extreme knockdowns take my breath away. The boat is knocked down sixty to sixty-five degrees quite easily by the heavy Southern Ocean conditions, but she does not seem the least bit endangered by this.

Running with winds heavier than fifty knots, I tend to hold *Promise* with the wind over her quarter and let her fly under bare pole, no sail on at all, or just a tiny amount of mainsail. She is happy as hell doing this and gives me a bouncing, gyrating ride of six to nine knots.

I wish not to sail into that kind of weather and consider doing so to be masochistic and downright ungentlemanly. Of course, she will not sail upwind, as she does downwind, with no sail on, but even deeply reefed, she does not beat well into extremely heavy weather. (Does any boat?) She presents a large amount of windage with her high freeboard, fat, roller-furled headstays, thick mast, and antenna farm aft. When I was caught on the edge of Bermuda's North Bank, I had no choice but to claw my way dead into a gale and twenty-foot seas. It was very dreary and slow work for *Promise*. In six hours of struggle, she made just five miles. It was one more lesson to include lee shores right along with the Four Horsemen of the Apocalypse as things to avoid.

There are two stages of coping with heavy gales in a small boat. As prelude, it is my experience and generally well understood by seamen that the major cause for damage in a storm is the seas and not the wind. The first stage in coping with heavy weather is to run off with it, not dead down, but with the wind coming over one quarter. The second stage occurs when this becomes dangerous, as evidenced by being pooped, seas breaking over the transom, and a tendency for the boat to broach. It is then high time to heave to or to drag warps, the objective being to stop the boat's motion through the water as much as possible.

Boats lie hove to in different ways. The schooners like it best head to the wind, the bow forty-five to fifty-five degrees off and perhaps held there by a sea anchor. With a little foresail and helm that is up, they will lie abeam to the seas, not at all nice but, in fact, not acutely dangerous. I have spent many storms and many days hove to like this in a schooner, making almost no way. She does not fight the power of the seas this way, instead tossing and rolling and giving with them. I can then wait out the storm, snuggling below in the cabin.

Promise, however, teaches me new lessons. Left under bare poles to her own ways, she turns her stern to the wind and accelerates until she screams downwind at one very fast clip. I have no sea anchor on board and don't think one would help much unless it were as big as the Ringling Brothers big top. She just does not like to lie hove to. She likes to run with the storm. No, not simply likes to, she actually insists on running with the storm. And so, what the hell, I let her. We have plenty of sea room out here, and she flies very agreeably under bare poles in the worst of weather. She is as comfy as a hammock swinging, if somewhat wildly, on the back porch. She is responsive and steers well anywhere from a beam reach to a dead run. The autopilot finds no problem at all steering her under these conditions. The most critical factor is to make certain there is enough sea room to run down into, and this is what makes heavy weather sailing relatively easy and safe in the middle of an ocean and difficult and dangerous near land.

The closest she will come to standing hove to is to head her fifty to sixty degrees off the wind under reefed main and storm jib; she leaves her wake abeam upwind while making a couple knots of leeway.

Today, as I write about how *Promise* performs, she makes 233.2 miles noon to noon, not seven miles from the record for this size boat set by *Crédit Agricole*. And she does it with little help from me. When not writing or navigating, and between two-hour waking checks, I am sleeping like a possum.

DAY 91 ≈

We are a cheerful little ship after two days of 209 and 233 miles. The days put the memory of the dreaded calms well back on the stove for now. The miles bring us three days ahead of the projected times for waypoints across the Southern Pacific Ocean, Tasmania to Cape Horn, and about 3,100 miles from the Horn. We could pass that great cape in eighteen days. That would be the last day of February, the shadow anniversary of my marriage to Manny. If this were leap year I would plan to celebrate, but instead I get another year celebration free.

We are now completing 60 percent of the voyage in 90 days and at that rate would arrive back in Bermuda after a total of only 150 days at sea, a record of all records for any solo sail around. But this kind of talk is as useless as a whisper in a gale. This distance remaining is about what a weekend sailor would do in the ten best years of his life. Much too soon to count the tomorrows.

DAY 92 ≈

I dread this continued return to the light and variable winds and cannot fathom how there can be so much of this brand of weather in this part of the world. I am supposed to be fighting the big winds and they are supposed to be roaring out of the west.

I find these days moving by like the legs of a spent runner.

Painfully, each moment interminable, droning the specter of defeat. But if the others are spent, too? If the others have no kick left either? Where was I when the wall stopped me? But I have no competitors to push myself against, none to help mark my performance. Oh, it is so much easier when there are others to measure against. I miss that grimace-to-grimace, one-on-one competition now. It would be pure joy to pour some violence into direct combat with another man.

Those were the days. Simple-minded purity of combat on a quarter-mile cinder track. I was eighteen and ran the quarter mile because I could run it well. But the distance intimidated me because I pushed too much too early and always finished five yards after my legs had no more in them. I did not have the mindset to pace myself. Oh, give me those eighteen-year-old legs and my fifty-four-year-old mind and I will really show you something, my friend.

Only the other runners could give me those final five yards or take them away. Three strides behind the leader or two runners ahead of me and I could feel myself folding inside. Too much to make up. Hopeless. The finality of defeat was as prophetic and as emasculating as the moment of death. But one step away, behind or ahead, there was evidence showing of the other's pain, shoulders hunching, chin too high, arm pump too low, and the miracle of unknown power flowed.

I convinced myself then that I ran in my own private consciousness and that the other runners were of no consequence. That was why, I told myself, I so enjoyed the individual events. They suited well my view of myself as being alone, out of reach of the others, a silent and aloof warrior who would flaunt my drive and skill and then bask in a kind of heroic brooding, separate and apart. Now I know how vital those other runners were to me. I wish they were here now to spur me on or to kill me off.

Ninety-one days at sea is a long time. The things of civilization are well back in my memory now, static and unchanged because I have not watched them. Nothing changes that I do not witness changing. Yes. That must be right. What has changed in these ninety-one days is only me. I remember me when . . .

DAY 94 ≈

The seas have built to ten feet in fifteen knots of northwest wind. *Promise* rolls along downwind at seven and a half to nine and a half knots. I crank the daggerboards down and dial the heavy-seas setting into Murphy. The boat sways and sashays like a loosely sprung Pullman car. Now that I am used to the serenade of cans and tools and supplies and what-all clacking in lockers, the boat has become a world-class sleeping platform for me. As I lie in the bunk, the constant, involuntary rolling and shifting of my body are not unlike what I think it would be like to live in the womb of a large, athletic mother.

But I watch the barograph with growing alarm. It shows our atmospheric pressure dropping at the incredible rate of one tenth of an inch of mercury each hour. By dawn it is 29.1 and still dropping. The seas are up to twenty feet, and the tops are being broken off by thirty-five to forty knots of north wind.

I tuck another reef in at two in the morning. Back below, I hear a too-loud and too-close sound of sloshing water and discover that the bilges — and *Promise* has big bilges — are filled right up to the floorboards. She has taken on a couple thousand gallons of seawater somehow, from somewhere. To put it mildly, this matter gets my full attention. The first priority is to get rid of the water. I engage the big, engine-driven pump and the electric pump, and I man a big hand pump. The water level drops. The bilges empty. And I can see we are not now making water at a high rate. Next, I hunt for the leak. Through-hull fittings? Hoses? What? I know the problem is in the large center compartment because the other four watertight compartments are closed off and no water has accumulated in them.

I sit and watch the center compartment for two hours. The water does not rise. Damnit, the water does not rise. This leak wants to remain a mystery. But it will have to haunt me later because another priority intercedes.

Now the storm rages over us, mocking my recent rage at the calms. This will surely raise the average of the Southern Ocean wind speed for us. Is it asking too much to have it blow that average, not too little or too much?

The rain is horizontal, and the drops sting when they strike flesh. The air temperature is in the forties. The seas are broad-side to us, making the ride a wild one. We are laid down often, and the pilothouse is a missile range of loose gear until I secure every pencil, book, and granola bar. By noon, the sea is a scud of spindrift like driven snow. The wind blasts out of the NNE with gusts to sixty. The barometer still falls and is passing 28.8 inches of mercury.

DAY 95 ≈

I am busy just holding on. We are under bare pole, no sail set at all, and yet we make good way in a beam wind. I could use the storm jib in some of the lulls when the wind drops to forty-five knots. But I am lazy as well as cautious and leave the sail in the locker. Incredibly, the barometer dives still and has passed through 28.55. (The average world barometric pressure at sea level is 29.92 inches of mercury.) The paper chart on my barograph has 28.5 as its lower printed limit. I wonder if this storm will pull the marker right off the chart. I have never seen the atmospheric pressure this low.

Promise is knocked down more than sixty degrees at least once every ten minutes, with gray, solid seawater boiling by the pilothouse windows as she buries her deck in the sea. The waves roar toward us at thirty knots or more — a very discon-certing sight. But *Promise* handles them quite well and we make seven and a half to eight knots on our easterly heading, still with no sail on. I plead with the wind to veer to the west and take the seas around with it. If it keeps coming out of the northwest and the seas keep building higher, we will be forced farther south, where the icebergs roam.

It is cold and raw and damp inside the boat. The diesel-fired heater is permanently out of work because each time we are hit with a knockdown on the port tack, the smoke pipe on the pilot-house roof is buried underwater and fills with seawater, which then fills the heater itself. The cockpit is awash. The deck is only occasionally visible through the breaking waves, spray, and spume.

I wear three layers of clothing to cope with this weather. Next to my skin is heavy, quarter-inch polypropylene thermal underwear, thick with nap. Then comes the padded, insulated bib trousers and jacket. Finally the heavyweight Musto and Hyde foul weather suit, insulated knee-high boots, wool watchcap and, sometimes, a ski mask. The heavy wool mittens keep me warmer than the fancy insulated gloves. They are attached by a string that, kid style, runs through the sleeves of my jacket to keep them with me when I must use my fingers. I wear light leather gloves underneath the mittens. I look like Hoyt when he was a baby and Manny bundled him up in a bulk of clothing like a straitjacket and strapped him, immobile, into a car seat that was bolted to the bridge deck of the schooner for our Maine fall cruising.

It is imperative that the foul weather jacket have a built-in lifeline harness because I would never take time to jam myself and all this bulk into a separate harness. It would be one more reason not to wear a lifeline, and I am negligent enough as it is. More than foolhardy it is not to wear a lifeline in these conditions. The power of the waves barreling over the deck often sweeps my legs from under me and keeps me always with one eye out for a good handhold close by. Especially at night, when the waves cannot be easily anticipated, it is extremely dangerous. What keeps me careful is the flash of an image of myself in *Promise*'s black and endless wake, helplessly watching her sail into forever.

I know I can handle my own death if it comes. I had to come to terms with that possibility, of course, before attempting such a voyage. But I feel now that in no way am I ready to die. There is just so much that remains to be accomplished. And I must get myself through this to be back home with Hoyt and Kim as they grow up, even to help them grow up. So enough talk of death. Attach that lifeline.

The glass bottoms out at 28.5. It has dropped two inches the past two days, nearly one full inch in the past twelve hours. This is not just a Southern Ocean storm, it is one helluva Southern Ocean storm.

Promise sails the night at five to six knots under bare pole, not one bit of sail on. It's a very rough and wet ride but not threatening to the gear. Dawn breaks with the storm still raging, winds over seventy, but it doesn't look as bad in the light.

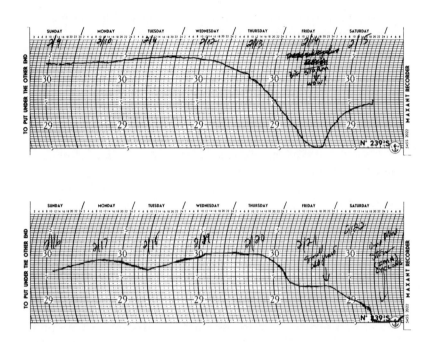

Tropical cyclone Ima may have struck Promise *twice with high winds and huge seas. The barograph bottoms out on the chart at 28.5 inches of mercury.*

I like the daylight hours better. During the morning inspection, I note we have lost two winch handles, a flashlight, and an EPIRB [emergency radio beacon]. I double-lash the poles to the deck forward and the running rigging to the cleats at the base of the mast. I set up the running backstays. I stow any loose gear below.

I remember that today the Whitbread fleet gets under way from Auckland for the third of their four-leg around-the-world race. These are big boats, many eighty-footers, with crews of twenty or more. They will average well over two hundred miles per day but will not catch me before the Horn on the way to their next stop, at Montevideo.

Promise has delivered an incredible performance, 175 miles noon to noon in the right direction under bare pole. In this wind she'll put the sailmakers out of business.

DAY 96 ≈

We are at 50° south latitude and 130° west longitude, more than halfway across the Pacific. We average more than 168 miles per day so far, seven knots. It makes me recall the article in *Cruising World* magazine predicting that *Promise* "might turn in some 175-mile days."

This storm, now in its third day, begins to abate, backing off to fifty-five knots of wind. As it does, the sky opens up around big, puffy, cumulus clouds. There is some sun. Oh, God, how the sun heals. The seas remain huge, at least fifty feet. Every ninth wave is a comber that rolls foam over the transom into the cockpit. Magnificent to watch. Easier to watch with the knowledge that the storm passes.

I have some time for the radio. I learn we have been going through tropical cyclone Ima. The real miracle is that the storm passed south of us, very deep in the high latitudes for a tropical storm, to bring the fury of its wind to our back rather than into our nose. What luck we have! I also learn that a fifty-mile-long iceberg is reported ahead and to the south of us, making a several-knot speed east, proving that even an iceberg can sail downwind. The only ice we see comes from the sky in the form of hail or snow, during the colder nights, with thin patches of skin ice forming on deck. I am happy to say our ice is not durable.

The cyclone leaves behind a six-hour vacuum of calm on the still-huge seas and my spirits nosedive.

Here we go again, back to that direct, almost mystical relationship between boat speed and crew spirits. At 0400 I give in to a deep depression, cold and tired and struggling to keep headway through the messy confusion of big waves and no wind. By noon I am cheered and bustling with activity as we sail at five knots on a light northeast breeze. At 1800, with the sun beaming and fifteen knots of wind blowing uninhibitedly over *Promise*'s transom, my only shadowy thought is that the euphoria must sometime end.

From barely controlled fury to uncontrolled, humming contentment on the whiff of a fair wind. Fate sometimes plays a strange role in this.

DAY 97 ≈

I feel like screaming my brains out and physically striking something when we are wallowing becalmed. Most of the time I do a good job of jailing the anger. This morning some escapes. About to light the stove, my arm suddenly breaks out of my control and slams a pot down hard on a burner. The noise is impressive. I don't feel any better afterward. And then the stove doesn't light and I think that payment for stupid behavior is extracted instantly. I find that, in fact, the stove has arranged with Providence to choose the exact moment of my fury to run a bottle of propane dry. Fate's lesson is not wasted on me.

On day 100, the boat sails so well it makes me horny:

≈ *Promise* sashays along under her wings in these light and lumpy conditions like a plump lady on a stroll with sex on her mind, her beam swaying from side to side in an exaggerated swing and her stern trying to catch up with a looping, smile-shape sideways path over the waves. The bow's motion is quicker, and she seems to be nuzzling and burrowing to find the slipperiest thrust forward. It is an exotic concert of movement, arousing and hypnotic, restless and comforting.

I begin to feel the climax of the Southern Pacific approaching. Cabo de Hornos. Cape Horn. The Cape. The sailor's ultimate challenge. My feelings are a confusion of anticipation, excitement, and anxiety. The Horn is not only the end of this ocean of extremes, it is the most important single event of the entire circumnavigation because of all that the rounding of it has symbolized for sailors through the centuries, because of its solid reputation for terrible weather, because of the ships and men lost there, and, for me, because it will put me back in my home ocean heading north to my home hemisphere. I feel ready to close my memories of these cold and dreary and inhospitable southern forties and fifties, ready to cross the great threshold.

DAY 101 ≈

Oh, how those tropics will feel. Again the glass drops and the cold wind rises. The air is full of wet on the edge of freezing. I am driven farther south. My fingers are slow to thaw back to feeling after working on deck. Inside the boat it is cold and dank. I eat more and it must be hot. Not good, just hot. If I have time, I heat everything I put in my mouth except my weekly can of beer.

DAY 102 ≈

Our last jib halyard is wearing rapidly and its furling gear operates sporadically. I lower the sail to the deck every three days now to check the wear, to lubricate the upper swivel, to alter the sail's luff length slightly to change the points of chafing. I also use the forestays'l instead of the jib whenever I can. The jib's roller-furling gear does not run smoothly. It jams and then spins free. I treat it like a piece of delicate art, roll the sail in or out slowly and gently by hand, and use the binoculars to keep an eye aloft when doing so. I am determined that Ted Hood's prediction of a couple weeks ago will not come true: that the one remaining halyard will not last me to Bermuda.

My wind instrument is now kaput. There are two wind speed and direction sensors mounted on the outer ends of the tower aft, so that one is always clear of the windstream of the sails. The starboard sensor failed when I entered the Indian Ocean. The other has now failed. I can judge the wind by the old sniff-and-feel technique. I have spent enough time to little avail on this instrument now, disassembling and cleaning and reassembling and installing spares. Well, screw it. We'll let the experts ashore take care of it.

Repairs and attempted repairs consume several hours of every day now. Belowdecks it is not really bad. I can't keep the two big alternators operating, but both generators run fine. The pumps work and the stove works and both satnavs work and the radios work — and that's about all I need to have work down there. On deck is another world. On deck everything is always in the process of failing, and only my vigilance keeps the failures at bay. The twice-daily inspection tours become even more critical.

I have now become quite content alone out here, taking each hour and each day as they come to me and not feeling lonely or sorry for myself. My ham radio, however, will not allow me to remain completely alone. And as I get farther east I can get back in touch with my ham friends in the Northeast. Just four days ago, I renewed contact with George, W2IBN, on Long Island. It was our first conversation since Christmas Day, two months ago. George has the perfect radio voice, deep and round, and, this time, edged with excitement. He and his rig put me instantly closer to Manny and to Bob Rice and make me think more of home. The radio has also added another element to my social life, the discovery that there is one more boat with me here in the Southern Ocean. I speak with her daily now. She is *Dream Merchant,* a sixty-foot steel schooner with seven aboard, bound for the inside straits and channels just north of Cape Horn. She left New Zealand a week before we sailed by there, but we are quickly catching up. I learn from her skipper, Gary Cross, that both boat and crew took a big beating from cyclone Ima. Since *Promise* is sailing some forty miles per day faster than *Dream Merchant,* I decide to aim for her latitude on the chance that I can sight my first human beings in more than three months.

The social life of this solo sailor is becoming downright hectic. I have a renewed radio schedule with my East Coast ham friends, eager to patch me into contact with home, I have my new neighbor to keep up with, and I have the immense specter of Cape Horn to wonder about. My journal is becoming a gossip column, and the new entries are a lively addition to the inevitable and never-ending descriptions of every facet of the weather, each storm and each calm, written up in yawning detail. The weather, of course, is not only my one constant and loyal companion, good and bad, but the single most important variable in my life, so it quite naturally dominates.

DAY 104 ≈

Wow. Someone else is actually having the same shitty weather we are. *Dream Merchant* is full of complaints and has slow progress in spite of her seven-person crew and the use of an engine as well as sails. Makes my ego swell. I am within thirty miles of their longitude and closing fast, but Gary is giving me confusing data on his latitude. His problem seems to be in plotting his position, and I begin to doubt I will find her visually.

This cold, cold climate at 54° south makes our stormy weather harder to endure. The frequent squalls are punctuated by sleet and hail. The sleet coats *Promise* with sheet ice. Most of the hail bounces merrily overboard.

I handle this storm, forty-five to fifty knots of wind over thirty-five-to-forty-foot seas, like a true professional: I spend much of it with my two skins of long underwear snuggling under wool blankets and a down comforter in my incredibly comfy dry cabin bunk. The wild and jarring motions of the boat are attenuated here, and I can at any time peek out of one eye to check the boat speed on the instrument at my feet, which, more often than not, reassures me that *Promise* knows exactly what she is doing.

I can barely contain my anticipation for the Horn, just four days away now. Islas Diego Ramirez, southeast of the Cape, should be my first view of land since Bermuda. How will I handle that?

DAY 105 ≈

A cold south wind signals the passing of this storm and cleans the sky for first the sun and then the full moon to shine over us. I am in paradise. The ham circuit gives me heartwarming chats with Kim and Hoyt and Manny and then Bob Rice. No question! I will take the Rice route north to the equator, shaving 380 miles from the planned route and — don't tell anybody yet — bringing me back to Bermuda on April 16 for a 155-day circumnavigation!

On my evening ham schedule with *Dream Merchant,* we find that *Promise* is now ahead but only by some ten to fifteen miles. *Dream Merchant* turns on her masthead light and *Promise* lights her spreaders (her masthead light has failed) on the slim chance that we can sight one another. Then I look aft, and there, when we ride a crest, I see a tiny yellow light riding on the waves astern *Promise*. This is my first sight of mankind for more than three months. That tiny yellow light. I get a powerful feeling from that little light which tells me I am, without doubt, a social animal.

One crew member aboard *Dream Merchant* is a New Yorker, Paul, who recalls seeing a television show about *American Promise* and particularly remembers Hoyt at his computer, with a tear in his eye, responding to a reporter's questions about his father's upcoming trip. Oh my, what a small world this is.

The hams certainly are noting me. I connect with old friend George and AI1W, Kent, in Woods Hole; K1DC, Don, and W1NZD, Bob, near my old Massachusetts plant; WA1SSI, Fred, in Marblehead; W1DEO, Herb, in Cape Elizabeth; W1TJW, Colin, on Cape Cod; W8VJW, Jay, in Ohio; WA9DKL, Dave, in Illinois; W3TIG, Mitch, in Pennsylvania; VP8WTW, Barry, in the Falkland Islands; W4NYN, Jack, in North Carolina; and W2NQ, John, in Salem, Oregon. John shows off his recording gear by playing my own transmission back to me. He demonstrates his speech processors and describes in infinite detail his rig, then he plays me recordings of his chat with the space shuttle and tells great jokes for thirty minutes. John from Salem is quite a show.

DAY 107 ≈
Noon, February 26, 1986, Wednesday, to noon, February 27, 1986, Thursday
55°33.69' south/77°15.17' west

We will arrive for our first landfall in 108 days early the morning after tomorrow. Islas Diego Ramírez. Seven to eight hours later we will arrive at Cape Horn itself. We will have both landfalls in hours of daylight, near perfect timing.

Cape Horn has no nickname such as the Cape of Good Hope's Cape of Storms, because it is its own best metaphor.

The lore surrounding this famed and feared Cape is legion. Rounding it is the sailor's ultimate badge of achievement. Its reputation is founded on foul weather, two of three days a gale, wrecked ships, and lost lives. Legend has it that Cape Horn allows passage only to those who are worthy, and it is true that a sailor does not approach it without having passed through an apprenticeship reaching into one's very soul. There is a hoary fraternity of Cape Horners, the small, gold left earring their odd symbol.

The Horn was first met in 1615 by two Dutch ships looking for a commercial route to the Indies. Captains Shouten and Lemoire named the great, stubborn cliff of rock separating the Atlantic and Pacific oceans after their home port, Hoorn, in Holland. For many years afterward, however, the route around the Horn was seldom used except by the great explorers. It took the lure of California's gold rush to bring sailors back to the challenge and make Cape Horn the "Boulevard to the Pacific."

The Frenchman Alain Colas wrote: "The Horn is not an enemy. It is not even an adversary in the sporting sense of the term. Rather, it is a symbol, a symbol of that which is difficult, of a certain anguish and fear to be overcome, of a great reward to be won, step by step."

For me, Cape Horn is the beginning of the final chapter in my personal odyssey begun as a dream aboard *Coaster* so long ago.

DAY 108 ≈

I am as skitterish as raindrops on a hot skillet, dancing around for a sail trim here, a sail trim there, light the big headsail, drop it again, crank the boards up, then down. There it is, the seven-knot speed around which we plan our Horn arrival. Go, *Promise,* go!

My whole consciousness is captive to thoughts of the Horn. The only digressions are gear failures. I repair a tear in the forestays'l and replace another block, this one blown apart by the MPS sheet. I discover the source of the clunking sounds I have begun to hear: the lower bearing on the main rudderpost has become very sloppy, allowing the post to flop back and forth a full quarter inch when the hydraulic rams pump in and out to turn the rudder. This is not a pretty sight, not easy on rams or bearings or autopilot, but because it doesn't look like immediate danger to us and because I have so many other things to attend to, I satisfy myself with tightening the bearing ring slightly and with wincing when the clanks resound through the hull.

The time comes close. I turn on the depth recorder and recompute, again and again, my arrival times. I wonder what in hell is going on with the weather as we beat on a ten-knot east wind. Will I see the Cape? In gentle conditions or a gale? One might think this is the night before the biggest day of my life. Well, perhaps it is.

The night is one of the most beautiful I have ever witnessed. Not one cloud blemishes the midnight-blue sky. The moon is just two days in wane from full. The Southern Cross is almost overhead. The three navigational planets and major stars are bright beacons. A shooting star crosses the sky every ten minutes. The air is cold and crisp and dry. It seems to me a long time since I have been under such a gorgeous, fathomless universe.

At one-thirty in the morning I see land: lights off to my port and almost abeam. They sparkle from one of the Chilean islands or peninsulas at the tip of South America, forty-five miles to the north of us. The night remains brilliantly clear, the wind light but steady from the south.

At 0415 dawn cracks and I see a whale-shaped land off my starboard bow. This is Islas Diego Ramirez, twenty-five miles away. At 0545 we are on soundings, four-hundred-foot depth. The Horn is just fifty miles away. The bright blue morning is planted high with puffy, white and gray cumulus. Visibility is forever, the wind fifteen knots now out of the west. I see a horizon filled with the mountains of Chile. They are snow-topped, and glaciers ooze down to the sea between the peaks.

It is coming together at Cape Horn: the visibility, the wind, the day. The long, long journey has reached its apex.

Is it possible I can actually see the Cape itself? Several large promontories are on the correct bearing. No, this is Falso Cabo de Horno. The real one lies still farther on.

A line of squalls suddenly appear and pass over us to obscure the shore, unload a downpour, and bluster with thirty
knots of wind. An ominous-looking black cloud boils above.
But I see clearly below it False Cape Horn guarding a phalanx
of black and jagged mountains. I do not feel invited for a visit.

A family of dolphins now escorts me to my reward. The sea
is choppy on long, lazy, ten-foot waves. The wind is west-
southwest at twenty knots, and *Promise* dances along under
her wings.

I am floating on a sea of utter contentment and pride. Every
so often I erupt into a yell of joy and punch the air with my
fist.

DAY 109 ≈
Noon, February 28, 1986, Friday, to noon, March 1, 1986,
    Saturday
56°06.1' south/67°45.67' west

We officially pass Cape Horn at a point one and a half miles
directly south, 67°16' west longitude at 1817 hours Greenwich
Mean Time. I am in the shadow of the great rock. It looks like
the head of a huge cat. The southern face of the Horn is steep
and jagged like lion's teeth, the back sloping and covered with
a manelike growth.

The three of us have a spontaneous celebration as we pass:
me, the will; *American Promise*, the great boat; and Cape
Horn, the legend. I remember three splits of champagne tucked
away in a locker and that my tuxedo is on board.

The impromptu party at Cape Horn plays before an audience
of two cameras, each loaded with three minutes of sound film and
aimed into the cockpit. "We have traveled eighteen and a half
thousand miles for this landfall and it is the sailor's ultimate landfall . . . truly a legendary place . . . and it is time to have a celebration, so that is exactly what we are going to do. Legend has it that
only those sailors who earn it get by this place, and so I guess we've
earned it because we are getting by. We are getting by. This one
(popping the cork from one split), this one's for me. And this one
is for *American Promise,* truly a great boat (the second cork comes
out and I pour champagne over the boat). Now this one (pop) is

for Cape Horn! I'll have your first drink, Cape. The rest is yours (I heave the bottle toward Cape Horn, about a mile away). NOW WE ARE GOING HOME!"

I spot a building and flag on a point just northeast of the Cape, Isla Deceit, and call on VHF channel 16. I get an answer. An Argentine takes our statistics in English and the rounding is officially recorded. Our time from Tasmania to Cape Horn is 31 days, 19 hours, 46 minutes. We are the second-fastest Australia–Cape Horn single-handed sailboat.

≈As *American Promise* stretches her wake away from Cape Horn, I am overcome with a solemn mood of nostalgia. The event is over, a memory never to be matched. This goal has for so long beckoned me that we had become friends. And now suddenly my friend is gone.

Our Cape Horn celebration gives us momentum. We make our turn north into the Atlantic as if propelled by a slingshot, sailing hard on a cold, southeast wind and averaging two hundred miles a day for the first three days, heading for a waypoint east of the Falkland Islands. Even the squalls are distinctively cheerful, repeatedly lighting our eastern sky with overfed rainbows that sit on the horizon like domes.

We intend to cut some corners from the traditional sailing route for this passage to the equator. The usual route spans 4,600 miles across the South Atlantic Ocean and takes about a month of sailing time. I hope to do the passage in twenty-six days, sailing about 4,250 miles. We will have 1,200 more miles of roaring forties kind of weather, then the variable winds of the horse latitudes, then the sailor's heaven of the southern trade winds, then the wall of the doldrums to break through. Once we reach the equator, the distance to our Bermuda finish line is as much as 3,420 miles if the traditional route is followed, as little as 2,700 miles if we cross the equator as far west as possible and drive a clean great circle route to Bermuda.

Right now, however, my attention is commandeered by the Falklands, just to the north of us, and by the isolated and ominous Beauchene Island, some ten miles south of East Falkland. I do not want to be drawn by the strong and unpredictable currents into any chance meeting with these rocky shores — the unfortunate fate of Richard McBride on *City of Dunedin* during the 1982–83 BOC Challenge race. Exhausted from a rough Cape Horn rounding,

McBride felt he was on a course to clear the islands and left the boat to his windvane autosteering for a nap. His nap turned into a deep sleep, and a wind change combined with currents to drive him hard onto East Falkland's Craigylea Point. The steel-hulled *City of Dunedin* miraculously survived the grounding, and the islanders came to McBride's aid, helping him rejoin the race.

I've heard that single-handed sailors die in one of three ways: falling over the side while taking a leak, running into the rocks while sleeping, and old age. It is my firm intention to employ the third method. I will, therefore, give the Falkland Islands a wide berth.

Following our first four Atlantic Ocean days of rough, close reaching and great progress on twenty-to-thirty-knot southeasterly winds, we run headlong into a wall of quick, alternating calms and northerly squalls that last for two solid weeks — two weeks of winds that either ignore us or belt us right on the nose and drive us up under the shelf of South America that hangs out to the east below Rio de Janeiro. I do not want to sail underneath this shelf, where a persistent lack of wind and the foul, southbound Brazilian current reign. But I stubbornly remain on the starboard tack because I know the wind should be blowing from an easterly direction, not the north, and I keep anticipating that it will do what it's supposed to do. This is one of my most stupid strategic errors of the voyage — doubly so, since by this time I really should know better. My noon-to-noon distances are disappointing enough, but my progress toward the waypoint on the equator is far worse. Day after day I put off the decision to come about and sail east, and day after day the wind disobeys orders and pushes me farther under the South American coast. In eight days, we sail more than 1,500 miles over the bottom and 1,234 miles noon fix to noon fix, but we cover only 900 miles on our great circle route. And we absorb punishment while doing it. My only consolations during these two lousy weeks are that both the climate and my ham radio schedule warm up.

DAY 114 ≈

We are sure as hell making payments on our good weather rounding Cape Horn and for the few days afterward. Our wind has been strong on the nose or not at all. Between the squall lines passing over us, we are left to toss helplessly, windless on a twelve-foot slop of sea. Very damaging to the gear and to my spirits and to our progress.

On the good side, the air has warmed considerably over the past several days, even though we are just passing into the latitude of the forties. I don't have an air-sensing thermometer now, and so I use the tip of my nose. Some time ago my little portable thermometer lost a battle with a flying winch handle, and recently I hurled the fancy, brass-encased, bulkhead-mounted instrument over the side when I scraped a skim of frost from its faceplate to see that it registered sixty-one degrees. I figure that now we have daylight air in the high forties and nighttime air in the high thirties. We are at 46.5° south latitude.

I am thrilled by the visit of several hundred terns today, darting about us in a magnificent array of organized confusion — more life than I've seen at one time for months. And I wonder that I have seen so few living things on this voyage, even birds. My one constant companion has been the albatross. Perhaps man has not yet found a profitmaking or sporting role for the albatross. He doesn't render to commercially valuable ingredients, doesn't make the grade as a delicacy, and flies too far from civilization to be good shooting sport. And so he is still around in numbers. Actually, I think it would be poetically just if the albatross became the very last appropriate game bird on earth and hunters were forced to sail alone into the Southern Oceans to shoot him. By the time they arrived on the hunting grounds, they would be well converted to naturalists and conservationists.

I am now very anxious to bid the albatross farewell and renew my friendship with the other of my wildlife buddies on this voyage, the flying fish — because he is an avowed resident of the warmest waters.

DAY 115 ≈

My ham radio is hot from use. I am in contact with several boats in the Whitbread fleet: *Drum,* the British contender, *Lion*

New Zealand, and *UBS Switzerland.* These guys are really screaming around the world, now heading for stopover number three at Montevideo, Uruguay, some six hundred miles east of us. The fleet leaders have essentially passed us and are estimating circumnavigation times of less than 120 days. It doesn't feel nice to be passed, but I would much rather go not so fast alone than go fast while being crammed into eighty feet of space with two dozen other guys. Poor *Dream Merchant* is the other case. She is still struggling to reach the Horn. When I think of her I feel better about our speed.

AI1W, Kent, patches me into home, and Manny reads me a sweet message from Hoyt, and I watch the sun drop into the sea with tears streaming over my cheeks.

DAY 116 ≈
Noon, March 7, 1986, Friday, to noon, March 8, 1986, Saturday 41°45.34' south/45°18.77' west

Just as the noon position fix and noon sextant sight are due, some dumb bastard's full cup of hot, steaming coffee jumps from the windward side of the chart table and bombs a blitz of brown running devastation across the log, chart, notebooks, computer, barograph, and other targets at random on the port side of the pilothouse. I actually catch the cup, one of those wide-bottomed untippables that truck drivers use, in midair as it speeds under my nose. I recover it empty and with no effect on the havoc, but the catch definitely makes me feel clever for a second.

The seas are as nasty as one will find anywhere, twenty feet high, close together, and steep as ravines. Below, *Promise* is her normal shambles of gear that has flown its appointed locations for the freedom of the air and captivity in crannies of the leeward side. The lashings of any gear or equipment of size or bulk need constant checking. From the cockpit, I feel a new, rhythmic thumping beneath me. I check compartment four and find that a spare hydraulic pump, weighing more than thirty pounds, has broken from its moorings and caromed into a five-gallon can of hydraulic oil and the already malfunctioning watermaker. The oil coats the compartment, making every object and surface at least twice as slippery as wet ice. I am a gross hazard to myself trying to lash the pump back in place, trying, even, to hold my own body down in this totally frictionless world. The greased pole is turned inside out and all around me; I am a ball bearing zipping around a well-lubricated race. Damn quick, I do my job and leave with my body bleeding in only three places. I throw some disposable diapers into the compartment after me; they are civilization's most effective absorbers of slippery stuff.

We take a seventy-degree knockdown every few minutes, and *Promise* ramrods her hull onto peaks of seas as solid as rock, frightening the mast and rigging into a frenzy of motion and vibrating my back teeth. It is a paroxysm of movement that, forced repeatedly on the human senses as it is, qualifies for the highest order of Chinese torture. I know that any person choosing to live this way is certifiably crazy.

I realize I can quiet the girl down some by reefing sail and reducing speed. But I am getting worse, if anything, in my singular drive to do anything that takes away a mile from the distance between *Promise* and home. I figure I am simply being given a farewell party by the roaring forties in the only way these inhuman latitudes know how.

We get some miles. But we have the equivalent of two east-west Atlantic crossings remaining.

I try to soothe my spirits in a hot shower. It helps but in a comedic way. As my soapy, naked body bounces off the bulkheads of the little shower room, I see myself as a lathered-up drunk in a phone booth.

This wind prevails till dawn, when it blows itself inside out and becomes light and variable, a breeze from the east, the south, indecisive in attack over a hundred-degree angle, making sail trim a boringly repetitive comedy of errors. We devise a solution and call it hanging laundry, all sails out every which way. Our speed ranges from three to five knots, and I am pleased it is not a wallowing zero. We sail out of the roaring forties now and for good; our slow and clumsy progress contrasts with the wild ride of ten hours ago like the rattle of waves on a beach after the passing of summer thunder.

DAY 117 ≈

We have the horse latitudes' light winds earlier than expected. The big, light, MPS headsail is up but unable to find
enough air to fill. We could have a full fifteen degrees, nine
hundred miles, fighting these light conditions, and that is bad
luck for us — a wider horse latitude zone and me with no
horses to throw overboard to lighten our load. I struggle to put
my brain in limbo to numb the rage of frustration boiling under the surface of my consciousness. I think the great grief I
feel is because I really can't see the end to the calms, and I
know we could, in fact, sit out here in one place until the end
of time, slowly eroding, coming apart, growing old. It is not a
dumb dream. It has happened before to sailors.

DAY 118 ≈

Deserted by the wind god, I sublimate my feelings of violence
by hard work. I take off the smaller, 90 percent jib and bend
on the big, 150 percent jib. This is a couple of hours of hard
physical labor, done in sunshine and enough heat to peel me
down to my shorts and make me feel as though spring has arrived. There continues to be good news on the troublesome jib
halyard and upper furling swivel: both are responding well to
my babying and look now as if they have every intention to finish the voyage with me. This news and the sun compensate me
for a day of wallowing, slatting, at one to four knots.

Just before sunset, after the sail-changing and another failed
effort to repair the alternators, the calm embraces us like death.
Nothing interrupts the cracking, crashing, clanging, unimpeded
roll from side to side. The sea is an oily, endless, undulating
desert. No birds fly. The clouds are stationary. The space is
lifeless. The senses are numbed blunt. My nerves tangle and
fray badly.

During the night, someone throws the horses overboard and
we sail again. A wind of ten knots from the northeast is plenty
of fuel for the big jib, and *Promise* leans into a seven-to-eight-
knot pace. As usual, the easier progress moves my world instantly from the lip of despair to the lap of comfort. We are
sailing well west of rhumbline, but sailing we are. I can feel the

pressure of the wind and *Promise*'s eager resistance to it, and
the energy the two produce together is as if it were being ex-
erted directly on my own nerve center. This is unadorned pleasure.

One time in the night I proceed through a sailing version of
the comical effects of vertigo. It happens because I am sailing
the boat a bit too high on the wind for Murphy's sake, and on
one slight change in wind direction, the jib backwinds and we
come about. This totally confounds the autopilot, which brings
Promise to a standstill, her mainsail and helm trying to bring
her up and her backed jib trying to drive her off. It takes me
two coming abouts and two jibes to figure out whence the
wind comes and to get her back on the rails.

At dawn, *Promise* still churns out the miles. I see myself grin
into the mirror over my bunk. What a sight! I look like a co-
median gone to seed, transformed into a desert island hermit.
My chipped front tooth (a couple of tooth caps were broken by
a flying line during my recent sail-changing rigors, and I replaced what I could with superglue) gives me a slap-happy
look. I remind myself of Alfred E. Neuman — "What, me
worry?" My hair is three inches long over my whole head, the
result of the growing out of the GI haircut I got just before departure, and this adds to the tone of happy neglect. The sight
has me laughing out loud until the laughter draws tears and
makes me laugh even louder and harder. I embellish this ridiculous image with a wildly bellowed monologue: "All hands on
deck — every manjack now — heave over more horses, sacri-
fice them all to the gods of the horse latitudes, keep the good
ship under way. No real horses, you say? Nonsense! Nonsense!
Then heave over the imaginary ones. We never run out of
imaginary horses, and they are so much more real anyway." I
run like hell up to the pilothouse to frenzy out our position and
to greet the new day with a boisterous cheeriness that is truly
an embarrassing contrast to the dark gloom of just yesterday.

DAY 119 ≈

The wind builds strength until by morning it blows forty
knots and better. We still sail hard on a northeast wind and

head for the Brazilian coast west of Rio, well west of our course rhumbline. The big jib becomes too much sail and does not set well when reefed down to a small area. The forestays'l does not carry at all on the wind. I put the storm stays'l on, hanking it on the inner forestay and sheeting it well inside the shrouds. *Promise* likes it better, but we average not much more than five knots. The seas are ten feet and sharp, the motion is ugly, and the hull slams with loud percussion and trembling aftershock. Not a gentleman's way to sail; you wouldn't find Bill Buckley sailing this way!

Bilges fill to cabin sole again. Pumps out okay. Still no sure sign of how water gets in. Must siphon through bilge pump or come in around prop shaft in heavy going.

DAY 120 ≈

Still forty-five knots north-northeast wind and seas like small cliffs. Painful ride. Boat pounds mercilessly. Still we average five knots. We sail hard on this wind. Storm forestays'l and reefed main. Forecast is two more days of this before wind veers east and southeast. We are too far west. Still aiming into that tuck of Brazil's coast where foul current runs and calms prevail. What's a calm? This shoots our Bermuda timetable to hell. Another lifeline stanchion breaks when the sea rolls over us. Mainsail repair tears out. Fire the seamstress. The port running backstay hauldown chafes through. The line flies leeward side like a crazed bird on a string. Hard to catch. Get thorough head-to-toe dousing but the sea is nice and warm now. I check — water temp. is seventy. Cannot run generator to charge batteries because too much heel, thirty-five degrees.

Amazing. In spite of this crap, day dawns pink and soft as nursery, settles into thin, high, gray overcast.

For first time in voyage, people ashore don't know where I am. ARGOS transmitter not operating for several days now. I open its box on tower aft to check the lithium batteries. This chore is like an aerial circus act gone awry; all the rigging swings while I try to stay still. My firm instructions from shore are to not breathe while close to lithium cells. Fumes are like knockout drops. Bad place and time to take inadvertent nap. Heave lithiums in sea and replace with twelve-volt lantern batteries. Kent and George will let me know whether this fix works if ham circuits allow them to tonight.

Come about and head east. Get away from Brazil.

DAY 121 ≈

Wind abates to twenty knots. I sneak out a few hundred feet of jib to keep storm stays'l company and *Promise* lifts herself up to eight knots. Still an unholy ride, though. ARGOS fix not a success. They still don't know where I am without my telling them.

Loud thumping from loose rudderpost really unnerves me. I spend much of day on this problem. Replace worn and leaking end seals on hydraulic rams. Tighten lower stuffing box seal around shaft. Tighten all screws and bolts in whole assembly and also those just nearby. Many are loose. Watching the post slap and jerk around is depressing. Why, then, do I sit in the hole of this compartment for minutes on end just watching this depressing sight?

Rain pounds down. Wind veers. Come about to head north, can make ten degrees. Should head thirty degrees to make waypoint a hundred and twenty miles east of Trindade Island, a lonely lump six hundred miles east of Brazil.

Never-ending beat puts me in permanent nasty mood. I notice wear all over *Promise*. The new jib just bent on is torn at the foot. Mainsail torn again too. Literally half of the running rigging cries to be replaced again. Have changed all of it at least once so far, much of it in the past several weeks. Chafing damage shows everywhere. Shows quickly. Even my set of foul weather gear is chafed through with holes from swinging around in the locker. The heads of screws holding the boom together keep breaking out, littering the deck. Rudder assembly still slops around, thumping, thumping. A hydraulic leak is still substantial. Bilges still regularly fill with a mixture of seawater and diesel oil. I pump every four hours. The pilothouse is working at the corners where bolted to the deck. Alternators still down. My bread doesn't rise. Wind instruments dead.

ARGOS still doesn't transmit to let those ashore know where we are.

DAY 123 ≈

My resolve and energy bounce back a bit with a new moon night so brilliant with stars I can read in the cockpit, yet light that camouflages the wear and tear. The wind rears back a bit but canters still from the wrong direction. It is hot now, and we are still thirty degrees south. The frigid days of the Southern Oceans are strangely distant. I take the caps off the dorade vents to get some air moving below. The wool blankets are folded away, and my long underwear fattens the dirty laundry bag instead of me. Dawn is bright and sunny, and I am suddenly up to doing some chores.

Chafed lines are either moved or turned end for end or replaced. Sails are patched and sewn. The sail and line stowage area in the forward compartment, turned into a tangle of random ends by the rough going, is ordered and lashed back down. The red binnacle light on the cockpit compass is repaired. Four cabin lights are repaired, two successfully. I fit a couple more small blocks to my Rube Goldberg rig of shock cord to retract the boom preventers automatically when not in use. I attack the ARGOS again and this time find the problem to be simple and obvious. Two in-line fuseholders have corroded contacts, dropping the battery voltage to half.

I project Bermuda now for April 16. Bob Rice, via ham radio patch, forecasts a storm for me, and as he does I see it clearly lingering over the horizon to our north and east. The wind is there, and we will get some of it.

DAY 125 ≈

I continue acting like a pregnant housewife in spring. The galley becomes showcase clean and organized. The tools are oiled and tidied and the workbench polished. Lines, many lines, get new whippings. Broken running lights are patched together again on the prospect that I may sometime soon want to light them. I finally free myself from the broken ARGOS by performing last rites on it. The generators are oiled and cleaned, the fuel line fittings are tightened, the hydraulic line fittings wiped and checked, the spare parts lockers are reorganized, and every surface of my little dry cabin is scrubbed so clean it smells like the inside of a lemon.

Promise loafs along at three to seven knots, rarely more. I finish reading *Anna Karenina*, the final book from my Bragdon library, and, as Peter Bragdon wrote inside the front cover, it is the "best ever book on love." It is a good time in the voyage for a book about love. I have thought about love often during the past 125 days alone. Soon, in just one more month, I will be back with my loved ones.

I have never been good at direct expressions of love in any of its forms. Don't have the skill. I think I can express love indirectly as in the show of respect, an action for the welfare of another, time given, bragging about one to others, but these are not often recognized as expressions of love. Maybe the problem is that I really don't need expressions of love for myself, even as I do need respect and the bragging of others for me. I have, in fact, felt much alone for most of my life — not unloved, simply alone. And so I have felt that I must and will cope with life without any help from others, and this has brought me to the state where love is a condition to be shared from a position of strength, in happy and positive circumstances. I feel that where I am threatened or in pain, it is best that I meet the threat and conquer the pain alone. For some strange reason, I do not expect others to feel that way and am pleased to comfort and help those I love in their time of pain or threat. If they want me to. And if they don't, do I love them deeper?

For me, expressing love for a man is easier than expressing love for a woman. Expressing love for a child is the easiest of all. I show my love for my brother by working hard beside him and grinning with him when things go well and by belting him on the arm when I feel affection for him and by poking fun at his little, unimportant weaknesses and eccentricities. We let each other know directly by faint praise and dense understatement, and these are well-understood ways. We let each other know indirectly by open and honest praise for one another to others. We never, never tell the other of this love, never, never talk of it at all. On the other hand, women are very difficult because they seem to want to talk about love. They are not content with just acting it out, but somehow think that giving it words, very specific words, has more impact, that actions, even the most intimate actions, must be proven with words. Expressions of love, then, are more intellectual for women than for me, and so I have troubles with them. But in spite of these troubles, if I had to choose just one, single person to be physically in my life, there is no question at all that that person would be a woman. Now the children! They are best of all because they don't intellectualize anything, and they think direct expressions of love such as playing ball and making faces and blowing bubbles are beautiful and meaningful.

I won't change much at this stage of my life, I know, but I do understand these feelings about love, and recognize them better after this time alone. I do know that love is more important than anything, when once I did not. I do know I am capable of love, when once I thought I was not. I do know I yearn to return to those I love, when once I left them for myself.

DAY 126 ≈

We sail into a hole of calm at nightfall. I watch the sun set on a placid world. The moon has waxed to half and is well up so that one skylight is replaced by the other. A breeze stirs from east-northeast and *Promise* takes it on the starboard tack, our course 359 degrees to the Trindade waypoint.

The night is breathtaking, and I am overflowing with joy at being a witness. An awareness that this is one of those lifetime moments that will always be remembered, never repeated, falls upon me. This moon paves a silver highway of light onto *Promise* and she is center stage. Billows of clouds, isolated and intense like smoke from cannon shots, shadow across the stage. The Southern Cross lies on its side, rising, and shooters spin their sparks, east to west. I wonder why? The boat leans softly on her bilge and pulses out six knots, and it is the easiest six knots ever felt.

It isn't easy to break the spell for my evening ham radio

schedule. Would George and Colin and Dick understand if I described my world to them now? No need to worry. The sky that gives me so much wonder now will not allow our radio waves to pass. I spend this night looking up out of the cockpit from a thin mattress, seeing, dozing, dreaming. Awake and asleep, my dreams are of love.

Promise and I straighten our track toward the equator as we cross north of the 30th parallel into the easterly trades. The wind blows just north of east, as if it were part of a fixed law. We aim along a series of great circle waypoints and sail exactly where we aim. Now our daily progress is real progress toward Bermuda. And the idea of Bermuda begins to exert subtle pressures on me. I begin an exercise campaign against a small tire around my middle, made obvious as I shed my clothes in the welcome heat. I note that my body tone is excellent between my neck and my lower rib cage, but quite sloppy at both ends. There is not much opportunity for leg exercise on the boat, so my midsection is soft. And my brain seems to have gone lazy as well. I have trouble recalling some very common facts from my life — names of people, descriptive terms, significant dates, even words to common campfire songs I used to sing. One night, singing loudly to the sky, I found I couldn't remember enough words to any song to make my way through it. Songs like "Moonlight Bay," for chrissake!

My compulsive reading continues to fill all the spare moments, but I run out of original material, except for drudgery like *Bowditch's Navigation*. By day 130 I have consumed the forty-five or so books on board, a rate of about one book every three days. Some I have read twice. Several are from the ten favorite books selected for my voyage by Peter and Dotty Bragdon, headmaster and mistress of Governor Dummer Academy, where I attended school thirty-six years ago. The books they chose are *The Adventures of Huckleberry Finn, Growing Up, Anna Karenina, John Brown's Body, Thursday's Child, American Caesar, The Rise of Theodore Roosevelt, The Killer Angels, Goodbye Darkness,* and *The Matarese Circle.*

The book that may have the most lasting impact on my day-to-day existence after I complete this voyage is Farley Mowat's *Sea of Slaughter.* I began the book early but could not stomach it at first. Too depressing. Too academic. It gripped me hard later, when I was more comfortable with my solitude and did not need a book so much for solace. In the context of the ocean wilderness that is my home, I am convinced that the human obliteration of the living natural realm — which Mowat describes in such painful detail — is a terrifying prologue to what the planet will become if we do not wise up. Human civilization, I can see, has never and probably will never improve on nature. Science may make bigger, juicier tomatoes and chickens that fatten for market in a few weeks, and technology may produce more powerful earth movers and cleaner smokestacks, but the net result is negative for nature. The benefits of such marvels are short term and for humans only, and we do not own this earth but share it with every creature, each plant, even each rock and every wave. We tinker in colossal ignorance. The earth is dying at the hands of our science and technology. It has been so since we learned how to multiply our efforts by too many of us crammed together and then by the machines we use and now by both our immense overpopulation and machines. I know these things are true and that they are frightening. I wonder how long it will be before we murder this ocean wilderness I now sail. I wonder how much damage is being done by my passing on *American Promise*. I take comfort in the thought of how small and insignificant is one solo sailor on such a wide ocean. I do destroy, but my destruction is small when compared to that of a fleet of warships or a forest of oil platforms. I am as one Indian with an ax in the woods compared to a team of lumberjacks driving D10 Cats and wielding chain saws.

DAY 135 ≈
Noon, March 26, 1986, Wednesday, to noon, March 27, 1986, Thursday
1°25.06′ south/29°38′ west
Still in the doldrums, but certainly back in the civilized ocean. Sight two ships today, a freighter heading east and a tanker floating high in ballast, bound west. Sight two small birds, one Portuguese man-o'-war, and a dozen or so flying fish. Paltry nature sightings at best. It still strikes me as strange how little bird and sea life I see. I pray it is because of the lim-

its of my vision and that the undersea is teeming with life. But the high seas wilderness is awesomely and surprisingly barren on its surface.

The heat now is oppressive, weighing the air down with haze and transforming *Promise* into an oven. Everything not in the shade is too hot to touch, and I am a fountain of perspiration. We are just about on the equator, bringing the sun directly overhead and about as close as one can come to it at sea level.

The breeze, light as it is, has the audacity to arrive from a most awkward direction and wag back and forth some fifteen degrees, slowly, like an old dog's tail. We do not point well. Whichever tack I choose is the wrong one. I fiddle too much with tacks and headings and trim and spend the night again in the cockpit, alternately snoozing and fighting to keep our way on. We are at the shear of the ITCZ, though, and I sense the wind on the other side almost within reach.

Several hours before dawn, I become serious about sighting Halley's Comet. I locate Sagittarius in the eastern sky as a celestial waypoint and prop my eyes open with a combination of determined anticipation and strong black coffee. The sky is mostly clear, and the lopsided silver egg of a moon has long set. Smudge pots of squall clouds blur the horizon, but the view overhead is sharp. Then I realize I don't know what a comet looks like. I am looking for a sight I think I won't recognize. Maybe just something different in the sky will do. I am still straining my eyeballs when the sky becomes washed dull by predawn light. I decide the hell with Halley. I'll view the sunrise instead.

But a large, leaden cloud formation moves mockingly to obscure the eastern horizon from me. No bright light of dawn gets through. The color is all on the clouds in the west, as if the earth has decided to spin the wrong way. Just as I am about to give my weary eyeballs their rest, the golden ball itself rolls into the open and ignites the whole rim of the world for me. There we go! I can decide later if I've seen Halley's Comet or not. Who the hell is going to argue with me?

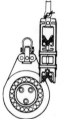 ~~ *12* ~~

I am reassuring myself that this final passage from the equator to Bermuda should be like the last, long, level straightaway to the tape for the leader of a marathon. *American Promise* and I have paced ourselves well, so we are not yet struggling and shouldn't have to struggle to make the finish line. The finish line. It is finally becoming our immediate goal. And we are beginning to smell it, to anticipate it just twenty-seven hundred miles away — about a tenth of the total distance.

Promise is bruised and sore but not slowed. Her one remaining jib halyard is holding out. Her sloppy rudderpost bearing is not getting worse. Nearly half her sails remain new in their bags. She has ample battery charging capacity left, two thirds of the diesel fuel and propane she began with, and food enough to start all over again. None of her problems is now critical. And I am stronger now, physically and emotionally, than when I began this voyage.

Twenty-seven hundred miles is not far when we have come twenty-three thousand. Fifteen days to go, and that is not long when we have been at sea now for 136 days. Not far and not long if we make it! I keep reminding myself that any one of those twenty-seven hundred miles or one minute of any one of those fifteen days could end it all for us. I keep reminding myself of the axiom that the more time one accumulates in a small boat at sea, the more likely one is to be beaten by it. It becomes simply a matter of the odds.

During this passage, I am clearly to be dominated by thoughts of finishing. I am also to be confused by mixed feelings about finishing. In fact, I realize I don't know what finishing will mean, other than the mechanical crossing of the Bermuda finish line itself. There is no question, however, that I am pulling for this finish line with everything I have, mystery and all. And the passage does begin well. We pull out of the doldrums and into the steady air of the northern trades the same day we cross the equator.

DAY 135 ≈

I fight another night at the helm for every meager mile. Sometimes we move at a tenth, a fifth of a knot pace. Murphy is helpless. I tend the helm. It is imperative that I keep *Promise* at the right attitude on the prevailing direction of those small puffs of breeze and keep her with some way on. When one of those sporadic puffs passes over us, we are lifted.

This night we are rewarded for my vigil. A steady, light breeze moves out of the northeast by early morning and gives us fuel for one to two knots, enough for Murphy to steer on and give me some needed sack time. I sleep in the pilothouse bunk, cheered by the sounds of water gurgling along the hull. By sunrise, we are sailing at six and a half knots. I know now we are through the doldrums, and I have myself a quiet, sleepy celebration.

We cross the equator at 0642 local time, 0942 Greenwich, and are now back in our home hemisphere.

DAY 136 ≈
Noon, March 27, 1986, Thursday, to noon, March 28, 1986,
       Friday
0°32.78′ north/30°47.83′ west

By nightfall the wind is solid at fifteen knots, and *Promise* is shaking out her doldrum wrinkles and kinks with eight to nine knots of speed, leaving no doubt at all about our having broken loose from the grip of the calms that are the signature of the ITCZ. This matriculation into wind is most welcome, of course, but it turns out not to be quiet and polite. The wind seems determined to prove something by continuing to increase to thirty knots, stirring up a washboard of six-foot waves with it. I feel that this is overdoing it; it is not at all necessary for the wind to blow thirty when fifteen is quite enough. In spite of the oppressive heat, I must close all the hatches because we are continually raked with heavy spray and often with solid water. The water temperature is 85° F. The ride below is turbulent, causing all matter not resolutely screwed down to spring up and slam down in a mocking demonstration of gravitational force. I don't know what the air temperature is, but I figure a thermometer taken into it from under my tongue would definitely rise. The flying fish are plentiful, and we have a surprise visit by a half-dozen petrels.

This day we come very close to completing our circumnavigation officially by crossing our outbound track in the Northern Hemisphere. The act of crossing the outbound track on return is called "tying the knot." We come within twelve miles of tying the knot when we are just north of the equator. For a while I think of altering our heading simply to post what could well be a solo, knot-tying circumnavigation record of 136 days. But my destination is not that point on the ocean. The dictatorship of our ultimate destination prevails, and we keep sailing as straight and as fast as we can for Bermuda.

After picking up the Northern Hemisphere trade winds, we have seven days of better than two hundred miles per day for a total of 1,491 miles in the week. That's averaging nearly nine knots in speed. We sail a close reach and cover more than half the 2,700 miles from the equator to Bermuda in that time. I am navigating to waypoints that arch along a great circle, the shortest possible route, and am splitting each of these waypoints with precision. I know our progress amounts to an extraordinary performance but prefer not to celebrate the good news aloud and frighten away the goddess of good fortune.

In these sailing conditions, my days are crowded with work and each chore takes longer to accomplish. The frustrations decrease in this rough going, but the workload increases. At least once a day for two hours I have to reef and slow the boat down in order to reduce our angle of heel from thirty to twenty degrees or less, so that the charging generators can operate safely. My sextant sights are so difficult to take in this constant, clumsy motion that I tend to neglect them and instead depend totally on the satellite navigator. The seas are only twelve feet high but just fifty feet apart, shorter than *Promise*'s waterline, and the result is like riding on a jackhammer.

DAY 138 ≈

All my careful maintenance programs and schedules, my personal hygiene, food preparation and consumption, exercise routines, creative thinking, and appreciation of nature are virtually cast aside for this miserable existence. It is simply hang-on-and-get-through-it time right now. The seas are not large. They are just very, very steep. The top of nearly every one of them sweep the deck with solid water. *Promise*'s motion is uncharacteristically quick, a motion that will jerk the jam off a cracker, so I eat my crackers dry. My one and mighty consolation, though, is a constant eight knots plus of boat speed.

It is Easter Sunday. The Christian world smells like spring and starch and soap. But I have decided against dressing myself up or organizing an egg hunt or even conjuring up a parade to watch.

This is a bad night. I get up for one of my rounds and find myself with a new problem that shakes my confidence. I am suddenly crippled by a pulled back muscle. When and how this happened I don't know. I do manage to carry out my normal waking routine of checking the sail trim and navigational position and general boat condition, but I do so hobbling very slowly, like an old man. *Promise*'s wild motion doubles my difficulties. My back knots up just with my hanging on. I am amazed at how totally intrusive a back pull can be. Even the most simple chore becomes painful and takes much too much time. If something goes wrong that requires a peak physical performance from me, we are in real trouble. Say, if I have to make another trip up the mast. Or change another sail. Or again renew a blown-out piece of running rigging or a broken fitting. It is times like this that remind me how fragile my position is, how close I am to the edge. It is times like this that remind me how this voyage hangs on a long chain of which I am the weakest link.

.   .   .

All the redundancy in equipment, systems, and supplies is absurd in the light of the basic fact: there is only one sailor. Just a single, frail human being. No backup. There is but one me and, unlike *American Promise* and her gear, I am not "high tech" anything or "leading edge" anywhere. What I am is supremely vulnerable, a maze of parts of questionable quality and condition, at risk to a big germ in the wrong place or a small break or sprain at the wrong time. I am aware that I am the Achilles heel of this operation, but, then, that is one of the big reasons I sail alone in the first place. Sailing alone is a kind of absolute, operational test of self. It is a no-recourse way to find out where one's weak parts are. The very worst discovery, of course, would be a failure that allows me to remain alive but renders me useless, a helpless witness to a slow defeat. A heart attack or a stroke could do this. But a bad back? Come on! Bad backs don't debilitate. Bad backs aren't terminal.

But there is not much one can do about a bad back except wait. None of the medical marvels aboard *American Promise* work on a bad back. Narcotics or painkillers might do something, but a solo sailor is one helluva lot better off with pain than with a drugged body.

My medical supplies reflect Manny's skill as an emergency medical technician. The boat is stocked about as well as an ambulance, with two trauma kits, a ten-pound case of prescription drugs (enough to be a floating felony in many countries), a substantial inventory of off-the-shelf drugs and supplies, and detailed instructions on diagnosing and treating most of man's ills and diseases. In fact, I have instructions and tools to remove a selection of my own organs, complete with staple guns to suture myself up after the surgery.

So far, though, I have used none of these supplies, outside of multitudes of bandages and miles of adhesive tape. Not even an aspirin. There are, it seems, no germs at sea. The only ones on board are the ones that came with me, and I get along just fine with them. A solo sailor's life is at least cough free. But I sense I am to pay a price for this radiant good health when I return to civilization, because no contact with people means no affairs with germs, which means I have the resistance of an innocent.

I am thinking more frequently about my return to civilization, but my thoughts are colored with uncertainty. I regularly project our Bermuda arrival date and time for the total voyage. They are

Ted Hood (foreground) and I.

Above: Ted Hood (left) and Per Hoel.
Below: The launching of *American Promise*.

Above: Thumbs up — but a few
days later a broken *Promise*
limped into Bermuda.
Right: Manny, Kim, and Hoyt
watch me sail out of Portland.

Above: A slow departure from windless Portland Harbor.
Below: I raise my fist in triumph as I complete the world's fastest nonstop circumnavigation.

Above: I am handed a bouquet as I sail into Bermuda after 150 days alone at sea.
Below: The Morgan family together again.

Hoyt and I sail *Promise* back to Portland.

happy projections now, but they are still always followed by the major qualification "if ever."

DAY 139 ≈

We are within thirty miles of our outbound track of last fall, and applying the averages of our progress reveals an arrival in Bermuda on April 13 for a 153-day circumnavigation. Hoo boy! The time and distances now really begin to shrink. Each day, each daily run, is beginning to make up a significant percentage of what remains to be sailed and triggers images of those two little guys nestled in my arms, the feel and the sight and the smell of them my world again. And dear Manny. And I think I will hug everyone I meet, the pretty and the hairy alike, and I will listen to the strange rumble of human sounds, joyously immersed in a rebaptism in the living world. In truth, I don't even know what it will be like or what I will be like. I do know it is much too early to taste the end, for it may not even be on this side of never.

I am naked much of the time now and can clearly see, no matter where I look, that small but resolute band of blubber protruding from my waist. To the honest exercise I normally get with the sailing of the boat, I have added a clerk's routine of pushups and situps and running in place to attack this rubbery growth. The exercising is clumsy and the results unclear. And I have to be sure that the damned movie cameras don't trigger and film my nudity because I don't like the thought of my private parts projected on the wall of Chris Knight's film studio. Of course, the film he makes could very well end up a desperate enough project to force him to resort to anything, even low-class, solo sex. But, no, Chris just doesn't have the proper mindset for X-rated work.

We pass over the 7th parallel with the trade winds keeping us on a close reach and continuing our extraordinary boat speed hour after hour. The air temperature drops to the sixties at night and the seawater has cooled to seventy-seven degrees.

Last night's ham radio klatch revealed some interesting and somewhat puzzling activity ashore. *Promise* and I must be watering a dry period for news, because interest in our voyage has reached the point where Manny is being invited to appear on the radio and on television to say God-knows-what. Actually, I am told some of her on-the-air remarks by my ham radio friends. Kent, AI1W, said she told a TV interviewer that she is going to give me a bath, a vodka-and-tonic, and a cheeseburger upon my return. She doesn't know I really won't need a bath. The truth of the matter is that it's up for grabs on how I will handle myself when I step ashore. For certain, I'm not at all prepared to appear on a stage of any kind; five months by myself in a confined space that constantly jumps around is no training for public appearances. I'm sure I don't even comprehend how many ways I have changed or what I have become over these months.

DAY 140 ≈

About 1,860 miles remain, eleven to thirteen days. My back is tolerable and getting better. Life aboard has strangely fallen into a kind of holding pattern. Time drags, and the days are long and uneventful. I am showing a short-timer's attitude toward the voyage now, simply watching the clock until it ends. What a shame. Like a prisoner and his calendar days before the end of his sentence. There are ten to twelve sailing days left to Bermuda. That I will be the first American to circumnavigate alone, nonstop, is almost certain now, which means the solo, nonstop record in elapsed time and boat speed will belong to *American Promise* and me. Even the record time for all solo circumnavigations seems probable. My only challenge now is to live through the next week and a half. That amount of time should seem very short after these hundred and forty days at sea, but it seems for some reason to be interminable.

My thoughts are of home and the worlds that await me there. I wonder how I will react immediately upon stepping from *American Promise* onto land. Will they expect me to say something? Should I say something? Is it possible for me to sneak into St. George's Harbour undetected, perhaps under the cover of night, and secretly get used to the presence of others before any official event is scheduled? Maybe if the welcoming group is large enough or casual enough, I could worm my way into it and just stand innocently gazing out to sea in search of myself.

Actually, this arrival is a once-in-a-lifetime opportunity, my one great chance to introduce bizarre, interesting eccentricities and to reemphasize those I have always wanted but lacked the courage to practice with real purpose. All the way to being a certified, happy screwball. Who the hell is going to say what? How can anybody complain? People may even demand it of me. After all, someone who spends five months at sea by himself is bound to lose his marbles to some degree, so it's not a question of *if* I return quirky, only a question of *how* quirky.

Let's see, what can I get away with? I think I would like to blame the voyage for my terrible memory for names. I would like my months of solitude to cause people to give wisdom and gravity to the stupid and obvious statements I make. I would like to fart in public and see people smile rather than frown. I would love to be given the license of a child to say exactly what I think when I think it. I would like to stare at, say, a woman's legs and get a patient, forgiving smile in return. I would like people to assume it quite all right for me to order a cheeseburger for dinner at a fancy restaurant. Wow! If I play this right, I'll be able to get away with almost anything short of bank robbery, and maybe even that, the way the legal system works.

I imagine a scene in St. George's. I step carefully off *Promise* onto the dock and bow deeply like an orchestra conductor and, with a condescending smile, slowly wave my arms for silence, then pull in a deep breath and commence to bellow my fal-setto-sounds-and-noises-but-no-real-words version of "John Jacob Jingleheimer Schmidt." Next, I jab the air violently and triumphantly with finger V's and, grinning hideously, leap back on *Promise,* piss noisily over the side toward the audience, slash the docklines with my rigging knife, and depart under full sail, all the while screaming abusive language at myself and tossing obscene gestures to the wind. That should do it.

DAY 141 ≈

I bake cornbread for my breakfast; it is quite good even if surprising in texture. Carved into the shape of a ball, it could be dribbled. I don't believe cornbread is supposed to be this way, but nevertheless it slides down nicely with gooseberry jam and coffee.

About 1,650 miles, ten to eleven days, to go. Today will be a full day of radio work if we can get the circuits. Manny wants a patch from me while some TV crews are filming at the house, and my ham happiness hour is expanding with a group from Bermuda led by Tony, VP9HK. I am becoming as much a radio talk show host as a sailor.

My inspection rounds reveal some working of the boom gooseneck fitting on the mast, a loosening of the pin holding the fitting together, and a slight bowing aft of the mast aloft from the upper spreaders. The loose pin is the most serious of these problems. It's the same one I had with the gooseneck on the hydraulic boom vang when it fell apart. Damned roll pins — difficult to service and impossible to inspect. What did the designer of these assemblies have in mind? To thwart crazed boom burglars in the night?

DAY 142 ≈

We sail a reach, apparent wind at seventy degrees. The seas are up at twelve feet. We make nine knots or more of boat speed. Constant spray coats all surfaces with a salt crust thick enough to measure with a ruler.

Flying fish are abundant, quite noticeably more numerous than at the same latitude of the Southern Hemisphere. I find many strewn about the deck and cockpit each day and hear the thwack of their collisions with the boat during the night. They make deck duty hazardous as they zip over *Promise* like scaly missiles, some weighing a pound and having the girth of a twenty-millimeter shell. They remind me of the enhanced respect for all living things, from plankton to people, my solitude has given me. Everything alive is precious, and each life is as important as any other. When I hear a flying fish come aboard at night and sense that he lives, I pile out of my bunk and rush up on deck to see if I can save him.

DAY 144 ≈

Some 1,062 miles, or about seven days remaining. This day passes with a very light south wind, and our speed wavers between one half and three knots. Something should blow on us by tomorrow, but this is a lost day.

I use the time to prepare for my arrival. I try to put the V-drive back together in case we need some engine propulsion to get into St. George's Harbour, but it is hopeless; I will sail in or thumb a tow. But the main engine itself runs fine and so I make fresh water, fifty gallons in three hours. I begin to think of visitors, and hoo boy, does that seem incredible to me! Living visitors! I begin another complete cleandown of *Promise,* end to end, inside and out. She really isn't that dirty, but I decide to make her look as if she has been on a day sail rather than a five-month sojourn. My theory is that I can determine the better of two sailors after a voyage by looking at their boats; invariably, the cleaner, neater boat belongs to the better sailor. I scrub down the topsides with a long-handled brush, reaching over the sides to get the hull shiny right down to the waterline. I scrub down the decks, the cockpit. I scrub the pilothouse. Not one coffee stain remains to be seen on the overhead. The more I scrub, the more I scrub. And the shinier she looks. The galley comes up so bright and clean, I am reluctant to use it again. The head looks and smells like an operating room. The two bright red generators look like display models. The job is satisfying. I feel good in spite of a poor noon-to-noon run of 106 miles.

It feels good to hear Bob Rice now, using position and weather references on Nantucket and Nova Scotia again after such a long, long time. Each day there are new signs that this voyage is coming to an end. I learn from my Bermuda ham friends that Manny and the children arrive there tomorrow. It's not easy to comprehend. Hoyt and Kim in Bermuda waiting for me!

DAY 145 ≈

We struggle to keep five knots of boat speed in light souther-
lies, veering to the southwest just as ordered yesterday by Bob
Rice. Occasional squalls help. When the black clouds bound
past us, we rejoice with eight to nine knots.

The signs of civilization are also out here, right with me. Tonight as I waffle over which tack will keep me closer on the
wind to Bermuda, a ship bears down on us from the northeast,
her lights growing brighter and higher on the same relative
bearing much too long. I turn my spreader lights on because
they still work and hold up the battery-powered port and starboard running lights. The ship passes just under our bow, and I
get a lump in my throat. Early in the morning we are accosted
by another huge ship, the freighter *San Andres y Providencia*
out of Islas St. Andes. This one muscles by not a hundred yards
astern and gives a blast of her horn. I realize this is the first hu-
man-produced sound I have heard directly for months, and I
wish it were something other than a ship's horn.

I can't believe Tony ate lunch with Manny and Hoyt and
Kim just a thousand miles away from *Promise* and me today.
Sunday, April 6. So close!

So close, but the wind does not cooperate, backing to the
northwest, three to eight knots, and putting Bermuda dead into
it. I can hear myself plead, "Come on, come on, let us through.
We've paid our dues, let us through." And I can hear my own
answer, "You are never paid up on your dues, my friend,
never."

While I am absorbed by a radio conversation with Tony,
who has Manny right with him, a huge freighter appears only a
hundred yards to our stern. She sees me. But the ship traffic is
too heavy. At dawn a container carrier crosses our bow, also
very close, heading west.

DAY 146 ≈

This is a milestone day for *American Promise,* the day she
ties the knot of the circumnavigation by crossing her outbound
track. It occurs at 1333 Greenwich Mean Time, April 7, at 24°
6′ north latitude and 56° 8′ west longitude. My circumnavigation is now complete in 145 days, 22 hours, and 22 minutes.

I release the spirit of Frank Shirley so that he can celebrate. All that is left for me is to tie the ribbon in a big bow by sailing into port.

By now, I am recalculating my arrival time almost hourly, and I am sailing harder than ever so that the next recalculation will be nearer than the last. This is as fruitless as any projection based on a small amount of short-term data. My guesses differ by fifty percent, two days at this point, which seems to be playing havoc with people ashore who intend to meet me and must schedule airline flights and hotels. I have been projecting my arrival time now for months, yet on day 148 I write: "508 miles remain and that equals ??? days." Later that same day, after bitching that no one, not even the vaunted Bob Rice, can really predict weather, I gloomily guess my arrival for late on April 13, four days hence, in spite of having but 452 miles to go and a daily average for the entire voyage of more than 170 miles.

I am barely holding my temper at bay, and can do so only because I can find nothing reasonable to target the anger at. This is simply more dues, I guess. Midnight finds the light wind back behind us, and I put the poles back on. This quiets some of the slatting and banging about. The northern sky is ablaze with lightning. A soft rain falls almost straight down on us. Damn, I am sick and tired of this. Adding to the lousy news, I lose radio communications because of the failed coupler power switch.

On day 149, only 374 miles from St. George's, I get some wind on the beam and some boat speed, eight and nine knots of it, and, as always, a new lease on cheer.

≈If we can keep this wind for a day and a half, we will be just fifty miles away from the human race. And then if we have to beat or if the wind abandons us again, I will jump over the side with a line and drag her home.

Even a very close call at being run down by a ship doesn't long dampen my optimism:

≈Huge, green container ship plunges through the seas aiming right at *American Promise* as if on a kamikaze attack. It is bright daylight. She passes so close I cannot see her bridge, which is hidden by the chilling and ugly sight of a looming rusty hull. Her speed leaves me helpless. I know she has no idea that I am in her path. She seems as impersonal and as controlled as an avalanche. Even though I know it is purely a matter of fate now, I scream a plea to her: "Please, please don't. Don't run me down."

DAY 150 ≈

I sight a white speck on the horizon, a steady white speck among the flashing whitecaps. Suddenly I know the speck is coming toward me, to greet me, to show me the way back into the human race. It is only now that I realize my lonely struggle is over, my voyage ended. I feel the welling up inside me, and tears burst from my eyes and flood my cheeks. With all the power of my lungs, I cry out my last declaration in solitude for a long, long time to come:

"You have done it, Dodge. Damnit, you have done it."

All my energy focuses on the white speck. It grows. Others follow. And in a shocking collapse of time I am surrounded by boats and people and having the most wonderful time of my life. *Promise* is galloping. I see so many faces. And then I begin to see the familiar ones. There is Hoyt. There is Kim. There is Manny. The voyage is over.

American Promise and I cross the starting line, three miles off Bermuda, at 1217 hours Bermuda time, 1617 hours Greenwich Mean Time, on Friday, April 11, 1986. Together we have circumnavigated in 150 days, 1 hour, and 6 minutes. We are the first solo American boat to sail around the world without stops. This is the fastest solo circumnavigation ever accomplished and the shortest nonstop, solo circumnavigation by 142 days. We have sailed 25,776 miles for an average of 171.84 miles per day — an average speed of 7.16 knots.

The long sail is indeed over.

~~~ *APPENDIX I*

Purpose. The objective is to accomplish a solo, nonstop, easterly circumnavigation by sail in 180 to 220 days. The boat design challenges are implicit: A boat to bear the rigors of six months' continuous sailing in varied weather conditions; a boat to average 6.25 knots or better over that span of time; a boat that will match the age and physical condition of the skipper; a boat that will accept the required stores and equipment and kindly give up those stores one day at a time; a boat that has as few structural and mechanical weak links as possible; a boat that is planned with redundancy in key systems and equipment; a boat that uses mechanical and electrical advantages, proven engineering solutions, yet can be sailed without them.

A key challenge is in the word "nonstop." There will be absolutely no physical contact made with shore, ship, or aircraft, no provisions or equipment received during the 27,000-nautical-mile voyage. Another key challenge is the 6.25-knot average speed required to complete the circumnavigation in 180 days.

Solo circumnavigations have been accomplished many times now, some by sailors whose exploits were not noted in the news. "Nobby's" book of lists had 84 single-handed circumnavigations by 1983. Joshua Slocum was the first recorded to sail alone around the world from Boston, Massachusetts, USA, from April 24, 1895, to June 27, 1898, in the 36-foot 9-inch LOA yawl *Spray*. Robin Knox-Johnston sailed around alone, nonstop, winning the first and only such official race held thus far. He was the only one of seven starters to finish. He left Falmouth, England, on June 14, 1968, and returned on April 22, 1969, for a time of 313 days and an average speed of 3.6 knots. His boat, *Suhaili,* which was hardly well suited for such a voyage, was a 32-foot LOA wooden ketch. Knox-Johnston certainly fulfilled the spirit of the challenge, but he did make brief stops and contact, physically, with land. Chay Blyth sailed alone around in a westerly direction against prevailing winds and currents and became the first recorded to do so. He departed from Hamble, England, on October 18, 1970, and returned on August 6, 1971, averaging 3.85 knots, in the 59-foot LOA steel ketch *British Steel*.

The documented history of solo, nonstop circumnavigations is rather sparse and inconclusive. A case could be made for no one's having successfully completed a circumnavigation alone that was truly without any anchorings or stops and all sailed in open water. The amazing feat of Robin Knox-Johnston, the one most clearly documented such voyage, might be correctly called "round-the-world single-handed without any port of call"; his time was 313 continuous days. There are a number of recorded unsuccessful attempts at a nonstop circumnavigation.

D. H. "Nobby" Clarke, the recognized authority on sailing feats and records and authenticator for Guinness Superlatives, Inc., has established the rules for circumnavigations, and his word on these matters has become absolute. The Nobby Clarke rules for a nonstop allow anchoring but bar any passing of food, water, supplies, or stores of any kind; the solo sailor must not touch land above the high-water mark. Clarke sets a tough standard. He disallowed a claim for a record, nonstop, solo voyage of 286 days by the Dutchman Pleun Van Der Lugt in 1981–82 because Van Der Lugt accepted the passing of photographic film and a birthday cake from another vessel while at sea. Clarke states that no American has accomplished a solo, nonstop circumnavigation. He judges that my 180-day target is very ambitious.

Several successful one-stop single-handed circumnavigations have been documented. Sir Francis Chichester sailed his 54-foot ketch, *Gypsy Moth IV*, from Plymouth, England, around and back with one stop in Sydney, Australia. Leaving Plymouth in 1971, his first passage was 15,500 NM in 107 days; the second was 14,500 NM in 119 days. He sailed the 30,000 NM in 226 days for an average speed of 5.71 knots. It should be noted that he was physically exhausted upon his arrival in Sydney and spent the best part of a month recuperating in a hospital. Alain Colas, in 1973–74 sailed *Manureva* (formerly *Pen Duick IV*), a 67-foot trimaran, over the same route as Chichester in 168 days for an average speed of 7.34 knots and 175 NM per day for the 29,600-NM voyage.

A combination of improved technology, the increased popularity of solo sailing, and the emergence of commercial sponsorships have caused some dramatic changes in the achievements of solo sailors over the past ten years.

Philippe Jeantot sailed *Crédit Agricole,* a 56-foot LOA aluminum cutter specifically designed for the job, to victory in the 1982–83 BOC Challenge from Newport, Rhode Island, and return in 159 days, a 7-knot speed average. This record stands. The BOC racers, ten of seventeen starters finishing, circumnavigated in four legs, with layovers in Hopetown, Sydney, and Rio. The OSTAR Trans-Atlantic single-handed race has also been a fertile proving ground for advancing technology in boat and equipment designs, although boats designed specifically for the OSTAR are not generally appropriate for a nonstop circumnavigation, a far longer voyage promising far heavier weather.

I believe the poetic giant among single-handed sailors, after Slocum, is Bernard Moitessier. His name is not well served in the record books, because records have not been his primary objective; he is simply listed as the first sailor to circumnavigate twice consecutively. But I believe he best symbolizes the spirit of the solo sailor. Moitessier appeared to be leading in the 1968 nonstop, around-the-world race (Knox-Johnston's ultimate victory), when, after rounding Cape Horn, he decided to head east for the second circumnavigation rather than north to the finish. Moitessier had become aware that his joy in sailing alone was not well served by "The Race" or by any race. On his arrival in Tahiti to end the longest continuous sail ever accomplished, Moitessier said, "Talking of records is stupid, an insult to the sea. The thought of competition is grotesque. You have to understand that when one man is months and months alone, one evolves, some say go nuts. I went crazy in my own fashion. For four months all I saw were the stars. I didn't hear an unnatural sound. A purity grows out of that kind of solitude." He had been at sea alone continuously for 301 days, 37,455 NM, and averaged 5.18 knots.

Although I have referred to records and the record books in my examination of this challenge, and although I do have the record-making time of 180 days as an objective, my fundamental purpose is most certainly not the record book. I have been intimidating myself with the dream of accomplishing the feat ever since sailing my old wooden schooner, *Coaster,* short-handed or alone, for two and a half years circuitously from Maine to Alaska in 1963–65. I was thirty years old when beginning that trip and learned as I went along. *Coaster* was a beautiful, Murray G. Peterson, gaff-headed, 36-foot LOA, 12.5-ton, thirty-one-year-old wooden boat. She leaked. She chafed. She was hard work. She was also strong and forgiving and would sail herself upwind for days without any self-steering gear, windvane or autopilot. She taught me a great deal. On the passage from Balboa, Panama, to Honolulu, a great circle distance of 4,776 nautical miles, she laid a track of approximately 5,500 NM in 49 days.

What I learned about myself from those years aboard *Coaster* formed a very important part of my self-knowledge. I learned how incredibly insignificant each one of us is in the whole realm of things. I learned that the very best each of us can possibly do in our lives is to be true to ourselves first and then to be as positive, as candid, as generous, and as demanding as we can to others within the tiny scope of our existence. The enormity of our ignorance is humbling. The immensity of nature is awesome and inspirational. There is something very precious in dealing with the quick and certain victories and defeats of sailing a small boat alone within the orb of such a humbling awareness.

I feel it is time to revisit that awareness and to retest myself on those basic challenges. I'm not sure how well I know myself now. I'm not certain I am up to the physical and emotional rigors of sailing alone so far and so long.

There have been successes and failures for me over the eighteen years since *Coaster.* But the sum total is on the success side of the scale of standard social measurements. The business I built with others, but feeling much alone in doing so, has prospered and paid me back with relative wealth, many fine friends, and a few precious relationships. I have an understanding and caring wife and we have two bright and beautiful children. My place in the customary order of things is secure. But the customary order of things is not enough. How much more is there?

It is time to try again to find out. There is so little time left.

The Voyage. The following is a general description of the voyage in terms of routes, distances, times, and expected conditions.

FROM	TO	GC-DIST	MERC-DIST
Newport (41.30N/72W)	Cape of Good Hope (35S/19E)	6,780	6,828
Cape of Good Hope	S. tip Tasmania (44.30S/146.40E)	5,245	5,924
Tasmania	Stewart Isl. (N.Z.) (48S/168E)	907	912
Stewart Isl.	Cape Horn (56.20S/71.30W)	3,871	4,457
Cape Horn	Trindade (22.40S/34W)	2,604	2,628
Trindade Is.	E. of Recife (7.15S/29.30W)	960	961
Recife	Newport	3,741	3,759
Total Nautical Miles		24,108	25,469

AVG NM/DAY	DATES	DAYS	PASSAGE	COURSE NM	TRACK NM
146	10/10–11/4	26	Newport–Equator	3,528	3,800
150.5	11/4–12/6	32	Equator–Cape Hope	4,649	4,817
152.4	12/6–1/9	34	Cape Hope–Tasmania	5,064	5,183
154.4	1/9–2/8	30	Tasmania–Cape Horn	4,527	4,633
146.5	2/8–3/12	33	Cape Horn-Equator	4,598	4,833
149.4	3/12–4/6	25	Equator-Newport	3,493	3,734
150	Totals	180		25,859	27,000

Circumnavigation General Recap Averages, 180-Day Target

ASSUMED TRACK	TOTAL NM	AVG. SPEED	AVG. NM/DAY
Great Circle Route	24,108	5.6 kts	134.4
Mercator Route	25,469	5.9 kts	141.5
Trad. Sailing Route	25,859	6.0 kts	143.7
Probable Route	27,000	6.25 kts	150

TRADITIONAL SAILING ROUTES FOR A
CIRCUMNAVIGATION

Newport to Cape of Good Hope:
October 15 to December 5–10
Depart Newport and make for the intersection of lat. 34N and long. 45W. Fair current and winds expected for close-reaching. In order to shorten time in the doldrums, take a direct track through the northeast trades to cross lat. 5N between longs. 20 and 23W. Southerly winds should be met around lat. 7N when one would sail close-hauled to make as much southing as possible and cross the equator between longs. 20 and 24W. Stand through the southeast trades close-hauled and, when these winds are lost, steer southeastward to cross lat. 30S at about long. 30W and thence cross the Greenwich meridian at lat. 40S. Then steer direct for Cape of Good Hope.

Cape of Good Hope to Tasmania:
December 7 to January 16–20
Easterly winds prevail around the Cape, making for several days of windward work, so one steers southwestward to the 40th parallel to pick up prevailing westerly winds and current. In crossing the Indian Ocean, one has one major tradeoff to make: Sail between lats. 39 and 43S with steady and moderate westerlies and relatively smooth seas, or sail a more southern route, lats. 50 to 52S, which is a shorter route but fraught with violent winds and seas, with heavy fog, with low, rocky islands, and with icebergs. Ice will be a potential danger now for the full distance across the Indian Ocean and the Southern (Pacific) Ocean; bergs are regularly

sighted anywhere below the 30th parallel and frequently sighted below the 40th parallel in sizes from 20 to 50 miles in length. The objective is to sail as far south as weather and ice conditions allow. Heavy weather with gale-force winds will be the most likely sailing conditions, but wind and current are at one's back. Pass well south of Tasmania at about lat. 46S and long. 147E.

Tasmania (s. Stewart I.) to Cape Horn:
January 17 to February 21–25

Pass south of Tasmania (lat. 46S and long. 147E) and thence between Auckland islands and Campbell Island on about lat. 52S. In crossing the Southern Ocean, one is still faced with the decision of how far south to sail, with the shorter, southern route carrying the probability of heavy weather, poor visibility, and ice. The southern route is between lats. 54 and 55S; the safer, more comfortable route is on the 47th parallel. Cape Horn is rounded close by at about lat. 56.30S. Sailing conditions for this Southern Ocean crossing should be similar to those for the Indian Ocean crossing, with relatively heavy weather at one's back.

Cape Horn (Trindade/Recife) to Newport:
February 22 to April 13–16

Pass Cape Horn at about lat. 56.30S in moderate to heavy easterly winds and strong favorable current. Make for a point about 80 miles southward of the Falklands Islands, thence to a point just eastward of lat. 35S and long. 32W. From this position, head NNE to about lat. 25S and long. 20W, thence northward toward Isla Fernando de Noronha, hoping for some southeast trades. On reaching lat. 10S and long. 30W, stand to the northward and cross the equator between longs. 31 and 34W. When the northeast trades are picked up, head for lat. 30N and long. 70W and thence on a great circle route as directly as possible to Newport. Variable light to moderate winds can be expected for most of this passage, with some weather work for the first portion, calms and light winds in the middle portion, and moderate reaching conditions for the latter portion.

Days for Circumnavigations Compared

Morgan nonstop objective	180 days
Blyth nonstop (record) '70	292 days
Knox-Johnston nonstop '69	313 days
Colas one-stop '74	168 days
Jeantot BOC three-stop (record) '83	159 days
Sailing estimates *Ocean Passages*, '64 ed.	230–260 days

Distances on Traditional Sailing Routes

DEPART	INITIAL G.C. HEAD	DIST. NM	CUM. NM
41.30N/72W	100	1351	
34N/45W	138	2177	3,528
5N/21.30W	192	2156	5,684
30S/30W	120	1582	7,266
40S/0	104	911	8,177
42S/20E	95	668	8,845
42S/35E	137	4396	13,241
46S/147E	122	827	14,068
52S/166E	148	3700	17,768
56.30S/71.30W	66	449	18,217
53S/60W	59	1602	19,819
35S/32W	49	864	20,683
25S/20W	326	1065	21,748
10S/30W	345	618	22,366
0/32.30W	313	2796	25,162
30N/70W	352	697	25,859
41.30N/72W			

Sailing Route Distances Related to Landmarks

DEPART	ARRIVE	NM	CUM. NM
Newport	Cape of Good Hope	8177	
Cape of Good Hope	S. Tasmania	5064	13,241
S. Tasmania	Cape Horn	4527	17,768
Cape Horn	Newport	8091	25,859

THE SKIPPER PRESENTED

Physical and Mental State. I am, in 1984, 52 years old, born 1/15/32 in Malden, Massachusetts. I am 6′3″ tall and weigh 180 pounds naked. My blood pressure is normally 117 over 70. I flew fighter airplanes in the U.S. Air Force from 1952 to 1957, graduated second in my Aviation Cadet class, and accumulated 1,010 flying hours. I was booted out of the University of New Hampshire for not earning good enough grades to compensate for being caught in the act of firing a cannon in the Dean of Women's bedroom while she slept. I graduated from Boston University, magna cum laude, in 1959. In my postmilitary careers, I have worked for "someone else" for just a total of four years. I had a successful three-year business career in Anchorage, Alaska, which paid for my first schooner and two and one half years of sailing her. I founded and ran Controlonics Corp., an electronics products manufacturer, for thirteen years until selling the company to Dynatech Corp. in 1983; Controlonics grew from four people in a garage to a very profitable, high-tech company with $26 million in sales in that period.

My general health is good. The following is a portrait of the critical factors and problems.

I suffer from cluster-type, migraine headaches that can, in cycles, become acute. These headaches can often be controlled by vigorous, physical exercise when the pain hits. Even in the most severe cycle, however, I can continue to function relatively well, and the combination of immediate, strenuous exercise, some "mind over matter," and a reasonably high threshold for pain allows me to cope with a headache in progress at critical times. My circulation is probably below average, as indicated by occasional numbness in fingers when gripping something hard over time in cold weather. Otherwise, I have a good, natural tolerance to cold.

My far-field eyesight is excellent, but my near-field eyesight is lousy, requiring glasses to read newsprint or chart details. My hearing is average.

My coordination is still quite good; I was a competitive athlete in several sports when young. My peak performance strength is well above average. My physical endurance is better than average, although now I do have a tough time running several miles at any reasonable pace. I can run 100 yards in less than 12 seconds. My wind has not been helped by a smoking habit, just now being broken. My bodily functions are normal. A lack of good manual dexterity should not be a detriment for this venture. I really need an average of eight hours of sleep a day but can grab it in short segments, can remain alert over a 24-hour period, and can store sleep. I do not wake quickly from deep sleep.

My general physical condition, although relatively good now, will be improved in a program of aerobics and weight-lifting over the next year.

My mental faculties are more than adequate. My emotional status is sound. I have a strong will and a singular determination to succeed. I do not easily give up. I can concentrate well over long periods of time and can focus a natural impatience on realistic objectives, satisfied with inches of progress if that is the order of the day or task. I know how to sort priorities and do not become confused by too many details. I know well the power of planning and time to reach an objective. I am very happy in my own company and can find loneliness a rather delicious feeling. And I don't suffer from seasickness.

Sailing Experience. I have experienced being at sea for extended periods of time while sailing *Coaster* from Maine to Alaska, 1963–65, either short-handed or alone. That was my first significant and is my most extensive sailing experience, although I've been "messing around in boats" all of my life. *Coaster* taught me as I sailed; I had some difficult times and a few close calls, but never had a life-threatening situation by my standards. I was totally immersed in the adventure, as is my way for whatever I'm doing, and never slept ashore for the two and a half years it took. *Coaster*'s keel crossed more than 25,000 miles of Atlantic, Caribbean, and Pacific bottom during those years. I stopped her now and again to replenish funds and make repairs.

Another Murray G. Peterson schooner has been in my life for the past fourteen years. *Eagle* is a seven-ton, 31-foot, gaff-headed, old-but-rebuilt wooden boat of exquisite beauty. I have sailed her only in the Northeast, from Chesapeake Bay to Penobscot Bay, but mostly along the coast of Maine I so dearly love. Much cruising has been with my wife, Manny, a very competent crew, and, more recently, our two children, Hoyt David, 10, and Kimberly Promise, 7. At least once per year, I have sailed *Eagle* alone for several days.

I am an excellent pilot; my dead-reckoning skills are superior. While on *Coaster,* which had no electronic navigation equipment, I learned to use the sextant with adequate results. I shot, but never truly mastered, the stars but did become very proficient navigating with the sun. As do so many solo sailors, I used the simple "noon-fix" solution to the celestial navigation problem with admirable success. Look in Bowditch, Dutton, or Mixter under "lifeboat navigation."

I am a damned good marlinspike seaman. I have a wide range of seamanship skills. I sail a boat very well and always without any panic. Although competitive by nature, I have not actively raced sailboats. I think "covering" is boring. Putting me in a seven-knot crowd around a mark is like putting a mackerel in a tree.

I have almost no experience with the type of boat that is specified for this circumnavigation. The largest boat I've sailed is my brother's 50-foot stays'l schooner, a behemoth for her length, and then I was only there as crew. I have sailed fewer sloops or cutters than Columbus. I have never sailed a boat with a windvane steerer or autopilot. I lack any decent experience with the advantages and the problems of roller-furling gear, of large winches to replace good old block and tackle purchase, of power-driven sail-handling gear, or of serious electrical systems. Only one of my schooners had electric lighting. I have no experience with a boat that does not leak and am looking forward to getting some. My persistent paranoia on *Coaster* was that the keel would drop off, and I was constantly sounding, pumping, and sponging the bilges to look at them, at least for a moment in time, happily dry.

I am competent, or reasonably so, with the maintenance and

operation of machinery; I certainly am no expert mechanic. I tend to the crude approach and pride myself on a level of "make do" rather than precise workmanship. I am more amazed at how well machinery works rather than disappointed that it doesn't. I'm not presently comfortable with a bottom-line dependence on electrical wizardry or internal combustion contraptions, but am quite pleased when they work because of a benign pleasure in doing things the easy way. I do have a basic understanding of electronics, now, and a belief in the performance and durability of quality-made electronic products (my business, right!).

I am a competent sewer of sails because a schooner chafes them like a file through a cake of soap. I think I can rough-jury-rig almost anything to keep it going.

I never take undue risks on a boat and never drink while under way. I do have to keep reminding myself of the importance of a personal lifeline. I have a natural instinct to keep a boat tidy and to be persistent in keeping all lines, gear, and stores in their rightful places. I have learned that a boat must, at all times, be ready for threatening circumstances and seldom let this lesson lapse.

My sailing skills, health, or mental preparedness should not be a barrier to a successful solo, nonstop circumnavigation.

THE BOAT'S SPECIFICATIONS

Foreword. These specifications are but a guide to assist the architect in providing a boat design that will be optimum for the mission. It is expected that the designer will have an understanding of the mission from prior experience as well as from a reading of my introduction with a brief history of solo circumnavigations, a summary of this planned circumnavigation, a general description of my physical condition and experience, and some spurious insights to my attitude about this whole matter. It is anticipated that the design challenge will be a joint effort between the architect and myself to produce the fastest and most durable boat we can together. I am not a boat designer, nor do I intend to try to act like one. My part of the effort will be strictly as specifier, editor, motivator, gopher, and bill payer. The design purpose for this boat, although very singular, will be fulfilled by mixing a complex recipe of many critically related factors. There will be numerous tradeoff decisions for the designer and me to make together. The design job will not be complete until the boat demonstrates she is ready for her objective; the designer will oversee the building of the boat and will participate in trials. The builder and all subcontractors performing work related to the hull, rig, and sail-handling gear will report to the designer.

I expect debate on the following specifications, even where I have been specific. I hope, however, that I have drawn a realistic and understandable frame of reference from which the designer and I can proceed.

This boat, well done and well sailed, will make history.

The Hull. This boat will be a 60-foot LOA cutter built of aluminum using aircraft-type construction methods, of cold-molded wood, of cored fiberglass, or of steel. The 60-foot overall length is selected because it has become, recently, the size limit rule for both the 1984 OSTAR and the 1986–87 BOC Challenge race around the world. Designing the boat to the rules established for the BOC Challenge, such as size and safety standards, will allow her to participate in this major single-handed sailing race if that course is followed. Her performance with me in my 1985 nonstop voyage will, I trust, make her a potential BOC contender.

This boat is not the proper one for expressing radical design innovations. The known and the tested design characteristics should prevail. She must be ready to absorb a knockdown without damage, for even as she is designed not to be easily knocked down, she surely will be several times. It would also be just fine if she were able to survive a 360-degree lateral revolution through the water, the ultimate knockdown.

Although predicting sailing conditions by percentages of wind strengths and points of sail for such a voyage is a textbook lesson in futility, an act of predicting the unpredictable, I have tried. The following estimations have been taken from courses plotted on recent Pilot Charts. The circumnavigation should find 3,062 NM of beating, 3,979 NM of close reaching, 6,419 NM of beam reaching, 7,857 NM of broad reaching, and 6,142 NM of running. The historical odds say that there will be an average wind speed of force 3.7 for the passage from Newport to the equator, with about 2.5% reported calms and 12% gale-force winds. From the equator to the Cape of Good Hope, one can expect an average of force 4.3 wind speed, 2% calms, and 5% gales. From the Cape of Good Hope to Tasmania, one can expect a force 5.3 wind average, no calms, and 40% gale-force winds. From Tasmania to Cape Horn, the expectations should be for force 5 average wind speed, no calms, and 40% gales. The passage from the Horn to the equator should show one force 4.1 average wind speed, 2% calms, and 20% gales. On the passage from the equator to Newport in March and April, one can expect force 3.9 average winds, 2.5% calms, and 20% gale-force winds.

The displacement weight factor of the boat is a decision that speaks directly to the overall design concept and will be the key, initial discussion between the designer and myself. I am not experienced with light displacement boats and have generally found myself defending heavier displacement boats. The relatively light displacement boats I have sailed have been stock, glass boats in the 30-to-40-foot range and have not pleased me. But, if *Crédit Agricole* is a role model, and she certainly was successful, light displacement certainly does work for a single-handed circumnavigation at high speeds and with safe passages. She displaces 11 metric tons, which makes her some 30% lighter than a comparable IOR boat, if heavier than an ultralight. She is described as being very beamy, with a flat exit and a sharp entry. If relatively light displacement is selected, a water ballast system such as *Crédit Agricole* has must also be considered. In *Crédit*, some four thousand pounds of water ballast can be pumped into the weather tank for trim or the tanks can be emptied in light airs.

In this key debate over displacement weight, I will, it is important to note, be generally defending the heavier boat. I would rather try for a compromise to deliver the conditional speed required with weatherliness and stability. I somehow feel that the alternative range is not heavy or light, but somewhere in the pound-at-a-time scale between.

Layout. She will be spartan belowdecks. There will be an enclosed area just forward of the cockpit for an inside helm, navigation station, wet hanging locker and, possibly, one berth. A one-burner gimballed stove may also be located here for heating coffee or soup. Visibility via deadlights should be 360 degrees. Since this will be a planned wet area, adequate drainage and venting should be supplied.

Forward of this area and behind a watertight door will be the galley and the head. This area should also be prepared as a wet area. A workbench will be included here with space for tools and spare parts. A locking, gimballed table will be in this cabin.

The sleeping area, whether forward of the galley or below and aft, will be one place where "no water shall ever reach." If there was anything I wished for on *Coaster,* it was a sleeping area that was dry and forever kept that way. This cabin will have a watertight door and natural lighting from skylight or deadlights. There should be venting provision for sailing in tropical waters. Two permanent bunks should be set, one for each tack. It should be emphasized that this area will be used only for sleep and relaxation. A locking, gimballed table with bench seat will be in this cabin.

The remainder of the hull belowdecks will be devoted to sail locker and rope and ground tackle stowage. I estimate space needs for these purposes will be approximately 350 cubic feet.

Stowage of Nonconsumed Items. The entire forward portion of the hull will serve as a sail locker. The sail inventory will include 4 mainsails, 2 storm trysails, 4 forestaysails, 6 jibs, and 5 spinnakers. This sail inventory will be accessible through a large deck hatch forward and through a watertight door belowdecks. The hatch should allow me to physically get below and to pull out and stuff sails as easily as possible; perhaps rollers along the hatch sides would help. Compartments should be supplied to separate sails in a specified manner. Space will also be required for 200 fathoms of ¾-inch rope and 100 fathoms of smaller-diameter rope as spare. A reasonable inventory of made-up lines will also be stowed here. Ground tackle, including a 100-pound CQR made up with a 100-fathom rode and a 60-pound Danforth made up with a 50-fathom rode, will be stowed in the forepeak. This entire forward area below will drain directly into the bilges through a heavy grate.

A generous wet hanging locker will be in the area of the inside helm to hold foul-weather gear and wet clothing of all descriptions and dimensions.

Dry clothing will be stowed in the sleeping quarters.

Space will be supplied for thirty books and fifty audio tapes in the main sleeping cabin. A working library of twenty-five books and space for charts (100) will be at the navigation station in the wet area with the inside helm. Space required for the navigation equipment is detailed in a following section.

One or two diesel generators will be below in the engine compartment. Also located here will be mechanic's tools, engine oil, and spare engine and generator parts.

Stowage of Consumed Stores. Space for 800 pounds of canned food, 400 cans of soft drinks, and 200 pounds of dry foods will be made in the galley area, or a working stock of these items could be stowed here with general stowage in the bilges elsewhere (not in the sleeping cabin).

The supply of fresh water could well involve a tradeoff of permanent tanks and a seawater desalinator. It is my understanding that desalinators are capable of making fresh water in fairly large multiples from diesel fuel. At least 100 gallons of permanent fresh water stowage will be needed. I know I can get along fine with one-half gallon of water per day if canned food rather than freeze-dried food is selected.

The capacity of diesel fuel tanks required will depend on the demand for fuel for battery charging and for water making. A capacity for 400 gallons would be the maximum.

Safe, vented stowage must be provided for propane fuel for the galley stove. I sure like the idea of a gas-fired stove, but don't have enough experience with the fuel to accurately calculate the amount required for the voyage. For purposes here, I recall my one three-month period with a gas range on *Coaster* and estimate use at 12 pounds a week for a total, with reserve, of 360 pounds. The bottles must add another 40 pounds or so.

A very rough estimate of the weights of consumable stores is: food, 800 pounds; fresh water, 750 pounds; diesel, 2,600 pounds; engine oils, 60 pounds; propane, 400 pounds; total consumable weight estimate, 4,610 pounds.

Navigation Station. The working navigation area, navigation instruments and equipment, communications equipment and sailing instrumentation are discussed here.

The nav station will be a key working area and should be spacious, with a large, chart-size table and cubbies to give access to the standard assemblage of plotting tools, a working library for up to 25 volumes, 100 charts, pencil sharpener, calculators, extra eyeglasses, hand-held bearing compass, and skullcap. The station must be very well lit, in daytime by ambient light and at night by artificial light.

There will be redundancy in primary navigation equipment.

Two satellite navigators will be installed and will be the primary navigation system. I do not plan to install Loran or Omega. The sextant will provide my backup. The satellite instruments will be located at the nav station. There will be one permanently installed and one portable IPIRB; the IPIRBs should talk to the SARSA/COSPAS satellite system.

At the nav station, there will be the mandatory, if relatively useless, VHF-FM two-way radio, possibly an SSB radio, but more important an amateur transceiver. The ham radio will be primary communications gear. A depth recorder will be included in this area. A weather facsimile receiver will also be here. A general all-band receiver will be included.

Sailing instrumentation will probably be provided with a microprocessor-based integrated system, such as the Brookes and Gatehouse Hercules system 190 or the new Datamarine Link system. The basic information on water speed, wind speed, wind direction, and point of sail (apparent wind) will be read out at both helm locations and, possibly, at the nav station. There will be magnetic compasses at both helms, even if a flux-gate electronic compass is installed, and telltale compasses over both bunks in the sleeping cabin. An alarm system with an audio output loud enough to soil one's shorts will be installed; similar to the B&G Hornet 4 sailing monitor, this alarm will be programmable to report selected changes in water speed, wind speed, and heading.

A cassette tape sound system, installed in the sleeping cabin with remote speakers to the inside helm area, will spice up my daydreams.

Four autopilots will be installed, one for each helm quadrant and each capable of handling all quadrants. Experience with the Autohelm 3000 is reportedly good (Jeantot, however, burned out two with his damaged rudder; the Autohelm 5000 didn't steer *Crédit* well). A windvane steerer (plan space for spare parts!) will be used for upwind and reaching work and downwind work in heavy air. My sense of windvanes is that they refuse to stay whole on boats very long. The two wheel steerers may be mechanical or hydraulic. There will be an emergency tiller should all else fail, although I don't know how it would be to steer a 60-footer in heavy weather with a stick.

I plan to film this voyage with videotape. Cameras will be

placed to view the cockpit and the foredeck. God only knows what they will record after a few months at sea.

Electrical Systems. This boat, it appears, will have a relatively high dependence on electrical power to operate the myriad instruments and equipment. But this boat will be ready for me to keep her sailing in the event of total power loss. I anticipate two banks of high-capacity, heavy-duty batteries in the engine compartment. A smaller bank of batteries will be in a sealed area higher up in the hull to provide emergency backup. Solar panels will be laid out on deck or housetops to charge batteries, specifically the emergency bank. The main engine and diesel generator will provide charging for the two working banks of batteries. Electric lighting will be distributed to provide good visibility in all working areas. Oil lamps will provide emergency lighting.

Galley. I am a nondiscriminating eater and a marginal cook. I can, literally, live on peanut butter and cheese sandwiches. I can make bread that remains chewable for about forty-eight hours from flour, powdered yeast, sugar, and seawater; I cook it in a pot on the stovetop.

The primary galley equipment will be a sink with hand pumps for fresh and raw water, a gimballed propane stove with oven, mounts for a backup kerosene stove (which I know can be fired with diesel oil), and a cool box. The cool box is a dilemma to me. The only ones I know to stay cool burn too much power; ice better not be available. Perhaps it's best to plan not to cool food. Adequate stowage for dishes and utensils is taken for granted.

The Rig. The cutter rig is preferred, jib, forestaysail, and mainsail. The prime objective here is to provide a rig that allows easy handling in a variety of weather conditions and is durable, or strong, under very heavy weather conditions. My past experience has been that light conditions are more of a problem than heavy conditions, but I've never sailed in the roaring forties and I was on a gaff-headed schooner that suffered more in light airs and was able to keep her bottom in the water even when carrying too much sail in heavy airs. I assume that the cutter will sail well under her staysail even when going to weather and that she will, with a good-size main and staysail, jib, or both headsails, make a powerful, easily handled rig. A storm trysail should make this a very adaptable rig under all conditions. It may be prudent to fit twin headstays to option two jib sizes. I will carry spinnakers, stayed or un-stayed, and will find someone to teach me how to set one. (It may sound bizarre, but in some 75,000 miles of sailing I have never set a spinnaker.)

The standing rigging must be very strong; a factor of safety of 2.75 to 1 might be reasonable. I suppose that a double- or triple-spreader arrangement is called for. The chainplates will tie into the floors and the mast chainplates or tangs should be commensurate. I understand that cutters generally carry running backstays for heavy weather work under the forestaysail, although I don't like them; can someone figure out how to keep the forestay stiff and the mast straight without them? Wire and fittings should be 316 stainless, right? And big. The spars will probably be aluminum un-less someone knows more than I do about carbon fiber. Please step the mast in the keel and not on deck. And, somebody, consider the days in heavy weather when I have to go aloft for repairs. I can climb the mast hoops on a schooner; what do I do on this rig? At least give me lots of spreader lighting over the deck and aloft.

I have summarily looked at a stowaway main and was im-pressed by how simple to handle it all looked, how difficult it ap-peared to replace a blown sail, and how hopeless it seemed to con-sider my making a serious mechanical repair at sea. The only way I would sail with one is if there were tracks on both sides of the slot so that sails could be set the "old way" when the system fails.

Running rigging will be wire with rope tails on the halyards and big braided stuff on the sheets. A compression strut will be used on the main boom in lieu of a topping lift. Both headsails will be roller furling; such gear performed, generally, without mishap in the BOC. The spinnaker will be given a fat, thin-walled pole (2) no longer than the base of the foretriangle, and there will be socks on all of those mysterious sails. The mainsheet deck block will be on a traveler, full width, so that a vang will be required only to serve as a preventer. Make the blocks oversize (no Cape Cod prob-lem, "small blocks and large lines," please) and put four parts of purchase on the mainsheet.

The layout of the deck will be a very important study in itself. Big, self-tailing winches will encircle the cockpit and handle all sheets and furling guys (except for the spinnaker?). A gang of track cars with heavy rollers will fairlead the running rigging from the mast area and foredeck. I would dearly like to handle, set, trim and furl all sails in place from the cockpit with the exception of the spinnaker. And, before I forget, please include a big hand windlass forward so I can kedge off; I will try not to use it. Of course, the deck will also be cluttered with a canister containing a life raft and, in case I break my no-kedge promise, a bagged rubber boat to carry ground tackle to deep water.

It is obvious that a great deal more knowledge has to be thrown at this whole subject of rig, rigging, and sail handling gear. Please remember that I am a fast learner whose major handicap will be, in 1985, 53.5 years of age. But I resolutely believe in the value of solid engineering to provide answers.

The Calendar. I am certain that this specification will appear primitive and incomplete, indeed, by July of 1984. For the sin of wordiness in it, please blame my word processor. Here is the schedule to be met:

<blockquote>
Departure around world   October 1985
Launching party   June 1985
</blockquote>

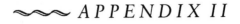

APPENDIX II

A CLIMATOLOGICAL DISCUSSION FOR A GLOBAL
CIRCUMNAVIGATION BY SINGLE-HANDED SAILBOAT
Bob Rice, *Weather Services International*

FOREWORD

Point-to-point routes for sailing vessels on the various world oceans have been historically well established through centuries of trial and error. Since, by definition, the sailing vessel performance is primarily dependent upon wind velocities, it follows that the routes have been established around certain persistent weather features and/or occurrences. Ocean currents also play a part, but there is a cause-and-effect relationship between prevailing wind fields and surface currents such that a study of wind will generally imply significant currents. Wind will remain the dominant factor in routing. These routes have been honed down by experience and, assuming a stable climatology, it is likely that little can be done to offer any large-scale deviation from these routes, at least for preliminary planning. In itself, this suggests a certain consistence in the weather patterns that can be expected to prevail over the world for a given time of year. This is particularly true when considering an ocean global circumnavigation, since the major portion of the trip must take place in Southern Hemisphere waters. There tend to be far fewer anomalous events in the Southern Hemisphere middle latitudes as opposed to the Northern Hemisphere. That portion that does take place in the Northern Hemisphere is mainly within Atlantic subtropic and tropic regions, where conditions remain relatively stable. As such, the route will see little of the large-scale deviations and anomalies seen over the midlatitudes of the North Atlantic and North Pacific. This is not to say that there will not be episodes of heavy or severe weather, but rather that the episodes will tend to be more predictable on a climatological basis in the Southern Hemisphere.

The geographical breakdown for discussing "normals" is

somewhat arbitrary. Typically, this can be done on the basis of climatological regions, e.g., midlatitude, subtropic, and tropic, or it can be discussed in terms of specific oceans. We will compromise and discuss the route by breaking it down into convenient legs encompassing similar weather patterns. Obviously the dominant weather sequences within these legs will vary with the season. The chronological period has, therefore, been roughly determined by the goal of a Newport departure during the month of October and a period en route of 180 days. Rather than stating that the period within each leg is to be a specific time slot, we have broadened the period on either side to allow for schedule deviations. The leg end points used have been estimated from the traditional sailing routes.

Specifically, these legs, and the time period within each leg, will be as follows:

LEG	DISCUSSION VALID FOR
Newport, Rhode Island (41.5N/71.4W) to 15N/30W	October/November
15N/30W to 15S/25W	October-December
15S/25W to 40S/0W	November/December
40S/0W to 50S/180W	November-January
50S/180W to Cape Horn (57.0S/70.0W)	January-March
Cape Horn to 40S/30W	February/March
40S/30W to 15S/25W	February/March
15S/25W to 15N/50W	February-April
15N/50W to Newport	March-May

Newport, Rhode Island (41.5N/71.4W) to 15N/30W: October/November

During the period October/November, or any time of year for that matter, there is one dominant weather feature controlling the circulations within this leg; the subtropical high pressure system, or the so-called Azores High. The subtropical high pressure is not a permanent feature, as such, but rather an area of prevailing high pressure. This means that while the feature will occasionally break down, and/or move out of position, the mean circulation will typically show a massive high pressure ridge oriented east-west along about 35 degrees north latitude, from west of Gibraltar westward to the coastal waters of North America. The mean center of highest pressure typically lies near 35N/35W but can vary considerably in real time. The mean strength and location of the Azores High varies with season, being farthest north with the highest pressure during the summer, while being weaker and farther south during the winter.

The anticyclonic or clockwise flow along the southern periphery of this mean high pressure ridge provides that persistent east and northeast flow across the Atlantic, south of 35N, which results in the quasi-permanent trade winds. The trades weaken somewhat during the October/November period but remain generally persistent nonetheless. These trade winds will typically extend southward from the mean axis of high pressure to south of 15 degrees north latitude. To the north of the mean axis, the clockwise flow results in the prevailing southwest and west winds of the midlatitude western North Atlantic. It will be noted in the discussion for subsequent legs that all the world oceans have a similar high pressure dominance in the subtropic region, all very important in the overall global circulation.

Aside from this dominant Atlantic subtropical high pressure, other features of note will consist of the migratory midlatitude highs and lows, the diminishing risk of tropical cyclones tracking northeastward in the western Atlantic, and a very low probability of storms moving westward through the southern portions of this leg.

Cyclogenesis, or the formation and development of extratropical gale centers, is becoming much more frequent in October, to become very active during November. The principal areas of cyclogenesis over the western Atlantic will be northward along the North American coast from the Carolinas to Newfoundland and Labrador. For our purposes, the primary envelope of concern will be from Cape Hatteras northward past Cape Cod and eastward to sea some 600 miles. As concerns the Atlantic south of 40N, another area of cyclogenesis will be developing near and north of the Azores and eastward into the Mediterranean, but this active region should not be a factor on the planned route. There is a related circumstance of a westward shift of the mean position of the subtropical high more into the central and western Atlantic during periods of cyclogenesis near the Azores. Typically, the risk of extratropical storm development along the route diminishes considerably, probably to insignificance, after passing 30–33 degrees north, not being too likely south of 35 north. Trailing cold fronts from storm formations farther west and north along the North American coast will occur, however, as well as those fronts brought southward by the storms that develop north of the Azores. As such, gale-force northwest to northeast winds will be possible at times southward to 20–25 north and on rare occasions right down to 15 north, the latter mostly in November.

Tropical cyclone (tropical storm and hurricane) frequency is fairly high in early October but diminishes rapidly by late October, becoming rather low for November. Typically, these late season storms develop mainly in the western Caribbean, with some also forming east of the Antilles. The frequency of storm development is decreasing, but there is a fairly high probability that if a storm does develop, it will track northeastward through the western Atlantic. Specifically, there will be about 20%–30% risk of a tropical storm or hurricane in the western Atlantic, west of 55 degrees west longitude during any given October, diminishing to 5%–10% in November. Speaking only of hurricanes, the risk drops to about 10%–15% in October and less than 5% in November. The highest risk for either tropical storm or hurricane will be prior to October 20. East of 55W the risk will drop to less than 5% for tropical storms and less than 2% for hurricanes. Tropical waves will track westward from the Cape Verde, Africa, region, but rarely show development into cyclone stage. These features can be associated with thunderstorms and/or squalls, however.

The result of these typical patterns will be to show the great possible variability of conditions in the route from Newport to about 35 north, and much less the remainder of the leg to 15N/30W. North of 35N, conditions can include gale-force winds from any direction, in association with storm development, but mainly from southeast to southwest and again from northwest to north. Most of the very strong easterlies will occur north of 40N. The exceptions to this trough will be associated with the possible tropical cyclone moving northeastward west of 55W. Since most of the migratory systems will be north of 35N and west of 55W, this will be the area of most variability, with some occasions of very light winds associated with migratory polar highs that move out into the region behind the storm systems. Aside from these incidents of strong storm-associated winds, the prevailing wind will tend to be west to southwesterly in the 10–25-knot range, in association with the subtropical high. South of 35N, the wind will tend to smooth out to a more persistent south and southwesterly backing with distance to east and northeast south of 30N. While areas of near calm conditions can exist, mainly in the 30N–35N range within the mean center of high pressure, relatively rare cold frontal penetrations will induce strong northerly winds south to 30N and rarely to 15N. South of 30N on to 15N there will tend to be persisting east and northeast trades in the 10–20-knot range, occasionally with higher squalls in thunderstorms, mainly near 15N.

All in all, it would be expected that the frequency of gale-force winds that might be encountered by the boat would be in the 15%–20% range along this route in October, mainly north of 35N, and somewhat higher, at 20%–25%, in November and again mainly north of 35N. The highest probability will be from extra-tropical developments.

Regarding any suggested deviations from the traditional sailing routes, there would seem to be little to be gained from any marked changes. An initial track more eastward from Newport might set the boat out of the western Atlantic storm track sooner, and away from the more probable area of tropical cyclone tracks, but the difference is probably not significant enough to warrant the distance penalty. Further, any attempt to move farther eastward, north of 35N, would pose the threat of becoming involved in the calms of the pulsating mean high-pressure center that might be encountered north of 35N and east of 40W–45W. Thus, while facing a higher risk of gale-force winds along the first third of the route, the overall wind field should be more reliable. The aiming point of 15N/30W cannot be argued with either, since, as will be seen below, it is desirable to cut across the equatorial regions as directly as possible to gain access to the South Atlantic southeasterly trades.

15N/30W to 15S/25W: October–December

This leg constitutes the passage through the tropics. In this region the dominant weather feature is the intertropical convergence zone, known as the ITCZ. In somewhat oversimplified terms, the ITCZ is that boundary between the two hemispheric weather regimes, specifically the meeting of the Northern Hemisphere northeast trades and the Southern Hemisphere southeast trades. The Northern Hemisphere northeast trades are associated with the clockwise flow (gradient flow reverses in the Southern Hemisphere) around the counterpart South Atlantic subtropical high, which will be covered in more detail below. During the Northern Hemisphere summer, the ITCZ migrates northward to a mean position along 10N, in response to the strengthening and northward movement of the Azores High and the corresponding weakening and northward movement of the South Atlantic subtropical high. During the Northern Hemisphere winter, the reverse situation brings it typically to just north of the equator, extending essentially east-west. During the October to December period, the ITCZ is migrating southward, such that typically during this period it would be expected to be located between 6N and 8N, also extending east-west. The zone is rather broad, however, and does show real time variation north and south as the two hemispheric subtropical high-pressure systems wax and wane on a synoptic or day-to-day basis. Winds within the resultant ITCZ pressure trough can be either light and variable or light westerlies. This region is the so-called doldrums, where the wind directional steadiness drops off to low percentages and wind speeds will generally be less than 5–10 knots at all times. The maximum cloudiness will generally lie south of the northeast trades, in the area of the light westerly flow. Areas of convection (showers and/or thunderstorms) move westward in this zone, frequently in organized clusters associated with tropical waves, but mainly in the Northern Hemisphere, north of the equator. While these waves sometimes organize into tropical cyclones, this would be mainly a late summer and early fall occurrence, particularly east of 55W. These waves or clusters generally emanate from the African thermal trough, and as this feature gives way to wintertime high pressure, the activity greatly diminishes. During inactive periods of the ITCZ largely clear skies can result, as well as in that region ahead of tropical waves.

The wind field within this leg then is dominated by the two subtropical high-pressure systems and their interaction, the ITCZ. Specifically, winds will be persistent northeast trades, of 10–20

knots for the most part, southward to about 9N–10N. South of
these latitudes the winds will become unreliable, generally light
and variable of less than 5–10 knots; frequently light westerly.
These unreliable winds will extend southward to about 1N–2N,
occasionally to about the equator, at which point the southeasterly
trades begin to attain dominance. From the equator southward to
10S, the southeast trades of 10–20 knots will dominate, tending
to show a bit more tendency toward east and occasionally northeast, at similar speeds, southward to 15S. Winds within the steady
trades both north and south of the ITCZ, while typically to the
10–20-knot range, will on occasion fall off to less than 10 knots
and occasionally be in the 25–30-knot range, but any winds over
gale force (34 knots or greater) would be considered quite rare
within this leg, particularly in view of the approaching Southern
Hemisphere summer. Some squall activity may be encountered in
the ITCZ but should be minimal at this time of year. Precipitation
in the trade belt is not common, although substantial cloudiness
will prevail.

Due to the generally light and variable wind flow within the
ITCZ, it is desirable to cut through it with minimum elapsed time
while also entering the regime of the South Atlantic trade wind
field east of Brazil. As such, there again appears little reason to
deviate significantly from the traditional sailing route, since it will
be necessary to ultimately avoid the area of light winds that will
be associated with the central region of the South Atlantic subtropical high-pressure system while swinging southward along its western periphery to maintain reliable winds.

In summation, this leg (and subsequent return northward
through the same area) will be considered the most stable of any
throughout the global circumnavigation, but at the same time will
likely turn out to be the most frustrating due to the probable calms
and flighty winds encountered through the ITCZ, the doldrums,
which are rightly noted and dreaded throughout sailing history.

15S/25W to 40S on the Greenwich Meridian:
November/December
The South Atlantic subtropical high-pressure counterpart to the
Azores High lies with a mean center near 30S/10W, or at about
midocean to the west of the southern tip of Africa. While the mean

pressure is about 1023 millibars at this time of year, there do appear to be fairly large variations from that pressure, indicating that the system does show instability. Data sources in the South Atlantic are quite sparse as compared to the North Atlantic, such that the stability, or lack of it, in the subtropical high is not as well documented as is the case with the Azores High. As in the latter case, the mean center of high pressure comes about with migratory highs that fill in and assume the position of the subtropical; that is, the mean center merely indicates the dominance of high pressure, not the same system. In the South Atlantic, these migratory highs tend to track eastward between the 30S and 40S parallels. The significance of this, being that while the traditional sailing route is probably correct in skirting the western edge of the mean center, there can be occasions of light and variable wind conditions in that latitude bracket; 30S–40S along the traditional route. The frequency should be less than farther east, however, certainly low enough both in terms of occurrence and duration to be of little significance for route planning.

During this spring period, the highest frequency of low-pressure movements will be eastward to the south of 50S, with an average of as many as 10–20 low-pressure centers per 5-degree equatorial square per month in the spring in that band between 50S and 65S. For the area more pertinent to the route, the majority of low-pressure centers will be tracking southeastward after developing along the South American coastal sections from about 20S southward. Thus the primary storm track, aside from the dominant high-latitude tracks, south of 50S, will tend to be along the coast from Rio de Janeiro, Brazil, southward to Buenos Aires, Argentina, thence southeastward toward the island group of Tristan da Cunha, or roughly 40S/15W, then joining the major storm tracks south of the Cape of Good Hope, south of 40S. These storms will be associated with cold frontal systems extending northward and rotating east and southeastward. The storm systems will tend to be weaker and less frequent than in the winter months, but there is not the great difference in strength/frequency that is exhibited in the North Atlantic. Thus, the route proposed, and accepted, would be expected to encounter storm systems moving southeastward along and west of the route, with frontal passages over the boat. In the Southern Hemisphere, the migratory low-pressure/high-pressure couples tend to move east and southeast with great regularity, without many of the complications of the Northern Hemisphere. Thus, it would be expected that there will be relatively frequent frontal passages over the boat during the transit from about 30S southward to 40S/o.

The wind fields encountered southward along this route should show mainly the influence of the subtropical high-pressure system, southward to about 30S, then a gradual transition into the polar westerlies, which will dominate at 40S. Specifically, this will mean east to northeast flow at 15S, generally in the 10–20-knot range, with very rare incidence of any wind from the west semicircle. Progressing southward, the more variable wind directions associated with the migratory high-pressure features (into the quasi-permanent subtropical high-pressure position) will be encountered south of 20S, where most any direction can be found from 20S to 30S, but rarely over 30 knots. The more dominant directions in that portion will tend to be from NW through NE to SE, however. Winds around frontal passages tend to be north to northeast ahead and northwest to southwest behind. Gale-force winds would be considered very rare north of 30S. To the south of 30S, the westerlies will start to dominate, becoming very persistent by the time of arrival at 40S. Under the influence of the frequent gale centers south of 50S and the high pressure to the north, the frequency of gales will increase, such that by the time that 40S has been reached, the risk of gales will be up to about 10%, and winds in the 25–30-knot class can be expected as much as 30%–40% of the time at 40S. The directions will tend to be in the western semicircle, as stated, south of 35S but with fair variability from NNW to SSW. Most likely winds will be NW to SW, however, at mean speeds of about 20 knots. Northeast to south winds will be rare south of 35S.

Cloudiness tends to increase southward, with a high percentage of fair skies southward to about 30S, then tending to decrease southward, so that typically a considerable amount of cloud will be in evidence south of 35S to 40S. Precipitation frequency increases similarly, with about 15%–20% probability of precipitations at 40S.

The persistence of westerly winds along and south of 40S gives rise to persisting high sea states. While the variability and relatively light winds of the lower latitudes would be expected to give mean seas in the 2–4-foot range for the most part, it would be expected that upon reaching the 40th parallel mean seas will be up in the 6–7-foot range, with rather frequent occurrences of 10–12 feet, mostly long period. Maximum seas at this latitude, in spring, will likely be on the order of 20–25 feet.

Generally the extreme northern limit of icebergs will be south of 40S; however, they can move northward to 45S–46S with little difficulty, and it should be advised that great caution should be observed when approaching 40S for any stray iceberg occurrence.

Again, there would seem to be little argument with the traditional sailing route in this leg: somewhat farther east and the winds become unreliable, while much farther east encounters with southerly trades (and the northerly Benguela Current) will exist along the coast of Africa. These south and southeast winds extend down the coast to the Cape of Good Hope. Thus, the plan to make the more graceful transition from southeast trades to polar westerlies will be better realized along the traditional route.

40S on the Greenwich Meridian (0 Degrees) to 50S on the Date Line (180 Degrees): November–January

This leg is the longest single leg to be discussed. It lies generally within the Indian Ocean, although starting in the South Atlantic, southwest of South Africa, and ending in the South Paciifc, to the southeast of New Zealand. As is true with most of the Southern Hemisphere, weather data and statistics are quite sparse, due both to the lack of land area and the greatly reduced density of ship reports from that seen in the North. As a result, the actual development, movement, and complexity of weather systems within the region are not as well known as their northern counterparts. On the plus side, however, is the fact that due to this same lack of land area, and the lack of major thermal transport streams, such as the Gulf Stream and the Kuroshio of the Northern Hemisphere, weather features tend to move with greater regularity and less complexity.

Typically, the South Atlantic subtropical high-pressure system extends eastward into the southern tip of Africa. Migratory high-pressure centers break off and develop over the waters to the southeast of Africa, then to move more or less eastward in the

30S–40S latitude region. These high-pressure centers will track eastward toward Australia. The anticyclogenesis and decay or re-development of these highs may be somewhat of a question (as will be the similar life of the storm centers discussed later) due to the lack of history and the real-time data in following the individual centers. However, there does exist the same tendency for a quasi-permanent subtropical high-pressure belt to exist in the southern Indian Ocean that exists over other oceans of the world in the sub-tropical latitudes. Some evidence exists that the frequency of closed high-pressure centers reaches a maximum southeast of Africa, near 35 east longitude and again near 95 east, both between 30S and 40S. The frequency of high pressure moving into Australia dimin-ishes considerably during the summer months, due to the persis-tence of thermal low pressure over that region. For the most part, the migratory highs move across the southern land areas and along the immediate southern offshore waters while thermal (and occa-sionally tropical) lows dominate the interior and north. In any case, the dominant weather feature north of 35S–40S will be the southern periphery of these eastward tracking high-pressure cen-ters. Remembering that the flow about high pressure in the South-ern Hemisphere is counterclockwise, this sets up a dominant wes-terly flow regime along 40S.

Augmenting this will be the dominant belt of low presure that lies along roughly the 60S latitude: the circumpolar trough. Migra-tory storm systems will typically develop during the summer and move west to east, or east-southeastward, between 40S and 50S, forming at times north of 35S. The highest frequency of extratrop-ical cyclone centers will typically be south of 50S, however, with about five a month on the average passing through points centered near 62S/72E and another near 63S/112E. Typically, the migratory storm centers moving eastward between 40S and 50S will be mov-ing at speeds of about 30 knots.

The regularity and relatively high frequency of migrating storm systems to the south of 40S will result in frequent frontal passages along the route, even in summertime. In fact, there may be little real difference in seasonal frequency, albeit with somewhat lesser intensity during the summer. It is felt that a route along 40S may on the average see as much as one frontal passage every two or three days. Typically, the migratory storms will have multiple cold frontal structures. It may be argued that some of these features are not true cold fronts in the classic sense but will be defined here as cold fronts at least as regards their effects. The effect on the wind will generally be shifts from northwest to southwest, rarely showing directions eastward from due north or from due south. Showers will accompany the shifts.

Of some significance to the route along 40S will be the development and movement of tropical storms and hurricanes from the subequatorial region. These storms typically develop in the 5S to 20S band to in turn move westward with gradual recurving southward, then southeastward. There are three major areas in which these storms develop. The first is in that region near and east of Madagascar, from about 90E to the Madagascar coast, from which they move south and southeast toward 40S prior to dying or becoming absorbed into extratropical systems. Another major area is north and northwest of Australia, to move south and southeast off the west coast, then the third being that region north and east of Australia on out past the date line. These storms also tend to move down toward the 40th parallel. Generally speaking, these storms will rarely maintain tropical strength and characteristics south of 35S, and by the time of reaching 40S would only rarely represent a threat to the boat at that latitude southward. Severe damage has occurred on occasion southward into New Zealand, particularly the North Island, and the dying tropical cyclone can intensify extratropical storms that do come within range of the boat. As a result, strict adherence should be given to monitoring all marine bulletins for tropical cyclones that may be present to the north. Their clockwise circulation pattern might briefly distort the prevailing westerlies along the route, but if such an occurrence did take place, it would be brief.

Aside from the rare tropical intrusion into the 40S region, the pressure distribution would mean high pressure persisting to the north of the route, low pressure to the south, with rapidly alternating ridges of high and troughs of low pressure near the route. It would be expected that the wind distortion around these features would be relatively small, such that the variation in direction would not be that great during the passage of the various frontal systems, probably staying in the NW to SW quadrant for the most part, giving the mean direction of westerlies. However, the consistent features combined with the long open fetch will give a high percentage of gale-force winds.

It is felt that the mean wind speeds along 40S will be on the order of 20–25 knots, with frequent occurrences of 40–45 knots. Along the projected route, gale-force winds may be encountered with a frequency as high as 20%–25% of the time through this seasonal period. Moving farther north will tend to lessen the frequency of high winds while adding to distance traveled. Moving southward becomes very hazardous due both to an even higher frequency of high winds and a high risk of icebergs.

The normal northern limits of iceberg occurrence run generally from about 40S just south of South Africa to about 50S near 75E, then back northward to about 45S from about 100E to 120E, then abruptly to about 60S after 120E. Bergs have been sighted as far north as about 33S from 10E to 40E, such that the passage south of the Cape of Good Hope along 40s should be performed with great caution. These figures would indicate that the route along, or near, 40S from about 45E on eastward would be safe from icebergs. However, it must be remembered that accurate ice analysis in these waters is only a very recent event, starting with satellites. Therefore, it is recommended that a route along 40S, subsequently southeastward to clear Tasmania and Auckland, should be made with great caution throughout the possible iceberg intrusions, but in particular those areas to the west of 45E–50E, and perhaps again from about 100E to 120E.

The lack of land areas and the subsequent long, uninterrupted wind fetch will give persisting high seas. It would be felt that the mean sea heights will be in the 6–9-foot range but with frequent occurrences of seas in excess of 20 feet.

Clouds and precipitation increase rapidly southward, with a route near 40S showing a high percentage of cloudiness and an increasing frequency of precipitation southward past 45S.

In general, it would be recommended to sail eastward to the north of 40S with a more realistic wind/sea configuration likely to be found between 38S and 40S, with the added benefit of a much lower probability of iceberg occurrence. Rounding the Cape of Good Hope should be performed near 40S, however, to avoid the prevailing easterlies that will lie off the Cape. Rounding the Cape at 40S should give persisting westerlies, but rigid surveillance for ice must be maintained. Thereafter, it would be recommended to turn more northeast toward 38S in an attempt to minimize the gale/high seas frequency and the ice, despite the distance penalty. Or, at a minimum, it would be recommended that the route be biased northward upon encountering high winds/seas/ice and to sail a route that compromises the activity on a real-time day-to-day basis. Consistency and persistence are such that it's probably reasonable to state that the best plan would be to round the Cape of Good Hope at 40S, then continue along 40S, adjusting within the first 5–6 days to the most comfortable compromise between prevailing wind/sea conditions and distance to be traveled, then continue eastward on that chosen latitude on the assumption that mean conditions will be repetitive and consistent.

If sailing eastward at a latitude north of 40S, then surveillance and monitoring of marine broadcasts (if any) for tropical circulations should be maintained, however. In any case, it will still be necessary to sail more southward to pass Tasmania, New Zealand, and Auckland to the south. Again, gale frequency will be expected to increase to over 15%–20% south of 45S.

It should be pointed out that if conditions along 40S suggest a northward bias is desirable, it would be recommended that the route should not go north of 35S in any case. This is due both to the increasing danger of tropical cyclone high winds and, conversely, the increasing probability of local calms and wind variations to easterlies as approach toward the mean axis of the subtropical high pressure occurs.

50S on the Date Line (180 Degrees) to Cape Horn (Approx. 57.0S/70.0W): January–March
This leg of the voyage, across the South Pacific, traverses a region of very sparse data, both climatological and real time. As a result, the mechanisms of the weather features are perhaps less understood than for any other part of the world. However, the relative apparent consistency of weather features that was discussed for the southern Indian Ocean appears to apply here also, the net result being a continuation of similar weather events as those detailed for the Indian Ocean.

The presence of the subtropical high-pressure system, so common to all the world oceans, is equally strong in the South Pacific, although with a tendency to break off into two separate centers of highest pressure. In summer, the western portion tends to have a mean position near 37S and elongated eastward from the Great Australian Bight to east of New Zealand, while the eastern Pacific has a mean position closer to 30S and near 120W–130W. Again, these mean areas of high pressure are accomplished by many migratory high-pressure centers moving eastward in the 30S–40S belt.

The mean position of the summertime polar front lies roughly east-west across the Pacific between 40S and 50S. Cyclogenesis occurs along this mean position, with resultant storms moving east to south-eastward with life cycles of over five days. A few storms will develop in the 30S–40S belt, but most will occur south of 40S. The storm or cyclone centers south of 50S are quite prolific and move steadily eastward throughout the summer. The storm frequency is such that there will seldom be a closed high-pressure circulation between the storms and their associated fronts. Rather, only flat or ill-defined high-pressure ridges will be expected. This results in a similar pattern as that described for the Indian Ocean: a mean wind direction of westerly and only rare occurrences of winds out of that northwest to southwest quadrant along the route. Statistics suggest a gale frequency along the route will fall into the 15%–30% range, and perhaps as high as 25%–30% approaching Cape Horn. Few data are available on mean wind speeds, but it is felt that 20–25 knots for mean speeds will be realistic, rarely less than 15 knots but with common episodes of over 50–55 knots. Almost unlimited fetch and persistent directions will give high mean seas, probably in the 8–10-foot range as a mean but with frequent occurrences of over 20. There seems to be little reason to dwell longer on these winds/seas, since the consistency of the weather features suggests little in the way of anomalous events. The term "roaring forties" would seem to be aptly applied.

Cloudiness will be a fairly dominant feature along the route, with average conditions being pretty much in the broken to overcast lower cloud range. Steady precipitation periods will be fairly well spaced, but showers may be rather frequent, associated with the numerous cold front/trough passage. The chances of steady and heavier precipitation will increase approaching Cape Horn.

Icebergs will become a constant threat from 170W right into

Cape Horn, on the rhumbline. Particular attention will have to be maintained from about 130W eastward. Historical data indicate iceberg sightings as far north as about 44S between about 120W and 105W, but east of 100W–105W most appear to be south of 53S–55S. Again, it must be emphasized that accurate iceberg data in these waters are not available, such that caution must be exercised at all times. From what is known of the currents, it would appear that the ice will drift northwest from the Ross Sea ice shelf, which is a prolific berg producer, then turn eastward in the Antarctic Circumpolar Current, running eastward near 50S. However, this also suggests that more ice can turn northward into the Peru Current, to the east of 100W–105W, than is indicated in historical data. Most bergs will likely stay with the Cape Horn Current, an easterly current offshoot from the Antarctic Circumpolar, toward Cape Horn. In any case, it is likely that most ice will be south of 50S, but vigilance must be maintained throughout. Using the more northern track suggested in the traditional sailing route minimizes the ice potential but may not necessarily eliminate it. Nonetheless, it would be strongly suggested that the plan of sailing eastward in the 45S–47S range would give significantly reduced wind/sea configuration and much reduced hazard of icebergs until turning southward to round the Cape. Even at those latitudes, however, the average conditions are still likely to consist of winds of 20 knots or more. Light air problems would not seem to be much of a factor at any point from the Cape of Good Hope to Cape Horn.

Cape Horn (Approx. 56.5S/71.5W) to 40S/30W: February/March
Returning into the South Atlantic during this period will provide general synoptic conditions about as given for the southward run earlier in the voyage. That is to say, the dominant features will continue to consist of the subtropical high-pressure system, the cyclogenesis from the Brazil/Argentina coastal sections, and the steady progression of low-pressure centers eastward to the south of 50S. For more detail on these features, we would refer you to the discussion of the route 15S/25W to 40S/Greenwich.

The passage around Cape Horn is not treated separately here, due to lack of knowledge about the exact route planned and of local terrain and preferences. However, it is noted that in the traditional sailing routes an east wind is referred to. Data available here, and consideration of the typical synoptic conditions, would indicate a westerly wind in the vicinity of the Cape. Therefore, if accurate, this would suggest some local effect in the immediate vicinity out of the scope of this report. Ice distribution about the immediate Cape area falls into the same category. As an aside at this point, a conversation with Mr. Brad Washburn, chairman of the Boston Museum of Science, indicates that a book has been written by a man who spent most of his life in the area, off- and onshore. The book is, I believe, *The Udder Side of the World,* by E. Lucas Bridges. This one region is but a fraction of the entire voyage but perhaps the most critical in terms of weather, ice, etc. Therefore, you might want to attempt to obtain this book for a firsthand look at the area, particularly considering the general dearth of knowledge overall in the Southern Hemisphere.

The prevailing winds along this route will continue to reflect the merging of the polar low-pressure belt and the subtropical high pressure, which is to say that north to west winds will be dominant. Specifically, the winds will move westerly after rounding the Cape, but with prevailing directions gradually becoming more northwesterly progressing northward. Some variation to other directions, in the east semicircle, will be evident in developing low-pressure centers moving southeastward from the coast, but such occurrences probably represent less than 10%–15% of the time. Gale-force winds will occur on the average of 15%–20% of the time south of 50S, likely decreasing to about 10%–15% of the time northward to 40S.

Otherwise, conditions will be much as outlined for the southbound leg, with one major exception. Icebergs move north and northeast with the Falkland Current and the West Wind Drift currents, so that the potential for iceberg encounters will exist throughout this segment of the voyage, although most prevalent south of 50S.

40S/30W to 15S/25W: February/March
15S/25W to 15N/50W: February–April
15N/50W to Newport: March–May
There is little real reason to document these legs in great detail since the encountered weather/winds/seas will be very similar to

the reciprocal routes discussed earlier. Trade wind strengths at the end of the season will be similar to those at the start, with similar directions and speeds at the same latitudes, as will be the potential areas of light/variable winds of similar latitudes.

There are a few deviations that can be touched on, however. The return route, farther west in the North Atlantic, will be somewhat less susceptible to light and variable wind conditions in the subtropic belt (near 35N). There is a slightly greater risk of tropical circulations developing north to 5N, to the east of the Antilles, but still a fairly low risk for this time period. The threat of the east coast cyclogenesis, north of 35N and several hundred miles off the Atlantic seaboard, is diminishing through April and becomes fairly rare in May, although still possible. Thus, the net result is for typical conditions to be similar in spring to those in fall.

Afterword

Knowledge generally combines practical experience with learning acquired from books. As such, we at Weather Services felt that it would be desirable to reflect back on the climatological route study prepared for Dodge and see how it compared with the conditions he actually encountered in order to give us a better-tuned look at the weather around the world. Of course, weather conditions normally show sufficient vagary as to make it somewhat dangerous to assign positive conclusions based on a single boat at a single point. The problem is compounded by steadily moving this point along day to day.

Since Dodge completed his historic voyage, we have had the opportunity to work with several boats in the 1986–87 BOC Single Handed Around the World race. They followed roughly the same path Dodge did, but made three stops en route. We worked with Ned Gillette and his crew of three, who rowed the boat *Sea Tomato* across Drake Passage from Cape Horn to Antarctica, and we are in conversation with other veteran BOC racers for some upcoming events. As a result, we have been able to augment considerably our experiences relating to global marine meteorology since the time we wrote the study for Dodge.

In general, it would seem that the study has held up pretty well in the light of all this experience. However, several conditions are better understood now.

The first and most important item is the higher frequency of light air or calms that can be encountered to the south and east of Australia and New Zealand. As it turns out, this is a favored area for blocking high-pressure systems to appear, which can stall out for relatively long periods of time in the area east of New Zealand. When they do so, light and variable breezes will persist within the envelope of high pressure. This was understood, but what was not anticipated was how far south these effects can penetrate. When they do, they make a mockery of the terms "roaring forties" and "screaming fifties." Dodge probably will agree that despite all of the incredible storm conditions he faced, the worst times of the voyage came in periods of light air. If he doesn't care to agree, I would suggest that as the other end of many radio contacts during those periods, I know better. The tendency for light air in this location is particularly bad, since it represents an area about halfway home and occurs just as the skipper has committed to the vast South Pacific.

The other two items referred to can be combined into one category: the frequency of winds on the east side of north. The occurrence of winds in the north to northeast segment is much higher than we would have expected. This occurs from two separate causes.

The more frequent cause is what turns out to be the "normal" sequence around strong frontal systems. Since a front comes along about every three days or so, this gets to be a pretty common event. A high percentage of the cold fronts will swing through with a wind sequence that backs from north-northeast to north-northwest ahead of the frontal boundary, then to west-southwest as a post-frontal wind. Then as the next front approaches, the wind promptly clocks back through northwest to north-northeast. Thus, rather than the high percentage of winds in the northwest-to-southwest quadrant, we actually find them more in the north-northeast to west-southwest or from about 030 degrees true to about 240 degrees true. This is particularly true in the 40S to 55S latitude range. This should not have come as so much of a surprise as it was, since in the Northern Hemisphere, winds frequently turn into advancing cold fronts as south-southeast rather than southwest. The Southern Oceans' reputation for westerlies probably obscured this truth somewhat.

The other source of east-component winds emanates from storm tracks coming down from the north. This sequence was addressed in the original study, but there we dwelled mainly on the storm track southeastward from the offshore waters of Brazil and Argentina. Certainly there is prodigious cyclogenesis in this track, but significant numbers of storms develop in the mid-Pacific. We referred to the tendency to split the subtropical high into two centers but failed to realize that this area of relative troughiness represented an area of potential development. Some of the rare intrusions of easterly winds into the Cape Horn area occur when such a storm moves southeastward into the coast of Chile. This is more common in winter, as regards Cape Horn, but southeastward-moving storms out around 120W are not uncommon. Of course, the clockwise rotation of these storms brings northeast winds down into the higher latitudes.

A quick comment on tropical cyclones. We referred to the Atlantic tropical storms or hurricanes as being low probability for November. Indeed they are, but it will nonetheless be noted that Dodge had to skirt around Hurricane Kate, which developed after he left Bermuda. Low probability, yes. Impossible? Obviously not. Also, referring to the tendency of tropical storms to transfer energy into an extratropical feature, it is considered that the worst storm episode that Dodge and *Promise* encountered around the world was the result of storm Ima dropping southward out of the Polynesians and mating with an extratropical low pressure.

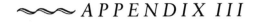 *APPENDIX III*

A PSYCHOLOGICAL PORTRAIT OF A SOLO
CIRCUMNAVIGATOR
William Nasby, Ph.D., and Randolph D. Easton, Ph.D.

Almost a year before Dodge Morgan departed on *American Promise* to sail around the world, he volunteered to participate in a unique study of the effects of prolonged isolation and stress. Morgan was given a battery of tests over eight days; among them were the Sixteen Personality Factor Questionnaire, the California Psychological Inventory, the Adjective Check-list, and the Millon Clinical Multiaxial Inventory. Out of the study came the psychological baseline and portrait of Morgan. That portrait could aptly be titled "thick-skinned individualist." The term thick-skinned captures many of the psychological attributes that allowed Morgan to withstand, far better than the vast majority of other people, exposure to prolonged isolation and stress throughout the voyage.

Extroversion/Introversion. Morgan directed attention equally toward the external world of events and people on the one hand and the inner world of thoughts and feelings on the other. A balance, therefore, of extroverted and introverted tendencies characterized this man who neither sought nor avoided the company of others. If he had strongly favored extroverted tendencies, Morgan would have found prolonged isolation unbearable.

Overall Adjustment. Several aspects of the study indicated that Morgan has achieved a level of emotional adjustment and maturity that ranged between very high and excellent. It was, therefore, no surprise that he reported leading a satisfying life.

The results also suggested that Morgan typically experienced less anxiety than most people. Either slightly less or considerably more of a predisposition to experience anxiety would have caused substantial problems for Morgan during the voyage. Exceptionally low anxiety often foretells lack of motivation to complete tasks. Exceptionally high anxiety can disrupt accurate and efficient performance.

Tough-Poise. Morgan also had a great deal of what is called "tough-poise," which describes someone who is alert, controlled, cool, decisive, and emotionally detached. High scorers, such as Morgan, approach problems analytically and rationally.

Morgan also deliberately understates the severity of physical symptoms and attempts to tough it out. For someone sailing alone over extended distances, this response can prove either adaptive or maladaptive.

A downside often accompanies elevated levels of tough-poise: being too distant and detached and appearing insensitive to the feelings of others. In Morgan's case, however, this problem did not matter much. Such an attitude is an asset for someone who had to face the adversities of solo sailing.

A low score would have concerned us far more. Excessive sensitivity, frustration, and moodiness often characterize low scorers. Indeed, when problems do arise, low scorers' emotions frequently run amok.

Independence. Morgan has spent his life pursuing independence; he cherishes self-assertion and self-sufficiency. Morgan also relishes playing the role of a nonconformist who does not readily accept the conventions, rules, and standards of others. Nor does he rely heavily on others for emotional support.

Morgan tends to enter situations that tolerate and, perhaps, reward assertive, aggressive behavior. Much of what he did before and during the voyage served a powerful motive: the need to exhibit, exercise, and extend autonomy. The best way to describe Morgan's code of conduct is "take charge of your own destiny."

Although he prefers to formulate decisions and tackle problems alone, Morgan usually realizes and admits when he is over his head. In such cases he not only accepts but also solicits advice from other people whose skills exceed his own. (His seeking expert advice on *American Promise*'s design and construction testifies to this.)

He does not, however, willingly accept interference from others. Such interference would probably evoke mistrust and hostility as well as occasionally trigger obstinate, rebellious, and unpredictable behavior. Those behavioral responses might create some interpersonal difficulties for him, but, as in the case of tough-poise, the possible liabilities of independence would arise primarily in social contexts. In a solo circumnavigation, the assets of independence far outstrip the liabilities.

Had Morgan attained a low or moderate score in independence, he definitely would have been in trouble. Low scores characterize passive, group-dependent, and chastened individuals. The Southern Ocean could destroy the low scorer, although such a person probably would have had troubles long before reaching it.

Discipline. Morgan highly values and uses care, self-control, self-discipline, persistence, and precision. He has unrelenting patience and uses organized and thorough approaches to solve problems. If a task requires long hours and continuous labor to finish, Morgan usually perseveres. He also anticipates problems and plans accordingly.

Maintaining steady progress toward a goal is tremendously important to Morgan; when progress stalls he can become somewhat rigid and inflexible. Those characteristics might have contributed to the distress he experienced while becalmed and when daily mileage did not meet expectations.

Abstract Thinking and Creativity. Tasks and problems that require abstract thinking appeal to Morgan, who can proficiently organize information from sources to form logical and meaningful wholes. He tends to grasp new material and new ideas quickly and can skillfully identify and analyze key elements of most problems. In addition, he can maintain alertness and concentrate for extended periods.

In prolonged isolation and stress, severe emotional disturbances and mental disorders, for example, major depressions or psychotic breakdowns, can often develop, causing intellectual functioning to deteriorate markedly. Even minor losses of intellectual precision and efficiency, of course, could prove hazardous to a solo sailor. For persons like Morgan who can think abstractly, the risk of intellectual deterioration because of emotional disturbance is not as great as for individuals who cannot think abstractly. Morgan can also think creatively and flexibly as well as abstractly, a strong combination, readily generating innovative solutions to problems.

Achievement Orientation and Motivation. Morgan aspires to accomplish difficult tasks as quickly and efficiently as possible and strives vigorously to attain challenging goals. Competition also appeals to Morgan, who seeks not just to win but to excel while competing.

Risk-taking and Exhibition. Test results showed that the following attributes characterized Morgan before the voyage: adventurous, bold, daring, energetic, enterprising, impetuous, intrepid, spontaneous, and uninhibited. The common denominator here is risk-taking. Morgan not only tolerates but actually enjoys activities and circumstances that contain elements of uncertainty, novelty, danger, and chance. Morgan obtained a high score in this area, indicating that he can face grueling and taxing situations well and that he does not tire easily. High scorers such as Morgan also formulate decisions quickly and confidently. (The quickness and confidence, however, do not guarantee correct decisions.) Interestingly, sports psychology indicates that competitive athletes generally obtain elevated scores, as did a group of Antarctic explorers that successfully completed its mission. An exceptionally high score in this dimension, which Morgan fortunately did not obtain, identifies persons who may foolishly and impetuously display a reckless willingness to risk harm and peril as well as an unrealistic lack of fear while confronting threat.

Risk-taking and the adventure of sailing alone, nonstop, around the world may have served another motive for Morgan, considering other data our study produced. The following cluster of attributes, which pertains to exhibition, also describes Morgan: colorful, dramatic, flamboyant, flashy, histrionic, theatrical, and unconventional. The presence of an audience certainly appealed to Morgan. Although he did not physically play to an audience, his exploit nevertheless drew, and continues to draw, considerable attention from not only the sailing and scientific communities but the public.

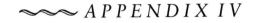 *APPENDIX IV*

THE DESIGN AND CONSTRUCTION OF
AMERICAN PROMISE

DESIGN TEAM

Head designer	F. E. "Ted" Hood
Project designer	Ted Fontaine
Mechanical designer	Melvin "Buddy" Duncan

CONSTRUCTION TEAM

Project manager	Grant Robinson
Yard manager	Arthur Fraser
Mechanical foreman	Leonard Frost
Electrical foreman	Frank Brennan
Head carpenter	Joe Baier
Head machinist	Fred Doughty
Head finisher-painter	Butch Dzengelewski

MAJOR SUBCONTRACTORS

Deck, Cockpit, Pilothouse: Walter Greene, Greene Marine, Yarmouth, Maine

Mast, Rigging, Furling Systems: Hood Yacht Systems, Marblehead, Massachusetts

Sails: Hood Sails, Marblehead, Massachusetts

Electronics and Instrumentation: Colin MacDougall, MacDougalls' Cape Cod Marine Service, Falmouth, Massachusetts

ACTUAL DESIGN PARTICULARS TAKEN FROM
FLOTATION WATERLINE

Displacement	77,515 lb.
Length overall	60'0"

Length waterline	56'9"
Beam waterline	15'2"
Beam maximum	17'2"
Draft	10'4"
Displacement/length ratio	203.52
Sail area/wetted surface ratio	1.96
Wetted surface displacement	77.24
Total wetted surface	819.52 sq. ft.
Ballast	22,500 lb. lead
Sail area, 100% foretriangle	1614 sq. ft.

AMERICAN PROMISE: NOON POSITION LOG

Days run noon to noon. This log shows the noon position at the end of each day, but the text gives the noon position at the beginning of the day.

DAY	DATE NOON END	NOON FIX POSITION	NM DAY	NM AVG.	CUM. NM	WX
0	11/12	32°22′N/ 64°41′W INM true east David's Light — leave Bermuda	—	—	—	SE 18-20 kt.
1	11/13	29°38.1′N/ 63°23.78′W	175	175	175	SE 20-22
2	11/14	27°01′N/ 61°46′W Feel lousy — lonely	175	175	350	ESE 25-30 Seas 12-15′
3	11/15	24°34.4′N/ 60°11.5′W Beat, wet — bumpy ride	184	178	534	SE 30-35 Seas 16-18′
4	11/16	25°54.3′N/ 59°18.8′W Head north to avoid Hurricane Kate	97	157.8	631	ESE 40-45 Seas 16-18′
5	11/17	24°39.7′N/ 57°06′W Kate hits Haiti/Cuba — we head south again	143	154.8	774	East 15-25 Seas 8-10′
6	11/18	23°23.8′N/ 54°38.1′W (Tired of beating into it!)	159	155.5	933	ESE 25 Seas 12-15′
7	11/19	21°47′N/ 52°18.4′W Getting used to being at sea	161	156.3	1094	SE 25-30 12-15′ seas
8	11/20	19°50.8′N/ 49°37.5′W Much diesel oil & water in bilges	190	160.5	1284	E 18-20 Seas 8-10′

DAY	DATE NOON END	NOON FIX POSITION	NM DAY	NM AVG.	CUM. NM	WX
9	11/21	18°25.3'N/ 46°58.4'W Much water & fuel oil pumped from bilges	173	161.9	1457	ENE 15-20 Seas 6-8'
10	11/22	17°07'N/ 45°18.2'W Light & variable east winds	123	158	1580	East 5-6 kt. Seas 4-5'
11	11/23	15°14.8'N/ 43°08.2'W Boat motion easier — sleep better	168	158.9	1748	ENE 5-10 Seas 5-6'
12	11/24	13°32.1'N/ 40°49.4'W Ideal sailing now in trades	169	159.7	1917	ENE-Trades 15-20 Seas 6-8'
13	11/25	11°35.1'N/ 38°33.7'W Still hard on wind — 2 weeks!	177	161	2094	ENE 20-25 Seas 4-5'
14	11/26	9°20.56'N/ 36°22.67'W Good speed hard on trade winds	186	162.9	2280	East 20-30 Seas 4-5'
15	11/27	7°32.93'N/ 34°12.06'W Getting used to life at 25 degrees heel	168	163.2	2448	East 20-25 Seas 4-5'
16	11/28	5°35.91'N/ 32°30.83'W First time on starboard tack! Still beating —	154	162.6	2602	E to SE, then S! 5-15 kt. Seas 5-6'
17	11/29	4°20.64'N/ 30°44.58'W Enter doldrums — variable wind	130	160.7	2732	S-SE 0-15 kt. Seas 5-6'
18	11/30	1°58.03'N/ 29°38.91'W	157	160.5	2889	ENE-ESE 0-15 kt.
19	12/1	1°00.9'S/ 29°43.7'W Cross equator — beautiful tradewind sailing	179	161.5	3068	ESE-Trades 20 kt. Seas 5'

DAY	DATE NOON END	NOON FIX POSITION	NM DAY	NM AVG.	CUM. NM	WX
20	12/2	3°59.53'S/ 29°33.98'W More easy going. I like it.	179	162.4	3247	SE 20 kt. Seas 3-4'
21	12/3	6°41.28'S/ 29°07.82'W Identical to yesterday	164	162.4	3411	SE 20 kt. Seas 3-4'
22	12/4	9°21.39'S/ 28°36.57'W More of the same fine going	163	162.5	3574	SE 25-30 kt. Seas 6-8'
23	12/5	12°30.82'S/ 28°14.4'W Sailing utopia — good for soul	191	163.7	3765	SE 15-20 kt. 4' seas
24	12/6	15°13.19'S/ 27°13.92'W Variable conditions keep one busy.	167	163.8	3932	S-E variable 5-25 Seas 3-4
25	12/7	18°05.63'S/ 26°07.57'W Note our good start so far! We are on reach!	184	164.6	4116	N-NE 5-20 kt. Seas 5-6'
26	12/8	21°23'S/ 25°46.28'W Voyage avg. speed up to 6.9 knots!	198	165.9	4314	ENE 8-18 kt. 10' swells
27	12/9	24°15.8'S/ 24°45.26'W This is old man's sailing — easy going!	182	166.5	4496	East 8-15 kt. 3-5' swells
28	12/10	25°38.72'S/ 22°46.04'W MPS — light sails to keep moving	136	165.4	4632	NE 4-8 kt. low swell
29	12/11	26°52.67'S/ 21°10.52'W Horse latitudes still	113	163.6	4745	NE light & variable low swells
30	12/12	28°19.79'S/ 19°59.04'W Struggle to keep way on	108	161.8	4853	Light, variable Calm to 8 kt. Seas low
31	12/13	30°05.65'S/ 18°50.36'W Poled out twin headsails	122	160.5	4975	Light westerlies Calm North — lights 8' swells

DAY	DATE NOON END	NOON FIX POSITION	NM DAY	NM AVG.	CUM. NM	WX
32	12/14	31°20.47'S/ 16°10'W Back to hard on wind	157	160.4	5132	SSE 6-16 10-12' seas
33	12/15	32°53.21'S/ 15°59.56'W Put heavy weather sails on	93	158.3	5225	SSE-10 kt.
34	12/16	33°36.42'S/ 13°49.64'W Finish heavy weather sail change	117	157.1	5342	Light SSE Seas 3-4'
35	12/17	35°19.32'S/ 10°14.36'W Effortless close reach! 8.5 speed avg. today.	205	158.5	5547	SSE/SE 10-15 Seas 4' swell
36	12/18	36°51.92'S/ 6°26.75'W Get ready for the Indian Ocean!	206	159.8	5753	S 15-20 kt. Seas low swells
37	12/19	38°07.67'S/ 2°54.97'W Homesick — fear of Indian O.	184	160.5	5937	NE to SW w/ passing front 10-30 kt. Seas 6'-up to 15'
38	12/20	39°25.23'S/ 0°38.5'E Easy going on reach	184	161.1	6121	SW 10-20 kt. 6' seas
39	12/21	39°56.19'S/ 3°13.43'E Caught in high-pressure zone	123	160.1	6244	Lt. variable South Easy seas
40	12/22	41°00.21'S/ 5°30.59'E In 40s, but they ain't "roaring"	122	159.2	6366	Lt.-variable S Low seas
41	12/23	42°04'S/ 7°58.55'E Still no *roars*	123	158.3	6489	Same as above
42	12/24	42°03.25'S/ 11°55.48'E High pressure still holds us	176	158.7	6665	S-SW 5-15 kt. Seas 6-8'

DAY	DATE NOON END	NOON FIX POSITION	NM DAY	NM AVG.	CUM. NM	WX
43	12/25	42°01.28'S/ 15°50.28'E We are S of Cape of Good Hope & have beaten the time of *Crédit Agricole*, BOC winner	174	159.0	6839	S 5-25 kt. 10-12' seas
44	12/26	42°08.05'S/ 19°45.25'E Now we arrive in the roaring forties	175	159.4	7014	West 25-30 kt.
45	12/27	42°09.63'S/ 24°23.23'E We sail under twin headsails hung out.	206	160.4	7220	North-NW 20-30 Confused 16-18' seas
46	12/28	42°06.05'S/ 28°31.67'E Wild world weather	184	160.9	7404	WSW 25-35 kt. 10-12' seas Build to 20-25'
47	12/29	42°19.74'S/ 31°59.93'E Front move through-wind veers 90	159	160.9	7563	NW 30-35/SW 40-45 Seas 15' up to 25'
48	12/30	43°48.58'S/ 35°34.82'E Several knockdowns occur	180	161.3	7743	NNE 45-50 kt. Seas 25-30'
49	12/31	43°31.04'S/ 39°40.05'E Big wind & sea, & we are full & by	178	161.7	7921	NNE 50-55 kt. Seas 35-40'
50	1/1/86	42°49.53'S/ 43°39.93'E Off the wind — reach under poles	180	162	8101	NW 25-40 kt. Sea 30-40'
51	1/2	42°09.17'S/ 47°33.69'E *Promise* rolls 90 degrees — ugh — 45 degrees each side	177	162.3	8278	35-40 kt. SW 20' seas w/10' chop on top
52	1/3	42°03.28'S/ 50°40.40'E Much putting out & stowing of poles	139	161.9	8417	NW to North to NE E 10-25 kt. 20' seas confused

DAY	DATE NOON END	NOON FIX POSITION	NM DAY	NM AVG.	CUM. NM	WX
53	1/4	42°09.31'S/ 55°37.8'E Close reach — no rolling — whew	221	163	8638	ENE to NE 20' seas
54	1/5	41°47.03'S/ 59°21.51'E Front passes — winds NE to N to W to SW, S	168	163.1	8806	Storm center passes, wind backs around Seas 20-25'
55	1/6	41°39.88'S/ 63°17.94'E Albatross constant companions	177	163.3	8983	SSW-15 kt. to SE 10 15-20' seas
56	1/7	42°06.92'S/ 66°18.77'E Plans begin for Pacific O. waypoints	137	162.9	9120	E to NE 10-12 kt. Seas 15'
57	1/8	42°27.31'S/ 69°45.59'E Fall gale beats on us & we on it	154	162.7	9274	NE 40-50 kt. 30-35' seas
58	1/9	42°10.93'S/ 73°33.75'E Gale still — we are knocked down 70 degrees numerous times.	170	162.8	9444	NE 40-55 kt. 35-40' seas
59	1/10	42°00.27'S/ 78°24.12'E Finally the wind behind us — we pole out.	216	163.7	9660	N to NW-W 30-40 kt. 35-40' seas
60	1/11	41°57.85'S/ 82°26.78'E To script — wind to south & light, then west & up	180	164	9840	W to SW 10-15 kt. Seas 15'
61	1/12	41°38.97'S/ 86°45.84'E Some good sailing, beam reach, some slatting	194	164.5	10034	W 15-20 &S 0.5 Seas 15-20'
62	1/13	42°03.08'S/ 90°46.55E Much chafing wear on lines. Boom vang adrift.	181	164.8	10215	Variable S-SW 5-20 Seas 15'

DAY	DATE NOON END	NOON FIX POSITION	NM DAY	NM AVG.	CUM. NM	WX
63	1/14	42°06.99'S/ 94°33.55'E Bright day — is this vacationland?	169	164.8	10384	North 10-15 Seas 10-12'
64	1/15	42°11.67'S/ 99°20.64'E Easy going, but we hit something hard?? A whale!	213	165.6	10597	North 10-15 to NW 25-30 Seas 10-15' up to 20-25'
65	1/16	42°09.76'S/ 104°24.76'E This would be a 235 NM day at 24 hours!	225	166.5	10822	North-NW 25-40 kt. Seas 20-25'
66	1/17	42°22.72'S/ 108°57.54'E Our average speed 7 kt. for trip so far.	202	167	11024	NW-W20-30 Seas 20-25'
67	1/18	42°17.81'S/ 113°17.04'E We hit a sustained 15 knots/18 momentary.	192	167.4	11216	West 20-25 to SW-5 kt. Seas 15-20'
68	1/19	43°14.62'S/ 116°42.33'E Jib furl line chafed & replaced & jib halyard parts-spare fitted	161	167.3	11377	West 6-8 Seas 15'
69	1/20	43°26.37'S/ 121°04.44'E Roll downwind square-rigged under poled wings	191	167.7	11568	West 20-25 kt. Seas 15-20'
70	1/21	43°24.62'S/ 124°30.77'E Very uncomfy going — roll is heavy	150	167.4	11718	West-SW-15-20 Seas 20-25'
71	1/22	43°45.74'S/ 127°51.14'E Gray day — we roll & make slow progress.	147	167.1	11865	SW-10-15 Seas 20-25
72	1/23	44°27.98'S/ 131°05.05'E More furling & halyard problems. Much chafing of lines.	146	166.8	12011	SW-S-10-15 Seas 20-25'

DAY	DATE NOON END	NOON FIX POSITION	NM DAY	NM AVG.	CUM. NM	WX
73	1/24	44°59.62'S/ 135°19.31'E I am in poor spirits.	183	167	12194	SW-15-20 Seas 15-20'
74	1/25	45°10.30'S/ 139°40.76'E A full moon shows & cheers me.	185	167.3	12379	NW-25-35 kt. 15-20' seas to 30 kt. south wind & 30' seas
75	1/26	45°13.67'S/ 144°11.83'E Halfway! High-pressure zone domi- nates.	191	167.6	12570	SW 10-45 kt. Seas 30-40'
76	1/27	45°24.69'S/ 148°12.75'E Leave Hobart, Tasmania meridian, in South Pacific	170	167.6	12740	S-30-40 kt. 35-40' seas
77	1/28	46°15.39'S/ 152°38.72'E Enormous seas! With 35-degree grades — more at peak	192	167.9	12932	W-20-25, then W-40-55 kt. Seas 35- 45'
78	1/29	47°22.29'S/ 156°42.78'E Generator problems — use main eng. alt.	180	168.1	13112	S-6-10 kt. Seas 20'
79	1/30	48°56.32'S/ 161°01.85'E I decide *not* to anchor for repairs in N.Z.	197	168.5	13309	SE-10-12 kt. Seas 20'
80	1/31	49°10.57'S/ 164°54.64'E Trop. Cyclone Winifred to north. We are almost becalmed.	153	168.3	13462	Lt. North seas 20'
81	2/1	49°11.18'S/ 168°44.5'E Very sloppy going, ugly conditions	150	168	13612	Lt. North seas 20'
82	2/2	50°14.21'S/ 172°23.79'E Light headwind forces us south	155	167.9	13767	Lt. NE seas 8- 10'

DAY	DATE NOON END	NOON FIX POSITION	NM DAY	NM AVG.	CUM. NM	WX
83	2/3	50°26.75'S/ 177°08.72'E	182	168	13949	NE-10-15 Seas 10'
83	2/3	50°40.50'S/ 178°02.41'W Internat'l date line — we live this day twice.	184	170.3	14133	" "
84	2/4	50°56.90'S/ 174°35.13'W Dolphin & whale show — we are becalmed.	132	169.8	14265	NE to calm
85	2/5	50°29.98'S/ 171°09.67'W While making water, discover eng. v-drive adrift.	133	169.3	14398	Light to calm
86	2/6	49°51.57'S/ 168°20.80'W Some south breeze to sail on	115	168.8	14513	Light-var. & south 5-10 Seas down-10'
87	2/7	49°45.24'S/ 168°20.80'W Becalmed much of day — high press. dominates	75	167.6	14588	Light & var.
88	2/8	50°07.6'S/ 161°53.14'W We sail some on a NE breeze — full & by — feels good.	176	167.8	14764	Lt. var. to NE 10 Seas 6-8'
89	2/9	49°20.42'S/ 156°38.33'W A bit of wind, and *Promise* lifts her heels.	209	168.2	14973	NE-15-20 Seas 8'
90	2/10	49°09.35'S/ 150°41.39'W A great run — close reach & flying great *233*	233	169	15206	NE-20-25 Seas 8'
91	2/11	49°04.42'S/ 147°08.79'W So much light wind in 40s & 50s???	139	168.6	15345	NE-15-20-dies to zip Seas 6'

DAY	DATE NOON END	NOON FIX POSITION	NM DAY	NM AVG.	CUM. NM	WX
92	2/12	49°03.17'S/ 144°03.88'W Struggle to get the knots — keep struggling	121	168.1	15466	Light to variable 6' seas
93	2/13	49°26.5'S/ 140°05.62'W These light winds give us a poor S. Pac. leg.	157	168	15623	Light & variable Some NW-10-15 Seas 8'
94	2/14	49°34.77'S/ 134°41.41'W Give us some wind, & we'll give you a run.	211	168.4	15834	WNW-15-20 kt. Seas 10'
95	2/15	49°04.49'S/ 130°16.6'W Battered by big wind. Barometer dives to 28.5".	175	168.5	16009	WNW-30-50 kt. Seas 30-40'
96	2/16	48°43.75'S/ 126°51.8'W From big wind to zip in an hour	136	168.2	16145	WNW-20 kt. Seas 35-40', then wind zips
97	2/17	48°49.73'S/ 121°39.5W Under wings we glide like a big bird.	206	168.6	16352	West 15-20 kt. Seas 15-20'
98	2/18	49°36.2'S/ 116°07.59'W Close reach and fast going	222	169.1	16573	NNE-25-30 kt. Seas 20-25
99	2/19	50°06.05'S/ 111°40.35'W Hung out and bouncing	175	169.2	16748	N-NW-15-25, then 5-10 Seas 20-25
100	2/20	51°02.78'S/ 107°54.55'W About ⅔ around in voyage	154	169	16902	W-SW-10-15 Seas 15-20
101	2/21	52°32.55'S/ 103°00.3'W Beautiful day & sail	203	169.4	17105	SW-15-25 Seas 20-25
102	2/22	52°52.85'S/ 97°44.5'W Jib refuses to furl — on poles we fly	192	169.6	17297	SW-20-25 Seas 25'

DAY	DATE NOON END	NOON FIX POSITION	NM DAY	NM AVG.	CUM. NM	WX
103	2/23	53°42.61'S/ 93°17.73'W Squalls punch us — jib furls if babied	167	169.8	17464	West 15-25 & 35-45 kt. in squalls
104	2/24	53°50.36'S/ 87°46.64'W Storm winds buffet us — rough going (Cyclone Ima!) Bare poles	196	169.8	17660	West-SW 45-70 kt. Seas 35-45'
105	2/25	54°52.12'S/ 82°30.58'W Storm over — contact w/schooner *Dream Merchant*	194	170	17854	South 15-20 Seas 30-40
106	2/26	55°33.69'S/ 77°55.17'W Broad reaching under blue skies	185	170.2	18039	South 15-20 Seas 20-25'
107	2/27	56°05.27'S/ 72°46.39'W We approach Cape Horn now/lt. going	154	170	18193	SE 5-10 kt. Seas 10-15
108	2/28	56°06.1'S/ 67°45.67'W Round "The Horn" in beautiful wx. WOW!	168	170	18361	S- SE 5-15 kt. Seas 10-15'
109	3/1	54°45.08'S/ 62°31.53'W The legend passed — we bolt north-ward (cold).	196	170.2	18557	SE 15-20 kt. Seas 10-15'
110	3/2	52°52.5'S/ 57°44.48'W Some squalls — we fly — & for home now	203	170.5	18760	SE 20-25 kt. Seas 10-15'
111	3/3	50°26.55'S/ 54°01.11'W The wind stays — our speed continues (cold).	201	170.8	18961	SE 20-25 kt. Seas 10-15'
112	3/4	48°07.68'S/ 51°41.84'W Our wind abates. Whitbread racers be-hind me	163	170.7	19124	SE 20 kt. to S 5-8 kt. Seas 8-10'

DAY	DATE NOON END	NOON FIX POSITION	NM DAY	NM AVG.	CUM. NM	WX
113	3/5	46°37.78'S/ 50°17.46'W	107	170.2	19231	Calm to NE 10-12 Seas 8- 10'
		Eastern wind forces us to westward of rhumbline.				
114	3/6	44°31.74'S/ 47°54.78'W	161	170.1	19392	E to NE 10-35 Seas 8-10'
		Sail hard on wind — & squalls bury us				
115	3/7	41°45.34'S/ 45°18.77'W	202	170.4	19594	East 35-45 seas Seas 20'
		Nasty going blowing hard up nose				
116	3/8	39°44.5'S/ 42°54.69'W	163	170.3	19757	E-ENE 40-45 Seas 20'
		Hammer to weather. We are too far west.				
117	3/9	37°58.07'S/ 41°32.3'W	124	169.9	19881	ENE 25-30 dies to N
		We tack and beat our brains out.				
118	3/10	35°44.5'S/ 41°24.83'W	134	169.6	20015	ENE 0-12 kt. Seas 4-5'
		Take off 90% jib-bend on 150% jib.				
119	3/11	33°10.64'S/ 42°32.5'W	164	169.5	20179	NE 35-45 kt. Seas 12-15'
		Use storm staysail, reefed main-hard on wind.				
120	3/12	31°55.11'S/ 40°10.95'W	141	169.3	20320	NE 35-45 gut kt. Seas 12-15'
		We are too far west — foul winds & Brazil current came bout.				
121	3/13	31°28.55'S/ 37°48.25'W	124	169	20444	NE 25-40 kt. Seas 15-18'
		We head east on STB tack — very rough going.				
122	3/14	31°12.38'S/ 35°13.8'W	133	168.8	20577	NE to ENE 25-40 kt. Seas 18-20'
		We still bash into it — tack to north.				

DAY	DATE NOON END	NOON FIX POSITION	NM DAY	NM AVG.	CUM. NM	WX
123	3/15	29°36.4'S/ 33°42.67'W Wind abates — stays from NE — 6 days of beating.	124	168.3	20701	ENE then NE 5-10 kt. Seas 10- 12'
124	3/16	28°48.02'S/ 30°54.25'W We beat east in light air.	155	168.2	20856	NE 5-10 kt. Seas 5-6'
125	3/17	27°13.58'S/ 27°59.32'W Still beat-STB tack — light airs	181	168.3	21037	NE-ENE 5-10 kt. Seas 6'
126	3/18	24°45.85'S/ 27°54.41'W We beat — some calms — can fetch Trindade Is.	148	168	21185	NE 5-10 kt. Seas 6'
127	3/19	21°28.03'S/ 28°01.13'W Close reach & good sailing. S. Atl. trades?	198	168.4	21383	ENE 15-20 kt. Seas 8'
128	3/20	18°09.82'S/ 28°21.29'W In and out of squalls — we boil along.	199	168.6	21582	ENE 15-20/35-40 in squalls Seas 8-10'
129	3/21	15°04.44'S/ 29°03.03'W Great sailing — close reach — much reefing & shaking out	190	168.8	21772	Same as above
130	3/22	11°38.64'S/ 29°41.14'W Punched by squalls — we really move.	209	169	21981	Same as above
131	3/23	8°02.14'S/ 29°32.52'W Approaching the ITCZ and fast!	217	169.4	22198	Same as above
132	3/24	5°10.54'S/ 29°45.34'W We hit the doldrums — some lt. NE wind.	172	169.5	22370	East 20-30, then lt. & variable NE Seas 8'

DAY	DATE NOON END	NOON FIX POSITION	NM DAY	NM AVG.	CUM. NM	WX
133	3/25	2°43.47'S/ 29°37.22'W Wind goes northwest, variable, slow going toward end of day.	147	169.3	22517	E 0-10/then N-NNW 5-8 kt. Seas 3'
134	3/26	1°25.06'S/ 29°38'W Light & variable to zip wind, doldrums — slow & exasperating	78	168.6	22595	Lt. variable N. Seas 4'
135	3/27	0°32.78'N/ 30°47.83'W Cross the equator & break out of doldrums into Northern Hemisphere	137	168.4	22732	Lt. NE to NE 8-10 kt. Seas 5-6' swells WX
136	3/28	2°32.9'N/ 33°25.03'W The NE trades are much earlier than expected!	198	168.6	22930	NE 25-35 kt. Seas 8' chop
137	3/29	4°47.22'N/ 36°20.21'W Close reach & flying — avg. 9.2 kt. today	221	169	23151	NNE 25-30 kt. Seas 8'
137	3/30	7°21.56'N/ 38°56.02'W Close reach still — extremely rough & uncomfortable!	219	169.3	23370	NNE 25-30 kt. Seas 10-50' apart
138	3/31	9°53.65'N/ 41°36.56'W Seas farther apart — easier ride — avg. 9.2 kt. for three days!	220	169.7	23590	NNE to NE 25 kt. Seas 10-80' period
140	4/1	12°15.82'N/ 44°17.54'W Wind finally veers & open up our reach — more comfy ride	213	170	23803	NE 20-25 kt. Seas 10'
141	4/2	14°59.18'N/ 46°48.17'W Same wind! Seas up a bit w/chop on top	219	170.4	24022	NE 25-30 kt. Seas 12'

DAY	DATE NOON END	NOON FIX POSITION	NM DAY	NM AVG.	CUM. NM	WX
142	4/3	17°27'N/ 49°10.58'W Sudden wind veer to SE — strength drops	201	170.5	24223	ENE 25 kt. veering to ESE-SE 10-12 kt. Seas 10' down to 6'
143	4/4	19°27.7'N/ 51°17.28'W Light & variable S winds slow us down.	170	170.5	24393	SE variable 0-12 kt. Seas 8'
144	4/5	20°49.48'N/ 52°29.49'W Very light winds & very slow going	106	170.1	24499	SE variable 2-6 kt. Seas 6'
145	4/6	22°28.24'N/ 54°10.68'W Light winds add to frustration by coming NW on nose!	136	169.2	24535	NW-NNW light & variable Seas 4-5'
146	4/7	24°24.58'N/ 56°20.31'W We "tie the knot" by crossing outbound track on return. Circumnavigation now completed.	166	169.w	24701	NNW-light-veering to NNE & NE 12-18 kt. Seas 6'
147	4/8	26°12.95'N/ 58°07.69'W Wallowing along under wings in wind 2–6 kt.	146	169	24847	South & light Seas 5'
148	4/9	27°45.82'N/ 59°55.95'W More light air struggle SW 10 knots. last 4 hours!	134	168.8	24981	South & light tc SW 10 kt. Seas 6'
149	4/10	29°56.35'N/ 63°01.7'W Progress on the SW wind. Hits hard NW at day's end	209	169	25190	SW/WSW/W 20-35 kt. Seas 12'
150	4/11	32°21.82'N/ 64°37.41'W Close reach. Finish at 1217 hrs. Bermuda time (1617 hrs. GMT)	167	169	25357	NW 18-20 kt.

ANALYSIS OF RECORDS ACHIEVED BY DODGE MORGAN (USP) DURING HIS SINGLEHANDED NONSTOP CIRCUMNAVIGATION, 1985–86
D. H. Clarke

YACHT: *American Promise*, 60'0 × 16'5" × 9'5" (18.29 × 5.00 × 2.87) Bermudan Sloop

ROUTE: From/to Bermuda, eastabout via the five southernmost capes. W-E(H4).

RECORDS BROKEN

1. Fastest solo passage from a North Atlantic post to (off) Cape-town by a monohull: Bermuda to Capetown, 7095 miles in 43 days 16 hrs 29 mins = 162.4 m.p.d.

    Comparison Philippe Jeantot (Fr); 56'0 (17.07)
    Crédit Agricole, 1982–3
    BOC Challenge: 7315 miles in 47 days = 155.6 m.p.d.

2. Largest monohull sailed singlehanded from North to South Atlantic.

    Comparison Previous   largest: 59'0 × 12'10" × 8'6" (17.98 × 3.91 × 2.44)
    British Steel, Chay Blyth (GB), 1970.

3. Fastest solo nonstop passage from Bermuda to Cape Horn: 18,511.9 miles in 108 days 1 hr 6 mins = 171.3 m.p.d.

    Comparison 11 monohulls and one multihull (trimaran) have completed nonstop circumnavigations (1969–1985). None achieved anything approaching the above average speed.

4. Fastest passage from Australasia to Cape Horn during a solo nonstop circuit. From the longitude of Hobart, Tasmania, to Cape Horn: 5690 miles in 32 days 19 hrs 46 mins = 172.4 m.p.d.

    Comparison See No. 3 comparison above. The fastest average speed achieved by a singlehander with stopovers (2); Philippe Jeantot (See No. 1 comparison above), from Sidney to Cape Horn: 5709 miles in 29 days 23 hrs =

190.6 m.p.d. It is interesting to note that in 1974 Alain Colas (Fr) managed to average only 173.8 m.p.d. from Sydney to the Horn in his $69'10'' \times 34'9'' \times 2'6''$ ($21.28 \times 10.60 \times 0.76$) trimaran *Manureva*.

5. Largest monohull yacht to round the Horn singlehanded.

    Comparison Previous largest, see No. 2 comparison above.

6. First American singlehander to round all five southernmost capes during a nonstop circumnavigation.

    Comparison The first American singlehander to round all five capes during a circumnavigation with stopovers was Mark Schrader, $39'11''$ (12.17) Bm. cutter *Resourceful*, 1982–3.

NOTES Dodge Morgan is the 66th singlehander to round the Horn ($+/-5\%$); the 13th to do so during a nonstop circum.; the 6th solo American Cape Horner and the 2nd American singlehander to round all five capes.

b. The five southernmost capes are: Good Hope; Leeuwin (SW Australia); South East Cape (Tasmania); South Cape (Stewart Island, New Zealand); The Horn.

7. Fastest 24-Hour run during a singlehanded nonstop circumnavigation: 236 miles.

    Comparison Previous nonstop circums offer no adequate comparison. The fastest monohull (3 stopovers), 1982–3 BOC/AA Race, Richard Konkolski (Czech), $44'8''$ (13.60) *Nike III*, 247 miles. Fastest multihull: Alain Colas (Fr), 1973–4, $69'10''$ (21.28) trimaran *Manureva*, 326 miles.

8. Fastest 7-day run during a singlehanded nonstop circumnavigation: 1494 miles.

    Comparison See No. 7 comparison. The fastest (3 stopovers), 1982–3 BOC/AA Race, Philippe Jeantot (Fr), see No. 1 comparison, 1552 miles.

9. Fastest speed for a singlehanded monohull circumnavigation: 25,670 miles in 150 days 1 hr 6 mins = average speed 171.1 m.p.d. or 7.13 knots.

    Comparison Previous fastest singlehanded monohull

speed: *Crédit Agricole* (see No. 1 comparison), 26,560 miles in 159 days 2 hrs 26 mins = 166.94 m.p.d. Fastest-ever speed for a solo circum: Alain Colas (Fr), 69'10" (21.28) trimaran *Manureva*, from/to St. Malo, W-E(H2), 1973-4, 30,067 miles in 169 days 4 hrs 11 mins = 177.7 m.p.d.

10. Fastest time for a singlehanded true circumnavigation: 150 days 1 hr 6 mins.

   Comparison See No. 9 comparision: 159 days 2 hrs 26 mins.

(Of particular importance is the precise wording of Records 9 and 10. It will be noted that neither refers to the nonstop category. The reason is seen in Record 11.)

11. First occasion when a nonstop circumnavigator has beaten both the time and speed of all previous singlehanded monohull records.

   (Note: Previous to this, nonstop circums. were necessarily regarded as being slower than circums. with stopovers for the obvious reason that a nonstop circumnavigator has to conserve his strength and avoid excessive wear to his yacht, since he cannot enter port to effect repairs, etc. Therefore of all the records which Dodge Morgan has broken, this is probably the most outstanding, and a remarkable "first.")

12. Largest monohull yacht to complete a singlehanded circumnavigation.

   Comparison See No. 2 comparison.

13. First American to complete a singlehanded nonstop circumnavigation.

NOTES Dodge Morgan is the 114th singlehander to circumnavigate (+/− 5%); the 13th to do so nonstop; the 21st singlehanded American.

   b. A true circumnavigation entails passing through two antipodal points which are at least 12,429 statute miles (20,000 km) apart. *(Guinness Book of Records)*

   c. All Cape Horn and circum. positions given are approximately correct, but cannot be guaranteed as reportings are constantly in flux. All the records quoted are believed correct, but are subject to claims or counterclaims.

d. All the records quoted for Dodge Morgan are supported by Argos readings.

e. Records 9/10 have been entered in the *1987 Guinness Book of Records.*

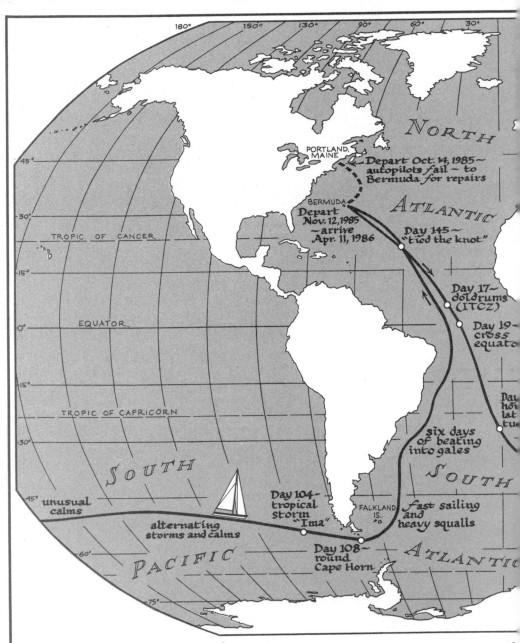

Labels on map:

NORTH

ATLANTIC

PORTLAND, MAINE

Depart Oct. 14, 1985 ~ autopilots fail ~ to Bermuda for repairs

BERMUDA

Depart Nov. 12, 1985 ~ arrive Apr. 11, 1986

Day 145 ~ "tied the knot"

Day 17 ~ doldrums (ITCZ)

Day 19 ~ cross equator

TROPIC OF CANCER

EQUATOR

Day horse latitudes

TROPIC OF CAPRICORN

six days of beating into gales

SOUTH

SOUTH

unusual calms

alternating storms and calms

Day 104 ~ tropical storm "Ima"

FALKLAND IS.

fast sailing and heavy squalls

ATLANTIC

PACIFIC

Day 108 ~ round Cape Horn

Dodge Morgan's solo, nonstop circumnavigation wit

October 14, 1985		Depart Portland, Maine
Day 3	42° N / 62° 30′ W	Both autopilots fail. Morgan must climb to repair failed halyard
Day 6	38° N / 54° 30′ W	Decision made to sail to Bermuda ~ the voyage becomes a failure
Day 12	Bermuda	*American Promise* is repaired
		~
November 12, 1985		Depart Bermuda
Day 17	4°20′ N / 30°44′ W	Doldrums
Day 19	0° / 29°44′ W	Cross equator
Day 30	28° S / 20° W	Horse latitudes